Strategic Assessment in War

Strategic Assessment in War

Scott Sigmund Gartner

Yale University Press
New Haven and London

For Diane

Library of Congress Cataloging-in-Publication Data

Gartner, Scott Sigmund, 1963–
Strategic assessment in war / Scott Sigmund Gartner.
p. cm.
Includes bibliographical references (p.) and index.
ISBN 978-0-300-08069-8 (paper)

1. Strategy. 2. War—Decision making. I. Title.
U162.G26 1997
355.4—dc21 96-39931
CIP

A catalogue record for this book is available from the British Library.

The paper in this book meets the guidelines for permanence and durability of the Committee on Production Guidelines for Book Longevity of the Council on Library Resources.

Contents

Acknowledgments

In writing this book, I was fortunate to have the help of a number of outstanding individuals, many of whom contributed a great deal of time and effort. I am particularly grateful to James Morrow and Allan Stam, both of whom read the entire manuscript several times, and whose suggestions significantly improved the final product. Robert Jackman, Randolph Siverson, Diane Felmlee, and Bruce Bueno de Mesquita read chapters and provided me with helpful comments.

I should also like to thank the following for their suggestions and support: Robert Axelrod, Marc Bennett, Scott Bennett, Douglas Dion, Elisabeth Gerber, Marissa Myers, A. F. K. Organski, Patrick Regan, Dani Reiter, Claire Rosenson, Gary Segura, John Shy, Jerry Sorokin, Scott Tarry, Jeremy Wood, and William Zimmerman.

Richard Andres, Bethany Barratt, Monica Barczak, Christian Erickson, Stacy Burnett Gordon, and Michael Wilkening provided excellent research assistance.

The research was funded in part by the University of California's Institute on Global Conflict and Cooperation, the Institute of Governmental Affairs, and the Academic Senate's Committee on Research at the University of California, Davis.

Chapter 1

Strategy and Organization

Life is measured by the rapidity of change.

—George Eliot

During World War I, the careers of British infantry officers whose units suffered low casualties were ruined because they were seen as lacking the essential *esprit de corps.* The fewer of their men who died, the worse the unit was doing: "A low casualty rate was taken as evidence that a regiment was shirking, and also led to dismissals."[1] If this seems like a rare phenomenon that was brought about by the unusually brutal and inane fighting of World War I, consider the following discussion between Generals Orlando Ward and George S. Patton during World War II, as described by the historian Geoffrey Perret:

> "How many officers did you lose today?" asked Patton. "We were fortunate," Ward replied. "We didn't lose any officers." "Goddamit, Ward, that's not fortunate! That's bad for the morale of the enlisted men. I want you to get more officers killed." A brief pause followed before Ward said, "You're not serious, are you?" "Yes, goddamit, I'm serious. I want you to put some officers out as observers," said Patton. "Keep them well up front until a couple get killed. It's good for enlisted morale."[2]

Shortly after this discussion, General Ward was relieved.

Although the relation between an observable wartime indicator, such as casualties, and evaluations of success might sometimes be surprising, numerical indicators like these strongly influence how decision makers assess performance in war. These evaluations affect such critical wartime issues as promotion, resource allocation, alliance formation, and whether to maintain or change current strategies.

This is a book about decision making in wartime and the role that battlefield indicators play in determining assessments of strategy. Leaders assess and, if necessary, alter their strategies based on information they gather from the battlefield through wartime indicators. These decisions can have enormous impact. Decisions on strategy play a significant role in determining a war's nature, as well as its duration, intensity, and ultimately who wins and who loses.

The maxim "to win the battle but lose the war" suggests the historic difficulty of assessing wartime performance accurately. Despite its importance and difficulty, strategic assessment in war has traditionally received little analysis, largely owing to the dominance of Cold War nuclear concerns.[3] Since World War II, "the study of war has almost exclusively been concerned with the subject of initial war outbreak."[4] The decreasing concern about nuclear conflict that has followed the end of the Cold War allows us to move beyond a narrow focus on the causes of war to a broader examination of wartime decision making.

How does the information generated by battle influence decision makers' assessments of the performance of their strategies? I argue that organizations form beliefs about their likelihood of success from what they observe during a war. We can capture these beliefs with what I call the dominant indicator approach: a general, organizational model that focuses on sudden and dramatic changes in the quantitative indicators on which decision makers rely to predict how organizations evaluate the performance of such implemented policies as strategy. The direction and rate of change with which these critical, "dominant" indicators move provides an estimate for an organization's likely policy assessments and behavior.

Some argue that organizations, and in particular military organizations, are insensitive to changes in their environment.[5] They believe that military organizations fail to learn from their wartime experience. My approach challenges these views. I think that experiential information, like that generated in the battle, affects all organizations' assessments of policy performance, but each organization employs a different informational lens to interpret these data. This means that different organizations might have different views of the same situation; because they are relying on different information for understanding the situation, they may talk past each other when discussing the effectiveness of their nation's strategies.

The quantitative data employed by decision makers to evaluate policy performance represent a largely untapped primary source for studying wartime decision making. Using these data, I examine how decision makers reacted to three different wartime strategic changes: the British response to Germany's unrestricted submarine warfare in World War I, British assessments of the effects of German submarine Wolf Pack attacks in World War II, and American evaluation of its success in the Vietnam War after the Tet Offensive. In addition, to get a sense of how the proposed approach works in a non-war situation, I look at the Carter Administration's decision to launch the hostage rescue attempt in Iran. In each case, I analyze the period before and after the adversary's strategic change to help us better understand how leaders assess the likely success of their strategies. Each analysis thus includes many actors and observations.

In each historical case I examine three arguments to explain organizations' strategic assessments. First, I test the proposed approach, which looks at the rates of change of dominant indicators employed by decision makers to assess their wartime performance. In particular, I examine how we can use the acceleration and change in acceleration of these indicators to make predictions about leaders' strategic evaluations. Second, I examine an alternative absolute value model that does not consider acceleration and change in acceleration of indicators and that closely resembles the standard "bounded rationality" organization approach of Herbert Simon, James March, Richard Cyert, and Anthony Downs.[6] Finally, I explore the parsimonious notion that nations simply alter their strategies after their adversaries do; what I call the action-reaction model. My study finds that the dominant indicator approach is a better predictor of behavior than the two alternatives and has a number of other significant implications.

The most important contribution of this effort is the development and empirical analysis of a new view of organizational assessment and decision making. But this book contains a number of other theoretical and empirical implications beyond that. First, the analysis suggests that organizations hold onto their assessment criteria more tightly than they do their policy preferences, which, as I shall show, challenges a central tenet of the Cult of the Offensive—a recent popular argument found in the security studies literature. This helps to explain why the British navy began World War II employing a convoy strategy, when most organizational arguments suggest that it should have preferred alternative strategies.

Second, the analysis helps explain why changes in strategy are widely seen as successful—as was the British implementation of a convoy strategy in World War I. Third, it shows that organizations can experience dramatic fluctuations in their assessments, as occurred with British naval assessments during World War II. Fourth, it helps explain the conditions under which organizations become internally conflicted and torn, as in the Johnson Administration during the Vietnam War. Finally, it helps explain the timing of decisions, such as why Jimmy Carter waited until April 1980 to initiate the rescue of Americans held hostage in Tehran. To understand better the context in which these arguments operate, we need to examine the process of strategic assessment.

STRATEGIC ASSESSMENT

Decision makers rely on critical numerical measures that strongly influence their policy assessments. These figures, or dominant indicators, represent systematic factors in the information relied on by decision makers. Sudden and dramatic movements of these indicators act as strong signals that decision makers' strategy is succeeding or failing. We can capture these sudden and dramatic movements by looking at record rates of changes in the decision makers' indicators. If an indicator moves in a record-setting rapid rate in the desired direction, it suggests that a policy is performing well and that we should observe decision makers formulating a positive policy assessment. Conversely, when an indicator moves rapidly in an undesired direction, decision makers are likely to see their implemented policy as leading to failure and prefer alternatives. Finally, if decision makers rely on indicators that move dramatically in directions that would lead to conflicting interpretations, an organization is likely to become "gridlocked" and unable to formulate a consensus policy assessment.

In Chapter 2 I present this argument for the dominant indicator approach in detail. My argument, however, rests on a specific view of the factors that influence organizations' strategic assessments. Before continuing, it would be helpful to identify six critical assumptions and propositions about strategic assessment that form the foundation of the dominant indicator approach. 1) Which strategy is best for a state depends on the other side's strategy. 2) An adversary's change of strategy needs to be detected. 3) In some cases, judging the success of a strategy is easy because there are obvious, easily observable indicators, but in many cases, judging its success is difficult, and there is no single, overriding indicator of success. 4) Random factors, such as weather and luck, influence performance on the battlefield. 5) Actors develop a feel for the level of noise in their indicators over time by examining earlier values. 6) Dramatic deterioration in performance provides the evidence that a strategy is failing and should be changed.

Warfare is, in part, an interaction of strategies. The interactive nature of war makes assessment difficult because it adds many players, and actors need to formulate expectations of how they expect their adversaries to react.[7] As a result, military strategy deals with "the actions of individuals who are conscious that their actions affect each other."[8] In the context of war, decision makers recognize that the behavior of one's adversary, ally, and allies' adversaries will fundamentally influence the outcome of the war and thus must be taken into consideration when making choices about how to fight it.[9] Rarely does a single wartime choice stand out as desirable, regardless of the anticipated actions of others. In game theoretic terms, there are rarely dominant strategies in war. That is, unlike a prisoner's dilemma game—where each player has an incentive to act the same (defect) regardless of what the other player does (a dominant strategy)—military decisions are a function of both the anticipated and the observed actions of one's enemies.[10]

Dealing with the interactive nature of war is seen by some as the key to wartime assessment. "In wartime, the essential problem lies in judging the results (and their significance) of interacting capabilities."[11] For example, before World War I, neither the German nor the British navy anticipated the German's use of unrestricted U-boat attacks on shipping. The German navy's implementation of this strategy occurred because the British navy bottled up the German fleet, and activity on the Western front stalled. British decision makers were thus facing a type of conflict where, because of their success on one dimension, their expectations about another turned out to be wrong. It is one thing to state that actors take into account their adversary's actions, but in the real world, how do they observe strategic change?

Nations do not usually announce changes in strategy, and strategic changes might not be easily observed. As a result, in some cases, a nation must estimate an adversary's change in strategy when the war begins to turn in an undesired direction. For example, in July 1940, the German Luftwaffe began to bomb Royal Air Force bases and other air-defense targets in Britain. In early September, the Luftwaffe switched from attacking British air-defense capabilities to bombing civilian targets in London. Thus the Battle of Britain became the Blitz. The only way the British could recognize that German strategy had changed was by observing how their adversary's behavior changed (even the Ultra code-breaking system did not help in this case). In this situation, the change was obvious, but in other cases, particularly when the battlefield is complex, strategic changes might be less clear. Thus, before an organization can form a response to an adversary's new strategy, it must first detect it. Recognition that an adversary has changed its strategy is the result of the strategic assessment process.

Once a nation determines that an adversary's strategy has changed, how does it know whether that alteration requires a response? One might state that a change in an adversary's strategy is likely to lead to an assessment of the *adequacy* of one's own strategy.[12] But what does an adequate strategy look like? And how can we, as analysts, determine when conditions are likely to lead decision makers to draw this conclusion? In order to determine whether a new strategy requires a response, nations and organizations need to use the information available to them to assess their strategic performance. This presents a number of serious problems.

In war, decision makers are suddenly deluged with information about a strategy's performance. "In a crisis, both data and policy outpace analysis."[13] The switch from peace to war leads to a dramatic change in the availability of information. "During wartime military organizations are 'in business.'"[14] The rapid pace of warfare places a premium on a nation's ability to decipher relevant information quickly and act upon it. A quick decision can lead to victory (Israel's attack on the Egyptian Air Force in the 1967 Six-Day War, for example), but it also can be disastrous (Egypt's decision to go beyond the Sinai passes in the 1973 Yom Kippur War). Like Centers for Disease Control officials evaluating a potential epidemic, if decision makers wait until the situation becomes clear, it is frequently too late for new actions to have any effect. Decision makers recognize this dilemma. In August 1990, when an adviser suggested that he wait to learn more about Iraqi intent before inviting American forces into his country, Saudi Arabian King Fahd replied, "The Kuwaitis did not rush into a decision, and today they are guests in our hotels!"[15]

It is not just change that depends upon assessment. Maintaining the status quo is also a decision that is driven by the assessment process. "Examining the decision to persevere in a policy involves some notions of the bases upon which the policy's continued desirability is to be evaluated."[16] In order to determine whether to persevere or alter policy, decision makers need to formulate assessments quickly with data that are far less complete than they would ideally prefer. As the former chairman of the Joint Chiefs of Staff, General Colin Powell, writes: "We do not have the luxury of collecting information indefinitely. At some point, before we can have every possible fact in hand, we have to decide."[17]

In a battle, when the front line moves, moving forward means that you are winning, backward, that you are losing. But although changes in the front lines of a linear ground battle might be clear indicators of success or failure, how do you measure the success of a strategic bombing or an antiguerrilla campaign? While there are various measures in these cases, there is no single, overriding indicator of performance. War has no scoreboard. Modern combat involves many battles in many places at once. Summarizing the net result of all this combat to assess your strategy is difficult. There is simply too much going on for an individual or organization to understand everything about how a side's forces are performing.

Instead of a score, in war there are many measures of performance, all of which provide confusing and competing indications of strategic performance. After the fact, it might be clear what measures were the right ones to look at to assess performance, but at the time that decision makers have to make their choices, the value of particular indicators may still be unclear. As Aaron Friedberg writes about British assessments of Germany before World War I: "It must be said that 'the facts' were not always so obvious at the time as they have come to seem in retrospect. This was not a case of people willfully ignoring a readily apparent, if unpleasant, reality. . . . Data were sometimes hard to come by, and measuring tools were imprecise and sometimes downright deceptive."[18]

The assessment process is also hindered by the emotional impact of the data; in war people die, regardless of the effectiveness of a nation's strategies. Although leaders ideally would prefer to fight a war where they achieve their objectives, suffer no losses, and expend no resources, they realize that this is not possible. Unlike what happens in peacetime, the presence of death and destruction tells a leader little about a policy's performance.

Once selected, the interpretation of these indicators is also problematic. Organizations know that such random factors as weather and luck influence their performance in the field. Indicators are noisy; they vary in ways that are unrelated to the performance of a strategy. The wartime environment makes the analysis of facts particularly difficult because of the inherent noise that accompanies all factual information. Carl von Clausewitz stated that a "great part of the information obtained in War is contradictory, a still greater part is false, and by far the greatest part is of a doubtful character."[19] Fred Ikle described the problems in using information for analyzing war termination, a decision-making process similar to strategic innovation, as one in which leaders must "decide which data to ignore as trivial and which to interpret as important signals. They must reconcile conflicting evidence. They must amalgamate into a single answer the most diverse indicators: reports from the battlefield, statistics on potential military resources, and impressionistic predictions of how friend and foe will bear the costs and suffering of further fighting."[20] War outcomes result from complex calculations that depend on a variety of unknown and hard-to-determine factors (strategy, leadership, *esprit de corps,* capabilities) and thus contain inherent uncertainty, noise, and chance.[21] "Battles are not pre-ordained. If they were, no one would bother to fight them."[22] Thus, it is not surprising that Clausewitz believed that information and its interpretation represented a key element in a war. "This difficulty of seeing things correctly, which is one of the greatest sources of friction in War, makes things appear quite different from what was expected."[23]

Despite this noise and uncertainty, decision makers still need to assess their performance in order to determine whether they are implementing the best strategies or deploying resources appropriately, whether they should sue for peace or press harder for victory. "When fighting starts it must often seem to a commander that everything is going wrong. His enemy pulls surprises, messages get lost, missions are misunderstood, supplies disappear, and dozens of other problems arise to hamper the quest for victory. All the while he worries about the progress being made."[24] How do actors draw inferences about the performance of their strategy in the face of this noise?

Actors compare current indicator values to past measurements in order to develop a sense of how to interpret their information. In this way, they begin to understand what constitutes unusually bad performance. For example, did the speed with which the FBI captured a suspect in the Oklahoma City bombing of 1995 suggest that U.S. domestic antiterrorist efforts were adequate? Or did the eighteen years required before a suspect was arrested in the Unabomber case suggest that these efforts were insufficient? Was the quick capture good luck or the long avoidance of capture bad luck for the FBI? In order to use this information to assess their efforts, FBI officials need to have some idea of the likelihood that "adequate" counterterrorist efforts will result in "speedy" arrests. In order to assess these situations, officials compare them with past situations.

Something must happen for a decision maker to determine that the implemented strategy is failing and needs to be replaced. It is not enough for the situation just to be "bad"; good strategies may also have negative results. For example, the surprise attack by the Germans in the Battle of the Bulge might have suggested to the Allies that they were pursuing a failing strategy and that they needed to implement a new way to fight Germany. Instead, the Allies waited for the outcome of the battle to become clear and saw it as a German "last gamble." In other words, although the surprise and losses of the battle were clearly undesirable for the Allies, the overall signal was that the Allied strategy was successful.

Strategic assessment is a complex and difficult enterprise. Given the enormous costs involved in defeat, leaders have a strong interest in implementing the best strategies available. As a result, strategic assessment is also a serious business. This book develops and improves our understanding of strategic assessment in war. But policy assessment is not limited to wartime.

POLICY ASSESSMENT

Although the empirical analysis focuses on decision making in war, the dominant indicator approach is general and can apply to non-war decision making. The need for decision makers to estimate, *ex ante facto,* before the fact (or decision), the effectiveness of their implemented policy is not unique to wartime situations. Herbert Simon argued that "in making administrative decisions it is continually necessary to choose factual premises whose truth or falsehood is not definitely known and cannot be determined with certainty with the information and time available for reaching the decision."[25]

For example, the Centers for Disease Control (CDC) try to estimate the effectiveness of policies intended to contain the spread of diseases before they become epidemics. They have scarce resources and attempt to direct them against diseases that have the highest potential of reaching epidemic status if they are not dealt with. In order to stop epidemics, massive investments of resources need to be made quickly, before the disease spreads. Sometimes the CDC makes a bad investment, such as when it targeted Swine Flu, which failed to spread at epidemic rates, resulting in warehouses of expensive, unused serum. In other cases, such as AIDS, where a disease becomes an epidemic, it would have been better if the CDC had expended more resources against the disease earlier. Because they cannot employ sufficient resources against all potential disease threats, CDC officials need to make judgments about the effectiveness of their policies before it is clear that an epidemic will (AIDS) or will not (Swine Flu) occur, so that they can reallocate their scarce resources.[26] The assessment problem is particularly difficult in wars and epidemics, where, even if a policy is successful, some people will die. In these cases, the pressure to make the correct decision quickly is enormous.

This general problem also has normative implications. For example, Stuart Hill has argued that the need for policies to be evaluated before outcomes can be observed should influence how democratic institutions are created. He writes: "If governmental decisions are expected to be responsive to citizen wishes, we must devise political institutions that draw on the laypublic's appraisal *before* a decision is made."[27]

EXAMPLES OF STRATEGIC DECISION MAKING IN WARTIME

On July 16, 1940, Adolph Hitler issued Führer Directive No. 16, which specified that the Luftwaffe should destroy all British military capabilities on land, sea, and air before the planned German invasion of Great Britain (Operation Sea Lion).[28] Hermann Göring translated these objectives into the strategy of using bombers to destroy all elements of the Royal Air Force. Göring stated: "As long as the enemy air force is not destroyed, it is the basic principle of the conduct of air war to attack the enemy air units at every possible favorable opportunity—

by day and night, in the air, and on the ground—without regard for other missions."[29] In July the Luftwaffe began the Battle of Britain. In order to bomb the RAF targets accurately, most of the Luftwaffe raids occurred in daylight, which facilitated bombing accuracy but which was also the most effective time for anti-aircraft efforts.

The German effort was enormous, employing a substantial portion of the Luftwaffe's planes. The effort was also extremely costly to both sides; in August alone the Luftwaffe lost 774 planes, or 18.5 percent of its total strength, while the RAF lost more than 25 percent of its fighter pilots.[30] Between August 24 and September 6, the Luftwaffe lost 380 aircraft and the RAF 290.[31] Losses were running too high for the Luftwaffe to sustain this effort, while at the same time the RAF's capabilities did not seem to be weakening fundamentally.

As a result, "the Germans changed their air strategy."[32] On September 7, the Luftwaffe instituted a strategic shift. "Attacks on Britain's air defense system through September 6 had given no indication that Fighter Command was weakening. Göring—at Kesselring's urging and with Hitler's support—turned to a massive assault on the British capital."[33] The Luftwaffe thus turned the Battle of Britain into the Blitz, as they altered their strategy from one of counter force to counter value and switched from attacking the RAF to bombing London. The Luftwaffe increasingly bombed London at night, which led to a much more sustainable loss rate than had their daylight raids against air-defense targets. Despite the improved loss rate, however, the Blitz was unsuccessful in destroying enough of London either to make the British sue for peace or to annihilate the RAF in its defense of London. As a result, the Nazis called off the Blitz and Operation Sea Lion and never tried to invade Britain again.[34]

Two aspects of the Battle of Britain and the Blitz deserve special attention. First, the Blitz represented a strategic change for the Luftwaffe because it switched its target category from air defense to London civilian and industrial targets. Second, the Luftwaffe performed two strategic assessments. First, they determined that the Battle of Britain was unsuccessful, and they switched to the Blitz. Second, they determined that the Blitz was not successful, and they ended it and called off Operation Sea Lion.

During both switches, basic German political objectives remained the same. Changes in strategy were driven largely by battlefield assessments rather than by the introduction of new goals. But sometimes changes in strategy result from the selection of new political goals. This was the case for the Americans in the Korean War.

During its first six months, the Korean War was a highly mobile, rapidly shifting conflict.[35] On June 25, 1950, North Korean forces crossed the 38th parallel and attacked South Korea. On July 1 U.S. troops arrived in Korea, where they began to retreat with Republic of Korea (ROK) forces to the Pusan Perimeter on the southern tip of the peninsula. On September 15, U.S. and ROK forces landed at Inchon, severed the North Korean lines of supply and communication, and crossed the 38th parallel northward. This effort was consonant with U.S. political objectives, which called for occupying North Korea and "rolling back" the communists. The Chinese, however, became fearful as U.S. and ROK troops approached their border, and on October 25 they attacked. By December, Chinese and North Korean forces had pushed the U.N. troops back down to the 38th parallel. At this point President Harry S Truman, with the support of the Joint Chiefs of Staff, altered U.S. political objectives from retaking North Korea to ending the war and returning to the prewar political status quo.

At the beginning of the war, the U.S. Army employed a strategy of annihilation and maneuver. Led by General Douglas MacArthur, U.S. forces attempted to locate and destroy communist forces. "Under MacArthur's direction, the army pursued a strategy of 'annihilation,' which was an attempt to destroy the adversary's military capacity to wage war. This strategy required that military forces seek out and annihilate the sources of enemy military capability."[36] This was a highly mobile strategy that exploited the American superiority in trucks, planes, and helicopters.

This strategy, however, did not work well with the new political objectives. Instead of penetrating into North Korea, the president wanted to end the war with a return to the 38th parallel. MacArthur, however, was not willing to change strategies. He believed that "Red Chinese aggression could not be stopped by killing Chinese, no matter how many, in Korea, so long as her power to make war remained inviolate."[37] As a result, there was a political fight, which Truman and the Joint Chiefs won. In April 1951, Truman replaced MacArthur with General Matthew Ridgway, and the United States began to follow a new strategy called attrition. In the attrition strategy, American forces dug in and used their superiority in firepower, rather than their maneuverability, to kill communist soldiers. Ridgway instituted a strategic "meat grinder, to chew up Chinese manpower at a rate even the Chinese could not afford."[38] The idea was not to locate and destroy critical sources of enemy material capability but rather to create a killing machine that would destroy vast numbers of communist forces. This would raise the costs of fighting so that the communists would negotiate and return to the prewar political status quo. The war thus became entrenched and positional, although even more deadly, particularly for the communists.

Two aspects of the American switch from a strategy of annihilation and maneuver to one of attrition and position stand out. First, this represents a switch in strategy because it consisted of a fundamentally different way of using a class of forces—in this case, infantry and armored divisions. Rather than attempting to find, circle, and destroy critical North Korean and Chinese war fighting material (supply depots, bases, factories, military units), the American troops largely contained themselves to a geographic region and attempted to kill as many communists who entered that region as possible. Thus, the strategic change resulted primarily in an alteration in operations.

Second, the American strategic shift was a direct result of a shift in U.S. political goals, not a critical strategic assessment. Unlike the German strategic change from Battle of Britain to Blitz, which resulted from a negative assessment, the trigger for the shift from annihilation to attrition was exogenous—a function of a new set of goals.

The Luftwaffe shifted its aims while the Americans altered the way they operated. In some cases, however, a new strategy incorporates a change in both the operations of forces and the specific aims pursued. The North Vietnamese 1972 Easter Offensive represents such a situation.

Between March 30 and April 8, 1972, the North Vietnamese Army (NVA) launched a conventional, large-unit, armored attack, called the Easter Offensive, across the demilitarized zone into South Vietnam.[39] The North Vietnamese decision to use major troop concentrations represented a fundamental strategy shift from their previous, small-unit, guerrilla-oriented strategy.[40] In this case the NVA changed both the way that it operated (from guerrilla to large-scale conventional attacks) and its aim. Unlike the guerrilla strategy, which aimed to whittle away at the South Vietnamese government's control of the state, the new strategy was a "massive conventional invasion that aimed to win a series of limited victories and lead ultimately to decisive victory."[41]

The North Vietnamese Army changed its strategy because it believed that its current strategy was leading toward defeat. The reason for the NVA attack was "to reverse the deteriorating battlefield prospects of communist forces. Despite the withdrawal of nearly all American combat forces, the North's influence over territory had waned, principally because the combination of Vietnamization and pacification had by 1972 become effective."[42] The Easter Offensive was the result of a negative North Vietnamese strategic assessment.

The U.S. response, a massive aerial bombing campaign named Linebacker, had greater impact than a similar, earlier effort (named Rolling Thunder) because of the interaction of the two strategies, U.S. bombing and the communist conventional attack. Robert Pape writes that "both Rolling Thunder and Linebacker demolished military-related targets in North Vietnam. Yet one failed while the other succeeded. The key difference lay in the connection between the air offensive and Hanoi's battlefield strategy. . . . Thus, the success and failure of coercive bombing depends not only on the assailant's choice of strategy, but also on the strategy employed by the opponent."[43] The two strategies influenced each other, which shows that strategies can be strategic.

Each of these cases represents a different type of strategy change: when the Luftwaffe changed from the Battle of Britain to the Blitz it altered its target category and thus its specific aims; when the American Army shifted from maneuver to attrition, it changed the way it operated its forces; and when the NVA used conventional forces to attack South Vietnam, it changed both its specific aims and the operation of its forces. In addition, these cases show that strategic change may come about as a result of a negative strategic assessment or from new political objectives. The concepts that these examples illustrate can help us to develop a better understanding of strategy.

STRATEGY

Modern discussions of strategic concepts tend to be both dominated by nuclear weapons and filled with an alphabet soup of acronyms, such as MAD (mutually assured destruction), MIRV (multiple, independently targeted reentry vehicle), and ICBM (intercontinental ballistic missile). Less visible from this mix is the fact that there is little consensus in the strategic-studies literature on the definition of basic concepts.

Modern thinking on strategy builds heavily on the work of nineteenth-century strategists Baron de Jomini and Clausewitz. Jomini divides war into five principal parts (strategy, grand tactics, logistics, tactics of the different arms, and the art of the engineer) and views strategy as the choice of where and with whom to fight, stating that strategy is "the art of making war upon the map."[44] Clausewitz states that "tactics is the theory of the use of military forces in combat. Strategy is the theory of the use of combat for the object of War."[45] For Clausewitz, strategy links military actions to political objectives.

Late twentieth-century notions of strategy have increasingly moved toward Clausewitz's idea that strategy represents a plan of military action. Bernard Brodie argues: "Strategy is a 'how to do it' study, a guide to accomplishing something and doing it efficiently."[46] This is similar to the definition used by the Joint Chiefs of Staff, who define strategy as "the art and science of employing the armed forces of a nation to secure the objectives of national policy by the application of force, or the threat of force."[47] In both cases, strategy is seen as a plan that connects means to ends.

These definitions share three problems. First, they are difficult to operationalize into clear, *ex ante* empirical measures. For example, Barry Posen (who, like Stephen Van Evera and Jack Snyder, uses the term *doctrine* instead of *strategy*) claims that the two key questions involved in defining doctrine are "*What* means shall be employed? And *How* shall they be employed?"[48] Yet he never clearly identifies how we should determine what constitutes a new strategy. The strategic qualities Posen examines—integration with political goals and the offensive or defensive nature of the strategy—do not clearly derive from his definition, making it difficult to apply his approach to wartime strategic change. Posen is not alone. It would be difficult *ex ante* to employ most definitions of strategy and determine what constituted a strategic change. The majority of strategic analysis looks at peacetime determinants of strategy. In these cases, a strategy exists solely as a written plan, and changes are observed when a new plan is written. In examining how adversaries react to wartime strategic change, we need to create a new definition, which focuses on more observable, behavior-based phenomena.

The second problem common to many definitions of strategy is that they are usually specific to one type of topography; that is, they apply solely to land, sea, or air operations. For example, both Allan C. Stam and Posen discuss such notions as attrition, maneuver, and punishment.[49] It is not clear, however, whether these concepts operate for naval warfare, and how one applies all three to both land and air warfare (that is, what is maneuver air warfare or punishment land strategy?). This is a common limitation in the literature.

Finally, most implementations of strategic definitions examine strategy at the national level—despite the presence of wartime debates about strategy and strategic assessment in virtually all military histories. These analyses are thus unable to capture critical political decisions. For example, in each of the post–World War II wars fought by the United States, there have been intense political and military debates about strategy, with significant political ramifications, including the firing of MacArthur in Korea, the decision of presidents Johnson and Truman not to seek second terms, and the timing of the end of the Gulf War. In order to capture these domestic decisions, we need a definition of strategy that can operate at the substate level.

Ideally, a definition of strategy should be empirically specific enough to differentiate between incremental changes and the implementation of new strategies, while at the same time general enough to apply to a variety of current and future weapons systems and topographies. It should operate at the substate level and allow us to capture domestic political debates. Building on the work of authors like Brodie, Posen, and Stam, such a definition might look like the following:

Strategy represents the way an organization operates a class of military forces to achieve specific aims against an adversary.

Three elements of this definition are particularly important. First, the definition addresses the organizational level of analysis. This allows us to capture substate, domestic political strategic debates. Although we might talk about a country's strategy, we are discussing the strategy implemented by a particular organization from this country. It would be difficult to discuss U.S. strategy in the Gulf War. Instead, one could say that the U.S. Air Force's strategy was to gain and maintain air superiority and to attack the Iraqi command and control apparatus, the army and marines' strategy was to threaten a coastal, frontal assault but in fact to assail Iraqi forces indirectly. In this example, we must identify at least three organizations and their respective strategies. Put simply, nations do not implement, assess, or fight over strategies, organizations do.

Strategy deals with the operation of a class of forces. A class of force describes the largest, militarily operational types of force, usually major weapons systems or organizational units, that a nation possesses. Examples of classes of forces are aircraft carriers, submarines, bombers, and armor and infantry divisions. Within each class, there might be many types of units and a variety of platforms, but a class represents the most general, meaningful notion of major military forces. That is, a class represents the most general way to say "country A used its *blank* to fight country B this way." The *blank* represent the possible classes of weapons systems. It might be that because of technological development, a class needs to be divided into two classes (say, attack and missile submarines). The thinking here is similar to the designation of brigade or division or corps as the best independent unit to assess and describe a country's army strength.

The "operation" of a class of force is what this class of force, as a group, does in order to achieve its intended aims. The operation of forces represents various critical aspects of how a class of force is used against an adversary. For example, the strategy of blitzkrieg combined together armor, air, and infantry units in new ways. Other countries, in other wars, had employed each of these weapons. The innovative nature of the blitzkrieg strategy derives from the combined operation of the forces.

Another way to think about this is to ask why some announced "changes" in strategy are later determined *not* to represent new strategies. Many have argued that the U.S. Army's employment of Vietnamization in the Vietnam War was not, as the military claimed, a new strategy.[50] They argue that, despite the military's proclamation of strategic change, how the Army fought did not change. Because the way U.S. forces operated did not change, American strategy did not change.

Strategy is a plan for pursuing specific aims against an adversary, such as the physical possession of an adversary's city, the destruction of an enemy's port, or the capture of an individual or group. By specific, I mean tangible, measurable objectives. The inclusion of specific aims as an essential element of strategy removes discussions of strategic style (offensive versus defensive, integrated versus disintegrated) from the discussion of strategy. This makes the notion of strategy clearer, and more operable, than the concept of doctrine employed by a number of recent scholars.[51] Strategies address how country "A" will use a class of military forces to destroy, capture, or in other ways influence a specific factor, be it military or civilian, of adversary "B." A strategy might deal with the daylight bombing of enemy cities or the massed attack of infantry on enemy infantry. In each case, the class of forces possessed by "A" and the aims (in this case, targets) of "B" are specified. But strategy does not include notions of military approach, such as aggressiveness, or efforts to destroy nonspecific intangibles, like enemy morale. Instead, a strategy that incorporated both aggressiveness and enemy morale might be the nighttime bombing of an adversary's cities, as the RAF did to German targets in World War II. In this case, a decrease in enemy morale was an anticipated outcome of the destruction of enemy cities, but the cities, rather than morale, were the specific targets of the strategy.

Strategy does not represent all types of military decisions. Micro decisions, like how to use particular weapons in particular situations, are called tactics. Whether to use bombers to attack civilian or military targets is a *strategic* decision. How each bomber attempts to avoid enemy anti-aircraft fire is a *tactical* decision. The distinction between these notions can be blurry, particularly because each decision type represents a range of choices on a military-political continuum.[52]

Strategy is part of a larger, military-political continuum, with micro-tactical decisions at one end and political decisions at the other. Many of the debates over strategy focus on how finely to cut this continuum, whether to include three categories (tactics, strategy, political) or more (the five used by Jomini, for example) or whether to divide key behaviors into strategy and tactics (the method favored by Clausewitz). Implicit in these discussions of strategy, however, is the notion of a continuum, moving from individual behavior (tactics) to national decisions (whom to fight).

Strategy represents the type of issues in the middle of the continuum: military decisions that have a major impact on how the war is fought. A particular decision might be on the border of tactics and strategy or strategy and political issues, but not both. Because of the political ramifications of military actions, politicians are often interested in strategic questions. "The problem is not only that the boundaries between policy, strategy and tactics are rarely clear, but that civilian leaders may insist on the right to control operations because of their political implications."[53]

Strategy plays a key role in a war's outcome, and some scholars consider the ability to adapt strategy to the circumstances of war as the most critical aspect of military leadership.[54] The ability or inability to innovate strategy when faced with changing circumstances can have a devastating effect. Strategic change in war led to the decimation of the Egyptians in the 1973 Yom Kippur War (when they switched from holding the Sinai passes to meeting the Israelis in the Sinai desert, thus altering the way their forces operated), while the lack of British naval innovation nearly succeeded in defeating Great Britain in World War I.[55]

In October 1973, the Egyptians had crossed the Suez Canal and taken hold of the passes close by. This provided them with both highly defensible terrain and proximity to their air-defense system, based back in Egypt. In this situation, the Egyptian forces could effectively fight the Israelis. The Syrians, however, were not faring as well and, in order to support their ally's losing efforts, the Egyptians left the passes and attacked the Israeli forces in the desert. Losing their advantages in terrain and air defense, they were quickly destroyed by the Israeli forces.

In World War I, British admirals refused to alter their naval strategy, despite the increasing losses incurred by British and Allied merchant shipping. Shipping losses were running so high by April 1917 that the British almost had to surrender because they could not support their forces on the continent. As Posen notes: "The bottom line is that the wrong strategy can endanger a nation's very survival. A military doctrine may also harm the security interests of the state if it fails to respond to changes in political circumstances, adversary capabilities or available military technology—if it is insufficiently *innovative* for the competitive and dynamic environment of international politics. If war comes, such a doctrine may lead to defeat."[56] Recent work strongly supports the belief that strategy influences war outcomes, duration, and costs.[57] Stam writes: "The interaction of two sides' military strategies has an important impact on the length of a war and on the costs that each side expects to bear as a result of fighting."[58] Strategic assessment and strategy change fundamentally affect basic elements of war.

Strategy and military capabilities also affect each other. Without certain capabilities, certain strategies are impossible, yet weaponry has no inherent capability without a plan for its use. Tanks existed in World War I, where they were dispersed in support of infantry, but the idea of combining tanks and infantry in the form of a blitzkrieg was not put into practice until World War II. The strategy of blitzkrieg greatly increased the capability of tanks. Blitzkrieg depended on tanks, but the tanks' capability was a function of the strategy in which they operated.[59]

At the same time, states can respond to minor changes in their adversary's behavior through the acquisition of more or new capabilities. Flame throwers helped U.S. Marines in World War II deal with Japanese bunkers. After the Battle of Biak, the Japanese strategy did not alter; they always attempted to hold the Pacific islands.[60] Similarly, the marine strategy of assaulting the dug-in Japanese remained constant. But as Japanese bunkers became stronger, the marines developed new capabilities and tactics to improve their effectiveness. Decision makers react to sudden and dramatic changes in their adversary's strategies by reassessing—and frequently changing—their own strategy. Minor changes, however, may be addressed by the addition of new capabilities. Strategy and capability thus work together to determine the force a nation can project and its potential response to adversary changes.

Strategy represents a critical wartime variable, influencing the outcome, duration, and costs of war. The importance of strategy does not pass unnoticed by national leaders. "We must concern ourselves not simply with weapons—and this distinction is crucial—but with their use and probable effect on the course of the war. These questions are uppermost in the minds of decision-makers."[61] Both military and civilian actors, as well as analysts, frequently view the choice of strategy as one of the most critical decisions made in war.[62]

The Cult of the Offensive—the name given in the late twentieth century to a popular argument about how doctrine is formed during peacetime—provides a useful starting point for examining what we know about how decision makers attempt to use the information available in war to assess their wartime strategies.

ORGANIZATION THEORY APPROACHES TO SECURITY STUDIES

In the 1980s, such scholars as Posen, Van Evera, and Snyder worked together to create a coherent view of strategic decision making and civil-military relations.[63] They argued that militaries develop a strong proclivity for offensive strategies as a result of organizational incentives and cultures and that under certain conditions these offensive strategies increase the probability of war. Analysts had previously argued that militaries prefer offensive strategies or that offensive strategies created first-strike advantages that increased the probability of war, but Posen, Van Evera, and Snyder's key contribution was to create a simple organizational explanation that connected the two arguments and that could be generalized to a variety of different situations.[64]

A central theme to this work is the notion that organizations, particularly military organizations, have fixed preferences in strategies—they always prefer offensive ones. Military organizations are thus unable to learn from their experiences. Posen writes: "There is little in organization theory or the civil-military relations literature to suggest that modern militaries prefer anything but offensive doctrines, if such doctrines are in any way feasible."[65] Van Evera concurs with Aaron Wildavsky's view of all types of organizations: "I started out thinking it was bad for organizations not to evaluate, and I ended up wondering why they ever do it. Evaluation and organization, it turns out, are to some extent contradictory terms."[66] Because organizational interests are generally assumed to change rarely or at most slowly, this also suggests that policy preferences change infrequently and that organizations have no need to evaluate policy. Instead, organizations use information solely to justify and sell their preferred policies, that is, for propaganda.[67]

Recently, there has been a "new wave"[68] of national security organizational scholarship that disagrees with the notion that organizations hold fixed policy preferences and that they do not learn from their experiences.[69] As Stephen Rosen notes: "Bureaucracies do innovate, however, even military ones, and the question thus becomes not whether but why and how they can change."[70] Some efforts to understand this innovation have focused on how organizations use information. Robert Jervis discusses the important role that indicators play in an organization's behavior. Arthur Stinchcombe examines how organizations move from information-poor to information-rich environments.[71] Along with Marissa Myers, I analyze how political objectives affect the indicators that organizations use to assess performance by studying the U.S. Army's switch from terrain occupied to body counts as a measure of success during the Korean War.[72]

This new literature, however, retains the traditional focus on domestic factors and tends to ignore the wartime environment.[73] In particular, security studies analyses of civil-military relations tend to focus on how civilian organizations control militaries. It thus poses the issue in the relatively narrow context of organizational oversight. This approach is representative of the larger analysis of political institutions. Terry Moe, Barry Weingast, Mark Moran, and others have criticized the political-institutions literature for myopically focusing on controlling "runaway bureaucracy."[74] This is particularly true in the security studies field, where analyses of strategic decision making focus on civil-military tension. This has created a lacuna in the security studies field. As a result, "What are needed now are comparative case studies drawn from primary sources and centered on organizational variables."[75] Wartime quantitative data provide an important and largely untapped source for analyzing strategic decision making.

Organizations do respond to a changing environment. The common wisdom in security studies is that military organizations are hidebound and tied to offensive strategies at all costs, but this book shows that they can learn and change strategy. Organizations and leaders use indicators to evaluate their strategies in complex environments and do respond to dramatic changes in those indicators.

My approach also explains why most of the literature reaches a different conclusion. It is hard to know when your strategy is failing. The course of combat in war is complicated, and often it is not clear how well a strategy is working. Given the interaction of strategies in war, making changes in strategy could prove disastrous. Military organizations need strong evidence that the current strategy is failing before they change to a new strategy. Most of the literature fails to account for the *ex post* problem we have as observers: we know which side lost and so wonder why the loser did not do something different. Determining which strategy failed is always easier after the fact than while combat is going on. As

Richard Overy says about World War II: "Explanations of Allied success contain a strong element of determinism. We now know the story so well that we do not consider the uncomfortable prospect that other outcomes might have been possible."[76] The reliance of my dominant indicator approach on *ex ante* measures can prevent this type of *ex post* bias.

Chapter 2

The Dominant Indicator Approach

I find the great thing in this world is not so much where we stand, as in what direction we are moving.

—Oliver Wendell Holmes

The purpose of this analysis is to create a theory of decision making that can help us understand better how organizations assess strategies in war, as well as provide some general insights into how organizations evaluate their implemented policies. Like others who apply organization theory to military politics (Posen, Snyder, and Van Evera), I am interested in understanding the factors that influence organizations' decisions.[1] But unlike these authors, I do not assume that organizational incentives facilitate leaders' misperceptions. Instead, I claim that the modern battlefield produces too much information for individuals or organizations to assess fully. So they reduce the available information to specific indicators. Additionally, the results of combat, and the indicators of performance, are influenced by a number of random factors, such as weather, in addition to strategy. In the face of too much evidence and random noise, actors must estimate how their strategy is performing. Under these circumstances, it is not surprising that actors reach contradictory assessments of strategic performance. From this perspective, they do not misperceive situations; rather, because of the variety of information sources available and the random factors involved in warfare, the results of combat can support diverse perceptions of the performance of a strategy.

I draw from both organization theory and rational choice perspectives to develop a general theory of decision making and policy assessment. This approach is relevant to a variety of decision making settings, but it is particularly effective at capturing the critical factors that influence decision makers' strategic assessments in wartime.

ORGANIZATION THEORY, RATIONAL CHOICE, AND BOUNDED RATIONALITY

My theoretical approach draws heavily from organization theory and concepts developed by scholars of rational choice and bounded rationality. I find that both rational choice and bounded rationality approaches lead to similar conclusions about how organizations use information generated by their experiences to assess their policy. Organization theory, rational choice, and bounded rationality each represent general approaches that scholars have adopted to explain a wide range of decision making. In addition to explaining a variety of decision types, there are diverse ideas regarding the meaning of each of these approaches.

Rational choice approaches form the heart of modern microeconomic and game theoretic arguments.[2] The rational choice approach postulates that actors make choices between policies that they expect to lead to particular outcomes. They have preferences over these outcomes and choose the one that they expect *ex ante* will most likely lead to their *best* outcome. *Expected utility* is the product of an outcome's likelihood and its inherent value or utility. Actors optimize; they attempt to maximize their expected utility. Actors attempt to choose the action that leads to their best outcome. They are rational in the sense that they act purposively, choosing among the available options to maximize their return.

Organization theory is the general approach to organization decision making pioneered by Herbert Simon, James March, Richard Cyert, and Anthony Downs.[3] These authors view organizations as having common, inherent characteristics that allow us to make generalizations about them across a wide variety of types. Critical to these authors' arguments is the notion that organizations face constraints, internal incentive structures, and conflicting objectives that influence their behavior. In order to explain this behavior, these authors, led by Simon, have developed the notion of bounded rationality.

Bounded rationality assumes that organizations are unable to make the optimal choice and therefore select something that is simply satisfactory. Organizational actors are "bounded": their internal structure constrains them from acting optimally. There has been a resurgence of interest in bounded rationality approaches. Jonathan Bendor writes that the central tenet of bounded rationality, "satisficing," is "alive and well in current research on decision making."[4]

At first, organization and bounded rationality arguments may seem to contradict rational choice views. However, I believe that bounded rationality and rational choice approaches are complementary; they work together to help us better understand how organizations operate. This becomes clearer when we examine some specific aspects of organizational behavior.

Organizational Interests and Mission

Organization theory identifies the incentives and mechanisms through which organizations function and how this constrains and directs their decision making. A critical notion to all organization-theoretical approaches is that organizations impose their identity on individuals through recruitment, training, and incentives. Leaders thus both represent and reflect their organizations. Individuals naturally have idiosyncratic interests and traits, but because organizational interests are systematic and general, a group and its leader's preferences tend to be correlated.[5] When he was at the Office of Management and Budget, Caspar Weinberger was called Cap the Knife because he was adamant about cutting budgets, which was the organizational objective of the OMB during the Nixon administration. After Weinberger became secretary of defense, budget director David Stockman referred to him as Cap the Shovel because he oversaw the United States' largest peacetime military buildup and was unwilling to cut the Defense Department's budget.[6] Caspar Weinberger certainly displayed individual characteristics, such as stubbornness and bureaucratic effectiveness, at both jobs, but in each position Weinberger also displayed the preferences and objectives of the organizations he led.

National security scholars like Posen, Van Evera, and Snyder built on the earlier work of organization theorists like Simon, March, Downs, and Cyert to argue that an organization's behavior derives from its pursuit of intrinsic interests.[7] These interests include such factors as autonomy, budget, prestige, and essence (the image that an organization has of itself).[8] I call these interests *basic organizational interests.*

In addition to its basic interests, each organization has an assigned objective. The objectives lay out the goals that an organization's supervisory agency (sometimes called the principal) expects the organization to accomplish. Organizations cannot simply do whatever they want. Instead, they try to make choices that will allow them to pursue their interests within the objectives imposed upon them. Organizations combine their basic interests with their assigned objective to form a mission. Missions provide organizations with operable goals upon which they can direct their efforts. Simon writes: "Most organizations are oriented around some goal or objective which provides the purpose toward which the organization decisions and activities are directed."[9] Missions represent what the organization sees as its purpose.

Organization and security scholars frequently state that organizations pursue their basic interests with a more-is-better approach. But what happens when an organization must make trade-offs between desired interests? We cannot guess how an organization will behave when faced with making a choice between maximizing budget and maintaining its autonomy.[10] Organizations frequently face these choices; a look at recent events at the U.S. Park Service will illustrate the trade-offs that organizations make and demonstrate the risk of assuming that organizations always want more of everything. Traditionally, the Park Service saw its mission as maintaining the major scenic, primarily western American parks.[11] In the 1980s, however, Congress increasingly used the Park Service as a conduit for pork-barrel spending by proposing a variety of largely urban park projects. Such projects as Steamtown, a train museum in Scranton, Pennsylvania, "designed to shore up the struggling downtown of this old coal and railroad center," promised to increase the Park Service budget by millions of dollars.[12] But because these projects threatened to move it away from its mission, the Park Service adamantly opposed them. Park Service officials repeatedly stated that "Steamtown and other such congressionally mandated projects were diverting the agency from its historic mission of preserving and maintaining great national parks like Yosemite and Yellowstone."[13] The Park Service requested 75 million dollars for the fiscal year 1992 budget, and Congress appropriated 200 million. James Ridenour, the Park Service director, defended turning down these funds, saying: "These proposals are great ideas, but they should not all be lodged in the National Park Service. Tourism is not our mission."[14]

The Park Service was not anti-budget. Had the funds been offered toward the maintenance of established western parks, the Service probably would have accepted the money. The Park Service turned down increases in its budget in order to maximize its organizational essence and to focus on its mission. Similar military examples include the U.S. Marines' efforts to halt the purchase of Osprey vertical take-off and landing planes and the U.S. Air Force's 1995 attempt to stop the acquisition of additional B-2 bombers.[15] As of 1995, 4.2 billion dollars had been spent on Osprey, a plane the marines said they did not want; each B-2 bomber, yet another undesired plane, cost approximately a billion dollars.[16] In both cases, the organizations feared that acquisition of the undesired weapons system would endanger other, preferred interests. In particular, the air force feared that the money spent on the B-2 would limit its ability to purchase new Y-22 fighters. Ideally, the air force would have liked to have both planes, but when faced with the choice, they preferred the Y-22. These examples show that organizations do make choices among their interests and do not always hold a more-is-better position. An organization's mission provides an analytical tool that captures how it makes trade-offs between desired interests.[17]

An organization's leaders choose the policy they think is most likely to achieve their organization's mission. During policy implementation, decision makers attempt to evaluate a policy's ability to accomplish its intended mission; they try to see whether their policy is working.

Broadly, decision makers evaluate policies in terms of mission for two general reasons. First, because the mission contains the organization's combined interests and objectives, decision makers believe that a policy that is good for the mission is good for the specific organization and, by inference, good for the larger organizational unit. Militaries view situations that are beneficial for their mission as also being of benefit for their nation. Kimberly Marten Zisk notes: "One factor influencing the calculus of whether or not innovation is a good idea is that military officers tend to see the health of their institution as a determining condition of the health of national security."[18] Thus, for example, if a strategy satisfies an organization's mission requirements, the organization is likely to see it as good for both itself and the nation.

The second reason organizations use their mission to assess policies is that abstract, high-level goals like "do a good job" and "win the war" are too broad to be well suited for either operational goals or oversight standards. Organizing to pursue an objective requires that performance toward that goal be measurable, and this requires clear, operable objectives. "High-level goals provide little guide for action because it is difficult to measure their attainment and difficult to measure the effects of concrete actions upon them."[19] More specific objectives, such as "be at this road by that date" or "earn this percentage of profit," are more easily measured criteria for evaluating success, both for the organizational agent and for its supervisory organization.

The problem of operationalizing high-level goals is not unique to war. The Apollo program's objective, as described in the speech by President John Kennedy, was to land a man on the moon safely and to bring him back afterward. But in practice, "safely" proved to be an amorphous concept, requiring translation into more operational concepts. Apollo chief engineer Glynn Lunney complained that "people would say things like, well the spacecraft's got to be 'good.' But what the hell does 'good' mean?"[20] Abstract, strategic goals are usually difficult to plan organizational activity around without modification into more specific missions.

High-level objectives, such as "win the war," are problematic for another reason. In war, decision makers want to know how well they are doing before the war is over. Victory and defeat by themselves are not useful measures of policy effectiveness. "Victory is an outcome of a battle; it is not what a military organization does in battle. Victory is not a characteristic of an organization but rather a result of organizational activity."[21] Victory might represent the key objective, but in order to make decisions, leaders need mechanisms and measures for evaluating their performance before the war's end.

Even when leaders win a war, they might evaluate their performance as poor. There are cases where a country has clearly defeated another with strategies that the winner later evaluated as poor. In 1941 German airborne forces defeated the British forces on Crete and took possession of the island. Yet John Keegan writes that Crete was "a highly ambiguous victory" and that the German leader of the invasion, General Kurt Student, noted immediately after the battle that Hitler was "most displeased with the whole affair."[22] And after Israel's "victory" in the 1973 Yom Kippur War, the Israeli government created a commission to study why the country had been surprised and why casualties were so high. These examples represent two situations where the winners determined that their strategies failed because victory was more costly than they believed it should have been. Thus, victory alone was not sufficient to guarantee that a strategy was seen as successful.

Within a nation-state, leaders may either share common high-level objectives (as did President George Bush and General Colin Powell during the Gulf War) or hold conflicting views (as did President Harry S Truman and General Douglas MacArthur during the Korean War). But even when leaders hold common high-level goals, they may evaluate themselves by different criteria. Because their missions contain specific, organization-level trade-offs, leaders frequently pursue different missions.[23] When organizations have different missions, they might rely on different types of information to assess individual performance. Graham Allison notes that "governments perceive problems through organizational sensors."[24] Because they look through a different organizational lens, two leaders who hold common high-level goals might reach conflicting evaluations of their nation's performance. Each might be unable to recognize that the other is using different criteria to assess the situation. In these circumstances, different organizational lenses might result in leaders talking past each other.

Scholars have generally examined this problem from two approaches. First, they analyze how principals create institutional incentives to encourage their agents to pursue their objectives. This issue is frequently called the "principal-agent" problem, and its analysis tends to draw heavily on a rational choice perspective (which I discuss later in this chapter). Second, scholars examine how internal constraints affect the organizational decision making process. This is the organization-theory approach, which frequently makes use of bounded rationality.

Bounded Rationality

Many organization theorists and national security scholars have argued that economic approaches to decision making, such as rational choice, fail to explain how organizations operate. "From the point of view of standard decision theory, it seems clear that organizations routinely and habitually make decisions without the kind of preferences that would satisfy the axioms of rational choice."[25] In particular, these scholars believe that decision makers are unable to evaluate all potential actions and thus fail to make optimal decisions; for these authors, the less cognitively demanding notion of bounded rationality better captures actual organizational decision making.

As mentioned above, in a bounded rationality approach, decision makers do not choose their optimal alternative but instead choose a policy that meets a threshold of satisfactory performance. Outcomes are not "best" but "satisfactory." In Simon's terms, decision makers "satisfice" rather than optimize; they choose options that are satisfactory but not necessarily optimal. Organizations thus satisfice because inherent constraints prevent them from optimizing.[26]

The inability to optimize is not a desired trait but the result of such organizational constraints as limited information, intense time pressures, and a limited cognitive capacity. Leaders satisfice because it is necessary, not because it is desirable. "No one in his right mind will satisfice if he can equally well optimize; no one will settle for good or better if he can have best."[27] Satisficing is thus the result of organizational limitations.

Bounded rationality theorists argue that organizations develop aspiration levels. These are utility thresholds (utility is a generic measure of value). When the aspiration level is met, the decision maker is satisficed and stops searching for alternatives. This approach results in two types of policies: those that meet or exceed the threshold and are thus satisfactory, and those that do not. "Any outcome which meets or exceeds the aspiration levels for each of the outcome variables is as good as any other. The person merely has to search through his acts until he finds one that yields one of these satisficing outcomes."[28] Decision makers thus make simple calculations about the expected utility of outcomes.[29] As soon as a choice is reached that meets or exceeds the necessary criteria, the search for new policies stops; even if this should occur before the decision makers have examined all the choices.[30]

Bounded rationality has two critical problems. First, it lacks a concept of "dissatisfaction." Organization theorists tend to focus on the positive aspects of satisficing. For example, bounded rationality works well in describing housing searches. Searches are costly, so people tend to look for a house that is "good enough." Prospective purchasers know that locating the best house might entail too much costly searching. They do not know how much time that search might entail—or even whether their ideal house exists. Therefore, when they discover a house that is acceptable, that meets their aspiration level, they satisfice and take it.[31]

This explanation captures the decision to stop searching for a house, but we would also like to know when a situation is sufficiently negative for a decision maker to want a new house in the first place, a condition I call *dissatisficed.* A dissatisficing situation is categorically the worst and thus is sufficiently negative to guarantee a search for new choices. A bounded rationality model that specifies the conditions under which decision makers are satisficed and dissatisficed is more powerful than one that only predicts when a policy is sufficiently good.

A second problem with traditional bounded rationality approaches involves aspiration levels. Organization theorists determine aspiration levels in two ways. The first is to specify some preset level of performance, an exogenous (externally defined) standard that represents satisfactory utility. This approach is problematic, however, because it is ad hoc and difficult to determine *ex ante.* Although sometimes the likely symbolic importance of an event is clear before its occurrence (the Dow Jones average reaching 10,000, say), frequently the significance of a particular value is unobservable until after the event. Furthermore, even if an event is perceived as likely to be important, the behavior one would expect at the critical value is often unclear. For example, the Dow's reaching 10,000 would seem to justify either a rally or a sell-off. Some may see a rally as probable because it suggests that an important, previously perceived symbolic ceiling was passed; others might expect a sell-off because an important goal was reached, and it is unlikely that a similarly salient mark will be approached in the near future.

In order to make predictions, concepts need to be measurable before the outcome of the decision we are attempting to predict. An *ex post* aspiration level is observable only after an event occurs and is thus not useful for prediction. We frequently do not know how to tell *ex ante* what an organization's utility satisficing threshold will be or how that is determined.[32] Furthermore, we might imagine that decision makers do not have to meet a critical level but just approach it. But how closely does the decision maker have to approach an important value for it to count? Setting a range compounds the problem because the range is also ad hoc or *ex post.*

Another approach organization theorists use to determine aspiration levels is to look at the highest absolute value reached on some measure of utility. Downs noted that for an individual, an aspiration level is "normally the highest level of utility that he has actually experienced in the recent past."[33] Record high levels of utility would satisfice decision makers; anything less is not acceptable. This method is better than choosing a preset level in that it is not ad hoc and it is definable *ex ante.* For example, all other things being equal, we might assume that someone would take a job that offered a higher salary than he or she had ever earned. However, relying on the absolute, record levels of utility has a number of critical problems.

Setting aspiration levels equal to absolute record values also means that as long as you are at that record value (you earn more than you have ever done), you should be content. In the real world this is not always the case. People frequently want to make more money as time goes on—they are not satisfied with making the same salary, even if it represents a record level of earnings for them. In order to avoid this problem Simon and March argued that aspiration levels rise over time: "When the situation is in a 'steady state' over some period of time, aspiration levels do not remain absolutely constant but tend to rise slowly."[34] If you are making the same salary as last year, you will be unhappy, even if it is the highest salary you have ever received. Unfortunately, although a common concept, this again transforms the aspiration level into an ad hoc measure; how do we determine what "some period of time" is or how much growth is enough? This approach raises the problem of ad hoc, preset aspiration levels and thus nullifies the quality that made the record–absolute value approach attractive.

Second, when using the record absolute value as an aspiration level, a decision maker whose strategic goal is to return to the status quo would never be satisfied with his or her progress. For example, if a Kuwaiti leader during the Gulf War had measured his utility by the percentage of Kuwaiti territory controlled by his government, he would never be able to break the previous record level of territorial control (100 percent), and he could only tie that level at the war's end. In this case, the use of record absolute values would not provide any insight into how decision makers assess a changing situation.[35] This type of threshold is thus not useful for assessing progress toward a goal, the key purpose of evaluative criteria. One way to deal with many of these issues is to incorporate the rational choice notion of subjective probability beliefs with an organizational approach.

Rational Choice

As stated earlier, a rational choice approach postulates that actors attempt to maximize their expected utility through the selection of actions that will lead to the best outcomes. Until the late 1960s and early 1970s, rational choice analysts assumed that these choices operated within a certain world. That is, they assumed that decision makers knew the likelihood of all actions with certainty. Such scholars as John Harsanyi and Reinhard Selten moved game-theoretic approaches beyond this constraint by introducing the notion of beliefs.[36] Beliefs are subjective expectations about how either another actor or "nature" is likely to behave. "Nature is a non-player who takes random actions at specified points in the game with specified probabilities."[37] The probability with which nature acts is a function of an underlying structure, some of which might be observable to the decision maker, but much of which is not.

The assessment process operates in a manner that complements these notions. Decision makers recognize that there are two worlds: one where their current strategy will succeed, and one where it fails. Unfortunately, they cannot determine exactly which world they are in. Instead, they must estimate—form beliefs about—future events. If they believe that the likely outcome of their implemented strategy is success, they will dedicate greater resources to it and defend it against critics. If, however, they believe that their implemented strategy will lead to failure, then they alter it and implement a new one. Since decision makers can never be sure which type of world they are operating in, and thus remain uncertain about the outcome of their strategies, their beliefs form a crucial element in their assessments of the efficacy of their strategies. We can thus think of strategic assessment as a process of belief formation, where beliefs represent best estimates about likely outcomes. Decision theory provides a precise way to describe this process.

Imagine a choice where nature moves first and places the decision maker in state "W" or state "L." In state "W" the organization's current policy "A" will lead to a victory. In state "L" the organization's current policy "A" will lead to a loss. The decision maker cannot observe directly the probability "P" that nature uses to determine whether the

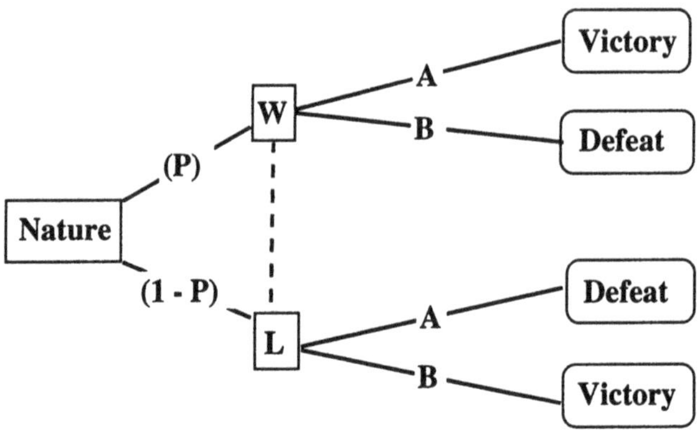

Figure 2.1 The State of Nature Game Tree

Legend
Nature = chance, moves with an unobservable probability distribution
P = true, unobservable probability that the decision maker is at node "W"
(1 − P) = true, unobservable probability that the decision maker is at node "L"
p = belief about the likelihood that the decision maker is at node "W"
(1 − p) = belief about the likelihood that the decision maker is at node "L"
A = current policy
B = alternative policy
Victory = the desired outcome
Defeat = the undesired outcome
Dotted Line = information set

actor is at state "W" or "L." Thus, in order to make a choice, the decision maker must form beliefs, "p," about "P," the probability that nature placed the actor in state "W." This choice is represented in figure 2.1.

In different states of nature, the same action has a different probability of resulting in a particular outcome. Decision makers would like to determine whether they are in state "W" or state "L" as quickly as possible to help them decide whether to remain with policy "A" or to consider innovating with policy "B." The dotted line in figure 2.1 between decision nodes "W" and "L" indicates that this is an information set and that the decision maker is unable to determine which node he or she is in. Decision makers hold exogenous beliefs abut the likelihood of alternative policy "B" leading to victory. They compare that belief with their expectations that implemented policy "A" will lead them to victory.

This decision making approach is general. Victory and defeat have been used to designate the clearly desired and undesired outcomes, but the basic argument applies to many different types of policy assessments, where choices can lead to differently valued outcomes. The model acts as a metaphor, helping us to focus on the key criteria decision makers wish to determine: their belief about the state of nature in which they make choices.

In many rational choice theoretical models, the state of nature has a specified probability. If decision makers know that the state of nature is determined by a coin toss, there is a 50 percent chance they are in state "W" and a 50 percent chance that they are in state "L." Much decision making, however, operates in a world of incomplete information. In a game of incomplete information, at least one decision maker does not know the state he or she is in. Eric Rasmusen notes that "in a game of incomplete information, Nature moves first and is unobserved by at least one of the players."[38] Under these circumstances, actors must form and update beliefs about the likelihood that they are in state "W" or state "L." As James Morrow states, beliefs "summarize a player's judgment about what has probably happened up to that point in the game."[39] Beliefs thus represent players' best efforts to infer from their past experiences information necessary to make decisions about their future. In order to solve a properly defined game, the probability with which nature moves would have to be defined. In applying the game as a metaphor, however, we must recognize that actors operate in an uncertain world where they must estimate the probability regarding their likely state of nature.

Actors update their beliefs about their current state of nature.[40] That is, they incorporate new experiences with old and formulate expectations of what they believe will happen. Early in his administration, President Carter believed that the Soviets were not interested in upsetting the status quo. After the December 1979 Soviet invasion of Afghanistan, he updated his belief of Soviet intentions. This belief included his previous views, as well as the probability that a non-imperialist Soviet Union would invade Afghanistan. As a result of this updating, Carter formed much more critical and skeptical views of Soviet global intentions. Robert Komer describes the updating process Carter went through and Carter's new tough stance, saying that "Carter, although he came in like a lamb, went out like a lion."[41]

Decision theorists and game theorists use Bayes's Rule to represent the updating process. Bayes's Rule requires that decision makers have a *prior belief* about the likelihood of an outcome. They then observe an event, to which they had assigned an expected probability of occurrence, given each potential state. On the basis of this new information, leaders update their view of the world and formulate a *posterior belief* about the likelihood of the outcome happening. More formally, Bayes's Rule applies a mathematical formula that determines the logical posterior belief, given prior beliefs and the conditional probability of an observed occurrence.

Bayes's Rule provides a formula for calculating posterior beliefs. But neither the rule nor most applications of it specify the empirical mechanisms that decision makers use to translate real-world observations into probabilistic beliefs.[42] That is, these types of analyses assume that decision makers have known, fixed probabilities for what they observe. For example, this would mean that Carter knew that if the Soviets were not imperialistic, then the likelihood that they would invade Afghanistan would be x. Given x, and Carter's previous beliefs about the Soviet Union, we could calculate his new belief that the Soviets were imperialistic. This new expectation would be an updated, posterior belief.

How do decision makers transform an observed event, such as a battle won or a primary lost, into beliefs about the likelihood of preferred outcomes? That is, if we do not imagine that decision makers have already formed fixed probability beliefs for all potential events, how do they create a probability derived from their experiences? Beliefs are critical to the formation of policy assessment, which in turn represents a vital element in the decision to innovate or change policies. I estimate decision makers' beliefs with an approach that combines elements from both rational choice and bounded rationality approaches.

Studies by David Kreps, Ken Binmore, and others argue that bounded rationality approaches and rational choice approaches are complementary.[43] Binmore applauds recent efforts to combine the two approaches and argues that the merger of bounded rational and formal approaches would have "many advantages" and represents "an important frontier for the discipline."[44]

Scholars like William Riker and Robert Jackman have argued that rational choice and bounded rationality approaches are "logically indistinguishable."[45] Critical to their perspective is the notion of procedural rationality. "Procedural rationality assumes that the process is consistent. Choice reveals preference because one can infer backwards from an outcome and a consistent process to what the goals must have been to get to that outcome."[46] This approach requires that the analysts posit *ex ante* the process that represents decision makers' behavior. Riker states that the key to bringing rational choice and bounded rationality approaches together is assuming that the choice contains the possible alternatives *as seen by the decision maker* at the time the decisions are made. "This assumption eliminates the unnecessary distinction between strict rationality and bounded rationality."[47]

Returning to figure 2.1, I assume that the search for alternative policies is costly, so decision makers undertake it only when they think they can increase their gain. However, I restrict my analysis to situations where this cost is always less than the difference between outcomes. That is, the difference in utilities between the certain outcomes "Victory" and "Defeat" is always enough to guarantee that the search for an alternative policy is rational. Thus, if decision makers were certain that they were in state "L," where their probability of reaching their preferred outcome "Victory" was zero, then it would always be in their interest to look for another policy. Anything short of a belief of zero means that decision makers would have to calculate the cost of a search and the gain that they expected. If decision makers were certain that they were in the state of nature "W" and that their current policy would lead them to victory, then they would never have an interest in alternative policies. The best they could do by searching for and implementing another policy would be to arrive at the same outcome, "Victory"; but doing so would include some non-zero cost for the search.

From this perspective, satisficing becomes a special case of optimizing in the face of a limited choice set. Or, as Jackman states, "Satisficing . . . is thus merely a shorthand label for optimizing under conditions of limited information and uncertainty."[48] Furthermore, many of the behaviors that appeared "irrational" to bounded rationality proponents may have resulted from the failure to include the factors critical to the actors who actually made the decisions. When specified correctly, some of these decisions may appear rational.[49]

Bounded rationality supporters argue that decision makers often fail to take all actions into account or to think in terms of long-term utility optimizing. Scholars like Riker have argued that a procedural view of rationality that specifies the beliefs and alternatives actually viewed by decision makers can incorporate those concerns into a rational choice perspective.[50]

In this book I examine how the information that decision makers choose influences their beliefs. Like proponents of bounded rationality, I assume that decision makers' choices and perceptive abilities are limited. But, like rational choice theorists, I argue that within these constraints (which we can explicitly specify), decision makers attempt to optimize their expected utility. In particular, decision makers form and update beliefs about their policies' chances of meeting their objectives. This method, which I call the dominant indicator approach, incorporates the "flavor" of organization theory in a procedural rationality model. The dominant indicator approach is compatible with both bounded rationality and rational choice approaches, and I employ terms from both methods in presenting it.

THE DOMINANT INDICATOR APPROACH

The proposition that organizations evaluate their performance might seem innocuous. However, scholars like Posen, Wildavsky, and Van Evera argue that organizations are indifferent to assessments. "Evaluation and organization, it turns out, are to some extent contradictory terms."[51] Some scholars go so far as to argue that organizations purposely structure themselves so as to preclude self-evaluation. They "auto-lobotomize."[52]

I argue that an organization's leadership continually evaluates performance in order to alter its behavior and maximize its likelihood of accomplishing its mission. Whether we identify this behavior as learning, Bayesian updating, cybernetics, or feedback, organizations assess and sometimes alter policies and resource distributions on the basis of their experiences. Put simply, organizations "keep tabs on their own performance."[53]

In order to assess their performance, organizations need to analyze information generated by their behavior. They may rely on a variety of different types of information to help them formulate beliefs about the likely outcomes of their implemented policies. Among the types of information they employ are quantitative indicators.

Indicators are quantitative, time-specific measures of complex information, and they are employed by a variety of organizations to assess policy performance. "Even a cursory examination of other historical examples suggests that a tendency toward the use of indicators is widespread across time and in different countries."[54] In making all types of choices, decision makers frequently rely on indicators. "People typically make predictions about the behavior of the economy and the behavior of individuals based upon a limited number of easily observable characteristics. We say that such a prediction is based upon an *indicator.*"[55] Indicators represent cognitive shortcuts employed by actors in the face of an overwhelmingly complex reality.[56]

Modern warfare generates many types of indicators, and decision makers usually rely on some of these to assess their performance. Naval leaders concerned with the effectiveness of a blockade might look at how many ships they were able to sink. They do not assume that each ship is equivalent, since some ships carry supplies that are more important than others. But as a general measure of the success or failure of a blockade strategy, the number of ships sunk represents a reasonable, useful measure of blockade effectiveness. This is especially true given that they cannot observe effectively the number of ships that make it through the blockade and reach enemy ports. But they do know that, all other things being equal, as the number of enemy ships sunk increases, their adversary is obtaining fewer supplies. This example closely resembles how the U.S. Navy operated in World War II. It measured the success of its blockade on Japan by the number of Japanese ships sunk. "Submarine skippers were simply told to sink ships, any kind of ships, or they would be relieved of command."[57] Ships sunk provided a measure of policy success, although an exact estimate of what supplies were destroyed was impossible to obtain. The number of ships sunk thus represented a quantitative measure of success—an indicator.

It is important to distinguish between quantitative goals, which are static, numerical descriptions of objectives, and indicators, which are variable measures of performance. For example, the Germans believed in World War I that if they sank about 600,000 tons of British shipping per month, they would win the war.[58] Similarly, during the Cold War, Secretary of Defense Robert McNamara identified the minimum amount of damage the United States needed to inflict on the Soviet Union for "assured destruction" as destruction of 30 percent of its population and 60 percent of its industrial capacity.[59] In each case, leaders defined objectives quantitatively. These numerical objectives may play a role in measuring success, but they are not themselves variable measures of policy performance. They are numerical specifications of what actors are striving for, not measures of how well actors are doing in getting there.

I identify the indicators that leaders rely on for evaluating their strategies as *dominant indicators* that together form an organization's *dominant indicator set.* Dominant indicators are the indicators decision makers consistently rely on when making decisions. They are dominant in the sense that they represent the most important quantitative data used by the group and, I believe, embody the primary forces that structure an organization's strategic assessment. As Aaron Friedberg writes: *"The indicators [make] discussion possible while simultaneously distorting and ultimately dominating it."*[60]

Dominant indicators represent an organization's central measure of performance. "Sinking enemy ships, seizing key ports, and establishing patrolled areas that friendly unarmed ships can safely use are linked to winning control of sea lines of communication. These relationships define measures that determine whether the military organization is performing the way it is supposed to perform."[61] Together, all the dominant indicators relied on by an actor form the dominant indicator set. This is the set of critical indicators that decision makers rely on when assessing policy performance.

War provides decision makers with a large array of potential indicators. Since a mission incorporates an organization's interests as well as its objectives, decision makers choose indicators that they expect to measure their policies' likelihood of achieving a mission. If an organization's interests were included in its mission, and decision makers ignored the assessment suggested by their indicators because they preferred another, previously chosen policy, then these decision makers would not be pursuing their organizational interests. Similarly, if a decision maker chose other indicators because they better justified a particular policy, he or she would not be attempting to pursue his or her interests as captured by the original indicators. It is thus in the decision maker's interest to choose indicators he or she thinks will measure how well the organization is achieving its mission and to use the information provided by these indicators to formulate his or her beliefs.

Leaders choose indicators that they expect to suggest that their implemented policy is successful. They thus react strongly when their chosen indicators show that their policy is performing badly. This view is similar to the one held by Randall Calvert, who gave an example in which it made more sense for leaders to rely on experts who shared their initial views toward a policy than on advisers who were either neutral or biased against them. He stated that "a decision maker with a strong predisposition toward one alternative might not benefit at all from having advice from an unbiased source, since regardless of its content that advice could not cause her to change her mind."[62] Calvert suggested that in some situations it was in an organization's interest to rely on assessment sources that leaders believed, *ex ante,* favored the organization's position. His logic was that if a favorably biased source suggested trouble, then the leaders were more likely to believe that their situation was grim than if they believed that the sources were biased against them or even neutral.[63]

If leaders choose indicators based on their organizations' missions, different types of organizations, such as military versus civilian, may rely on different indicators to assess their performance.[64] Even if the various leaders draw from the same general pool of information, they are likely to rely on different types of data for evaluating their policy's effectiveness. That is, leaders are drawing from an overwhelming amount of information on the basis of their specific organizational mission. Different organizations have different missions and may choose different information sources. During policy implementation, those sources may suggest fundamentally different beliefs about the likely success of the organization's policies. Because the organization sees the health of the larger unit, such as the nation, in terms of the success of its own policies, organizations are capable of drawing significantly different conclusions about their general likelihood of success.

Anthony Downs states that the "specialization of tasks common to every large organization inevitably leads to specialization of information, so that every official (or set of officials performing the same task) possesses a different 'bundle' of information from every other official. Therefore, even if all officials had identical goals and identical modes of perception, they might arrive at divergent conclusions about what the organization ought to do."[65] Thus, organizations that share common high-level goals might see fundamentally different operational situations. When discussing the success of their nation's policies, these actors might be talking past each other—failing to recognize that they base their assessments on different types of information that is providing conflicting assessments.

Critical to this approach is the assumption that decision makers hold onto their set of dominant indicators more tightly than they do their individual policy preferences. In order to pursue their organizational interests, decision makers must maintain either their means of evaluation or their policy as a constant. Otherwise, they are unable to determine what is in their self-interest. "The behavior of both individuals and organizations changes constantly. However, during any given period when some elements are changing, others must remain stable, or there will be a loss of identity."[66] Because the mission contains the organization's trade-offs between organizational interests and objectives, indicators represent the status not just of the implemented policy but of the organization. If neither the objective assigned to the organization nor the trade-offs between organizational interests changes sufficiently to change the mission, organizations will retain the measures they use to assess success.

Scholars like Friedberg and Robert Jervis argue that empirically decision makers employ few variables when making decisions.[67] I assume only that the collection and acquisition of information is costly, so that dominant indicator sets are finite (because actors have scarce resources). Another limit on the size of dominant indicator sets results from decision makers' efforts to deal with the problem of noise.

Noise, Time, and Uncertainty

Indicators are time-specific measures (such as ships sunk per month). Empirically, an organization's choice of a time frame is frequently easy to determine. James March and Johan Olsen write that in "many human situations the most easily identified property of objects or events is the time subscripts associated with them."[68] This easily observed condition, however, represents a complex set of organizational expectations.

Decision makers choose an indicator's time domain in order to deal with the problem of noise. Noise represents fluctuations that are not a systematic result of the policy's performance. They might be a result of randomness, instrument unreliability, or measurement error. For example, in the rapidly changing, highly ambiguous environment of war, "it is often impossible to distinguish between signals and noise."[69] In order to separate noise from signals and capture a broader sense of change, organizations attempt to create systems that are insensitive to small, apparently random changes. The time domain determines how long decision makers will collect information in order to separate the systematic elements of the message from the stochastic. An indicator's time period thus represents an organization's best estimate of the anticipated noise problem.

Organizations not only need certainty, they need action, the time frame in which an evaluation can have a beneficial effect. As was the case of the Kuwaiti emir discussed in Chapter 1, if the decision makers wait too long, the knowledge gained might come too late and be of no use.

Organizations trade certainty for time on the basis of both their needs and their anticipation of the signal-to-noise ratios inherent in their data. This puts them in a paradoxical situation. On one hand, the longer the time period over which decision makers collect information, the more certain they are of their assessment. But on the other hand, the shorter the time period assessed, the more useful the evaluation is likely to be. Arthur Stinchcombe stated that the "basic device for reducing random error is to take a mean (or a median or percentage); the larger the number of observations over which the mean is taken, the smaller the residual random noise. . . . The dilemma is to produce the most recent mean possible, compatible with its being sufficiently noise free to indicate what is happening."[70]

Indicators are time-specific measures. The indicator's time domain reflects decision makers' trade-off between their need for timely assessments and their expectations of the likely signal-to-noise ratios in their data. Since indicators contain intrinsic time domains, we want to understand some of the factors that influence decision makers' choice of time period.

Let me briefly summarize the argument so far. Organizations are interested in pursuing missions, which contain their organizational interests (such as budget, autonomy, and prestige) as well as their assigned objectives. To pursue these missions, they choose policies. They select information with which to assess their policy's performance. Among the types of information are indicators: quantitative indices

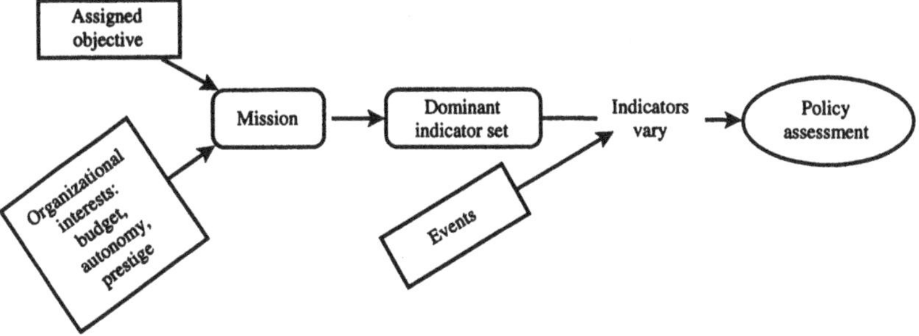

Figure 2.2 The Dominant Indicator Approach

with an intrinsic time base, such as the enemy killed per month. Indicators critical to leaders' decisions are dominant indicators. A dominant indicator's time frame represents a trade-off between decision makers' need for certainty, which is a function of noise, and action.

I argue that decision makers' dominant indicators provide a mechanism for observing how their experiences influence their policy assessments. Events, such as wartime experiences, make the indicators vary. The indicators act as a gauge, measuring the success of implemented policies. As the dominant indicators' values change, so do decision makers' beliefs about the likely outcomes of their policies. When their beliefs change, decision makers alter their assessments of their policies' performance. The complete dominant indicator theoretical framework is presented in figure 2.2.

The indicator-based theory provides an approach for capturing the effect of environmental factors on decision makers' assessments. It is not enough to state that by simply looking at an organization's dominant indicators, we can predict decision makers' assessments. We need to determine what type of indicator movement translates into specific policy assessments. I argue that a sudden and rapid change in indicators profoundly influences decision makers' policy evaluations. Thus, the key is dramatic indicator change.

Change and Policy Assessment

Decision makers react to sudden changes in their environment. A number of security studies and organization-theory scholars have argued that dramatic environmental shifts lead to fundamental changes in beliefs. Posen writes: "Intervention may stem from a recent disaster, or some sudden change in the perceived costs of war."[71] March argues that "if the environment changes rapidly, so will the responses of stable organizations; change driven by such shifts will be dramatic if shifts in the environment are large."[72] A 1993 analysis of international relations stated that "it is the *speed* of change that may create the condition wherein decision-makers might be expected to react in precipitous manner."[73] Common to these arguments is the notion that rapid changes have a profound effect on decision makers.

We can capture sudden and dramatic environmental change by analyzing the movement of an actor's dominant indicators with a mathematical function. Although a mathematical measure of the rate of change of indicators might capture the effects of actors' experiences on their policy assessments, the mathematical model itself is not likely to represent the exact process the actors use. This does not mean, however, that actors do not recognize the influence of rates of change on their decisions. As we shall observe in the empirical analysis in later chapters, actors frequently point to the rate of change as suggesting that strategies are succeeding or failing. When discussing the degradation of a small Pacific island's culture, Angel Cabeza, director of cultural affairs at the National Forest Service in Santiago, Chile, stated that "what is being discussed is not change, but the velocity of change."[74]

If decision makers react strongly to rapid change, the next step is to link changes in their environment to specific strategic assessments. In particular, it is critical to determine the type of change necessary for decision makers to be dissatisficed and satisficed. For this analysis, decision makers are dissatisficed when they perceive that the situation is out of control and becoming worse at an increasing rate.[75] When decision makers are satisficed, they perceive that the situation is going well and getting better at an increasing rate. Note that these definitions are different from those used in most bounded rationality approaches. Instead of determining the aspiration levels that satisfy decision makers, I am attempting to identify the conditions in which we should expect to observe or not to observe change in assessments. Thus, for me, dissatisficed translates into "extremely high probability of observing change," while satisficed means "extremely low chance of observing change." I can thus make these notions more applicable to both rational choice theories and empirical analysis.

It is necessary to create a system that translates an indicator's movement into decision makers' beliefs. While some scholars, such as Charles Doran and Wes Parsons, A. F. K. Organski and Jacek Kugler, and James Schampel, have looked at the velocity with which structural variables change, I do not think that velocity by itself captures the serious conditions necessary for satisficing and dissatisficing.[76] In particular, given noise, decision makers know that indicators will rise and fall (leading to changes in velocity). Actors will ignore this fluctuation, associating it with the anticipated noise. Dramatic change for the worse will capture their attention precisely because it is unlikely that such changes would occur if the strategy were working. I believe that in order to capture this perception of dramatic change, we need to examine the acceleration and change in acceleration with which an indicator moves.

When the situation is accelerating in a desired direction, and the rate of acceleration itself is increasing, actors will perceive this as ideal. Everything is going well at an increasing pace. When the situation is accelerating in an undesired direction and the rate at which it is moving is also increasing, actors will see this as the worst situation possible. This situation is out of control, deteriorating at an increasing rate. Acceleration and changes in acceleration of indicators thus influence actors' beliefs of satisfaction and dissatisfaction.

Indicators can increase or decrease. The relation between the direction of change and substantive interpretations of the situation depends on whether an organization is trying to *maximize* or *minimize* its indicator. An air force might attempt to maximize the number of enemy planes destroyed. In this case, the mathematical and substantive interpretations are positively correlated so that an increase in the indicator is good for the organization. Conversely, an organization might attempt to minimize the number of its own planes lost. In this case, because the mathematical and substantive relation is negatively correlated, a positive increase in the indicator is bad for the organization. For heuristic purposes, in this discussion I assume that actors are trying to maximize indicators and that an increase in an organization's dominant indicator suggests that the policy is performing successfully (the approach applies equally to actors who attempt to minimize their indicators).

Indicators can change at an increasing or decreasing rate. The situation might become progressively better or progressively worse, depending on both the desired direction of the indicator and the actual change. Thus we can discuss the rate of change and the rate at which the rate of change itself alters. Because the indicator is a time-specific unit (ships sunk per month, say), it is itself a measure of velocity. Thus, the rate at which an indicator changes is acceleration, and the rate at which that change itself alters is the change in acceleration of the indicator. Indicators can accelerate in a positive or negative direction or not change at all; similarly, the rate of acceleration can increase, decrease, or remain constant (as in the case of gravity). Combining both the acceleration and rate of change in acceleration of an indicator results in nine possible conditions, shown in table 2.1.

Decision makers always prefer a policy that is going well to one that is going poorly and a policy that is getting better at an increasing rate to a one that is getting better at a decreasing rate.[77] Conversely, leaders always prefer a policy that is going poorly to deteriorate at a decreasing rate rather than at an increasing rate. Expanding this notion to all nine possible conditions, we can create an ordinal ranking of the assessments as determined from the acceleration and change in acceleration of an indicator. This ranking is shown in table 2.2.

Two of the probabilities deserve special attention. In the long run, a situation that is going poorly but getting worse at a decreasing rate (P^3) might lead to a better situation than one that is going well but improving at a decreasing rate (P^7). In the short term, however, the situation described by P^7 is superior to that of P^3. If monthly profit is up 10 percent but had previously increased by 20 percent, this might suggest a slowdown that will lead not just to decreased profits but to

Table 2.1 Indicator Movement and Substantive Interpretations

Acceleration		*Change in Acceleration*	
Direction	Interpretation	Direction	Interpretation
+	Performing well	+	Getting better at an increasing rate
+	Performing well	o	Not changing
+	Performing well	—	Getting better at a decreasing rate
o	No change	+	Getting better at an increasing rate
o	No change	o	Not changing
o	No change	—	Getting worse at an increasing rate
—	Performing poorly	+	Getting worse at a decreasing rate
—	Performing poorly	o	Not changing
—	Performing poorly	—	Getting worse at an increasing rate

loss. But a situation where a loss increases by 10 percent but had previously increased by 20 percent might suggest that in the long run the company will make a profit. Leaders generally think in terms of short time spans, and organizations prefer making a profit at a decreasing rate now to incurring a loss at a decreasing rate. Thus, I hypothesize that decision makers focus on short- rather than long-term gains and evaluate P^7 as superior to P^3. Research by Cyert and March supports this view, showing that decision makers tend to rely on short-term data when assessing situations.[78] Another way to think about this is to say that decision makers recognize the unreliability of long-range extrapolation and tend to focus on short-term criteria for evaluation.

Ideally, decision makers who want to maximize their indicator would prefer the greatest rate of change attainable. But given that they are unsure of the maximum potential rate of change, I argue that the best that decision makers can expect is to experience record rates of change as measured by their dominant indicators. The use of record rates is consistent with the general theoretical thrust of the classical work on organizational satisficing. As discussed, Simon and March have developed bounded rationality models that rely on record absolute values to determine aspiration levels, and there is no reason that

Table 2.2 Indicator Movement and the Probability of Success

Acceleration	Change in Acceleration	Ordinal Probability of Success
Performing well	Getting better at an increasing rate	$9 = P_9$
Performing well	Not changing	$8 = P_8$
Performing well	Getting better at a decreasing rate	$7 = P_7$
No change	Getting better at an increasing rate	$6 = P_6$
No change	Not changing	$5 = P_5$
No change	Getting worse at an increasing rate	$4 = P_4$
Performing poorly	Getting worse at a decreasing rate	$3 = P_3$
Performing poorly	Not changing	$2 = P_2$
Performing poorly	Getting worse at an increasing rate	$1 = P_1$

we cannot substitute record rates of change. Movement of an indicator in a negative direction that sets records in both acceleration and change of acceleration represents a dramatic change for the worse and is a strong signal that the current strategy is not working. Random noise is unlikely to produce such a dramatic change. Thus, these conditions are reliable signs that the situation is out of control; it is going poorly and deteriorating at an increasing rate.

If an indicator suggests that the policy is performing well and getting better at record rates, then I believe that the actor will be completely satisfied with that policy, that is, satisficed. Conversely, if the indicator suggests that the policy is performing poorly and deteriorating at unprecedented rates, then the decision maker will be sufficiently dissatisfied to search for an alternative policy—dissatisficed. In a rational choice perspective, I am arguing that decision makers' subjective probability beliefs about being at state "W" approach one when their indicators suggest that a policy is improving at an increasing record rate, and zero when their indicators suggest that the policy is decreasing at an increasing record rate. A successful strategy is much less likely to produce record poor performance and record deterioration in performance than is an unsuccessful strategy. Information that separates the plausible hypotheses leads actors to update their beliefs.

Bounded rationality and rational choice approaches provide complementary notions of evaluation. I use concepts from both approaches to develop a theoretical model of policy evaluation. This theoretical approach to predicting and understanding policy assessment results in three basic hypotheses.

First, I hypothesize that decision makers will be satisfied with their policies, and not search for alternative ones, when they experience record rates of positive change in their dominant indicator.

H1 If one dominant indicator suggests that a policy is performing well and getting better at record rates, and no other indicator in the dominant indicator set suggests that the policy is performing poorly and deteriorating at record rates, then the current policy is satisfactory to decision makers (it satisfices), and they will fight to maintain it.

Record rates of change are thus a sufficient condition for satisficing. Because the policy is as good as it can be, there is no need to look for alternative policies. We can also think of this in terms of optimizing. Given the limits on the choice set and the cost of acquiring additional information, when an actor's indicator suggests that the situation is accelerating in a desired direction and that the rate itself is increasing, the actor is likely to decide that she is in a state of the world where the implemented policy will lead to a desired outcome. Thus she will have a positive assessment of the policy and be uninterested in spending scarce resources to search for alternative policies, which could at best only equal this performance.

Conversely, we also know that the least desirable category is the one in which a policy is going poorly and getting rapidly worse. Thus, an organization will be dissatisficed with a policy that reaches new record rates of this least desired category. This leads to the second hypothesis.

H2 Decision makers will be dissatisficed with the situation and search for an alternative policy if one indicator suggests that a policy is going poorly and getting worse at record rates, and no indicator suggests that the policy is performing well and getting better at record rates.

When a decision maker is dissatisficed, the organization will search for an alternative policy. In other words, the decision maker is likely to decide that he is in a state of nature where his current policy's probability of reaching a favorable outcome approaches zero and that it is worth expending resources to search for alternative policies.

Indicators in a dominant indicator set can move in any direction and at varied rates. Thus, it is possible for at least one indicator to suggest that a strategy is performing at its best while another indicator is suggesting that the policy is performing at its worst. I hypothesize that this situation leads to organizational chaos and gridlock; where the organization is too conflicted to reach a consensual preference about the policy's performance.

H3 If at least one indicator in a multiple indicator set suggests that a policy is performing poorly and getting worse at record rates, and another suggests that the policy is performing well and getting better at record rates, then the organization will become gridlocked.

In this situation, the dominant indicator set captures the conflict between the primary forces within the organization. At this time the organization becomes internally conflicted, and I would expect to observe a great deal of bureaucratic infighting and personnel change.

Three aspects of these hypotheses deserve additional attention. First, the indicators are not weighted. Although organizations may emphasize and discount information, the dominant indicators must be highly salient factors in leaders' assessments. If they are not, then the theory is wrong. Jervis states that empirically actors rarely weight variables.[79] If there is an actor-defined, *ex ante* weight for the indicators, such as an index or ratio, then the index or ratio is itself a dominant indicator.[80]

Second, I argue that if the other indicators are not setting record levels of change, a single indicator might be sufficient to change an organization's assessment. Thus, a clear signal that a policy is performing excellently or horribly dominates an organization's assessment process as long as the other indicators all suggest more moderate situations. However, differing indicators play a critical role when one indicator suggests that the policy performs as well as possible and the other suggests that it is performing as poorly as possible (H3). Under this condition, the assessment process breaks down and the organization is unable to make an evaluation. Finally, I specify the procedure for determining the rates of indicator change in a technical note at the end of this chapter. In addition to the dominant indicator model, I look at a standard bounded rationality approach and the argument that policy change by one actor leads to policy change by another.[81]

EMPIRICAL ANALYSIS

I compare the dominant indicator approach with two alternatives, the standard organization model—which I call the absolute-value model—and the action-reaction model: the argument that actors respond to changes by their adversary.

The absolute-value model states that when indicators set absolute records, decision makers are satisficed, and when records are not set, they are dissatisficed. The absolute-value model closely resembles the organization model proposed by Simon, March, and Downs. This model incorporates the standard organization approach with an indicator-based type of argument and contains two hypotheses.

H4 When a dominant indicator sets a record absolute value in the desired direction, decision makers will see this as satisfactory performance and will want to maintain their policy.

H5 When a dominant indicator establishes a record absolute value in the undesired direction, decision makers will not be satisfied with their performance and want to change policies.

This approach is similar to the dominant indicator approach except that it uses the absolute (original) value of the indicator (for example, planes shot down per month) instead of acceleration or change in acceleration. The critical difference is the value of the indicator necessary for complete satisfaction or dissatisfaction.

A variant of the absolute-value model that is closer to Simon's approach, but less appropriate for analysis here, would be to say that decision makers are satisficed when their criteria set record values and dissatisficed at all other times. Since this model specifies only when decision makers are not satisficed and does not include a concept like dissatisficed, it would not be possible to apply it to predictions of gridlock. In addition, since there are comparatively few observable strategic assessments, an approach such as this, which made a prediction for each unit of analysis, would yield a large number of false predictions. This is the opposite of the action-reaction approach.

The action-reaction approach represents the simplest hypothesis: that decision makers assess their current strategy as unsatisfactory after an adversary changes its own strategy.

H6 A change in one country's strategy leads its opponent to become dissatisfied with its own current strategy.

This hypothesis simply states that adversaries react to each other. This hypothesis is similar to arguments made by Zisk and others and is complementary with the spiral model developed by Jervis.[82]

Each of the three models employed argues that organizations respond to environmental change. These alternative models disagree about the specific nature of that change, but each argues that particular types of information will lead decision makers to alter their policy assessments. The Cult of the Offensive argument claims that militaries never alter their assessments on the basis of environmental factors. It claims that the dependent variable, strategic assessment, should not vary for militaries (the argument does not present a consistent rationale for when it should vary for civilians). Thus, it is unreasonable to conceive of this argument as an alternative explanation for organizational policy assessments.

The dominant indicator, standard organizational, and action-reaction approaches specify the conditions required for particular policy evaluations. An empirical test should determine three things: how well the model predicts preferences, when we observe preference shifts, and when we observe that there has been no assessment change. The dependent variable in this analysis is the policy assessment. It is not policy change. Strategic shifts result from complex processes involving organizational politics, power, and preferences. In order to determine what the organizational preferences are likely to be (keep the strategy, dump the strategy) we need to create a model of how organizations assess their implemented strategies. These preferences can then be combined in a bureaucratic model of politics, such as that employed by Bruce Bueno de Mesquita, David Newman, and Alvin Rabushka to predict strategy shifts.[83] The proposed approach is thus complementary with bureaucratic models that attempt to predict policy changes but not a substitute for them.[84]

Both the proposed and alternative explanations attempt to predict when decision makers will be satisficed with a situation. Organizations tend to express their discontent more visibly than their satisfaction. Unless another actor challenges the current policy, satisficed decision makers rarely express their preferences. Ideally, a test would incorporate a continual, observable indicator of policy assessment. Because such an indicator is unavailable, research is necessary to determine organizations' evaluations. The ability to determine an organization's assessment may be tied to how adamantly it states its position. Again, organizations tend to express their unhappiness more visibly than their contentment, so historical analyses are more likely to reveal dissatisfaction than satisfaction.

The indicator-based approach includes actual decision making behavior and a representative model of preference formation. I determine the decision makers' mission and dominant indicator set from official records and other primary sources, memoirs, official histories, and secondary literature. This approach also allows me to look at nonevents. When I predict that decision makers will be satisficed and not want to change their policy preferences, I do not expect to observe policy preference changes. Similarly, when I predict that an organization is dissatisficed, I would expect to observe signs of its unhappiness with the implemented policy. By looking at the correlation of indicator behavior and performance evaluation, I can test how accurately this model predicts both events and nonevents. One of the reasons that looking at nonevents is so difficult is that histories and sources tend to be connected to specific events. This approach provides a more effective way of analyzing wartime behavior than the traditional security studies models, which tend to focus only on change.

It is important to determine not only the dominant indicator set that each organization uses to evaluate a strategic policy but also the organization's interpretation of the indicator's direction. Occasionally, as we saw earlier, an intuitive assumption about whether an organization wants to minimize or maximize an indicator is wrong.

Ideally, we wish to use the indicators and data that decision makers employed at the time they were forming expectations about the likelihood of certain consequences of their strategies. Although the *ex post,* historical figures may be the most accurate representation of what actually happened, they are not the best indicators for constructing decision makers' *ex ante* expectations. The "wrong" figures that leaders relied upon better represent the factors that influenced them than the "corrected" numbers later determined by historians. In addition to using the figures decision makers employed, we need to break the data down into the time periods that they relied on at the time they made decisions.

As mentioned earlier, decision makers choose the indicators that they believe will best reflect a policy's performance in pursuing their missions. These beliefs form the starting point from which they evaluate their implemented policies, and are exogenous to my approach. "Policy analysis always begins somewhere, not *ab nihilo* as when God created the world. . . . [Decision makers] seek to improve their idea of present conditions, policies, and objectives by obtaining more information about them."[85] If indicators are unimportant, then the selection of indicators is inconsequential. If, on the other hand, indicators determine strategic preferences in the ways I argue, then indicators play an important role in wartime decision making. It is only by establishing that indicators are important that one can begin to find the selection of dominant indicators valuable.

TECHNICAL NOTE

Changes in indicator acceleration and the rate of acceleration are represented by the second and third differences, using a technique similar to the discontinuous derivative procedure recently employed in a number of political science analyses.[86] Because the indicators themselves are time-specific measures, they already capture the velocity of indicator change; they are represented by y'.[87] For example, y' could be the number of sorties per week. The cumulation of y' would equal y, that is, the total number of sorties.

In order to calculate the *acceleration*, y'', I subtract the value y' at time$_t$ from the value at time$_{t-1}$ ($y'_t - y'_{t-1}$). I calculate *changes in acceleration*, y''', by subtracting y''_t from y''_{t-1}.

For example, if we are examining the number of planes shot down, the cumulative total of the planes shot down by time$_t$ would equal y_t, the number of planes shot down in a month would represent y'_t, the difference between the value at month$_t$ and the previous month would be y''_t (the acceleration), and the variation between the acceleration for month$_t$ and the previous month would be y'''. If the numbers of planes shot down over three months were {2, 4, 7}, and the first month was time$_t$, then y''_{t+1} is $4 - 2 = 2$, y''_{t+2} is $7 - 4 = 3$, and y'''_{t+2} would be $3 - 2 = 1$ (we would be unable to calculate values y'''_{t+1}, y'''_t, or y''_t because of insufficient observations).

In both the dominant indicator and standard organization models, record values, whether of rates or absolute, must be greater than all previous values. A tie means that the observed value has previously occurred and neither model would predict satisficing behavior. Because I argue that decision makers deal with noise by aggregating information and that we can observe their *ex ante* expectations of the noisiness of a situation by observing the time periods they choose for their indicators, I make no ad hoc corrections for noise.

It takes two observations of a time-based indicator value to measure acceleration and three to measure changes in the rate of acceleration. A record is the highest positive or lowest negative value following the initial positive or initial negative figure. Thus, the earliest a record change in the rate of acceleration can occur is in the fourth observation.

Chapter 3

British Antisubmarine Decision Making in World War I

Convoy was as old as organized naval warfare.

—John Keegan, *The Price of Admiralty*

The major naval threat to Great Britain in both world wars resulted from German U-boat attacks on British and Allied merchant ships. The U-boat attacks killed merchant marines and destroyed food, raw materials, and vital war supplies and damaged or sank the ships. During World War I, a serious debate developed in Great Britain between military and civilian leaders over how to respond to the U-boat threat.

Both civilian and naval decision makers viewed two main strategies as potential responses to the U-boat problem: convoy and sea patrol.[1] In a convoy strategy, naval escorts accompany merchant ships in order to protect them from enemy attack. With a sea patrol strategy, the navy attempts to protect merchant ships by clearing ocean sea lanes through regular patrols. The key British debate concerned whether and when to change strategies from sea patrol to convoy.

Most scholars view the British shift to a convoy strategy as the most important naval decision of the war. For example, Paul Kennedy writes that no "individual advances in design and equipment were as important in defeating the U-boats as the operational decision to adopt the convoy system."[2] Actors involved in the decision at the time, like Prime Minister David Lloyd George, saw Britain's response to the U-boat threat as critical to the entire Allied war effort.[3]

Although there is a consensus on actions that took place in the decision to switch to a convoy strategy, there has been little analysis of why the debate occurred at all or, given the debate, why strategic change occurred in April 1917. The standard story of British antisubmarine warfare in World War I is straightforward and supports the views of civil-military relations held by such scholars as Posen, Snyder, and Van Evera. A detailed analysis, however, suggests that the situation was more complex than the standard story maintains and that the dominant indicator approach predicts the timing of changes in civilian and military preferences better than other decision models. Evidence further suggests that when evaluating quantitative data, British decision makers focused on rates of change rather than on record absolute values. Thus, the World War I antisubmarine case not only supports the model's predictions, but the behavior observed seems similar to the process described.

THE GERMAN STRATEGY

Before the outbreak of World War I, neither the Germans nor the British expected that German U-boats would attack merchant ships. German naval thinking and resources before the war had focused on their dreadnoughts—enormous battleships with far-reaching guns. German naval command was interested in challenging British control of the seas, and there was general agreement both in and outside Germany that a large fleet of dreadnoughts was necessary to sink an adversary's fleet. The purpose of the U-boats was to help support the dreadnought fleets.

Knowing that they could never gain dominance over the British navy, the Germans attempted to create a "risk fleet." This fleet was supposed to be sufficiently powerful to deter the British fleet by threatening to sink enough ships in a climactic naval battle (which the Germans could lose) that a third fleet (like the Americans) would be capable of challenging British naval superiority. The British would fear losing a potential second naval battle with their weakened fleet and would be unwilling to risk their global naval dominance and thus would not risk an encounter with the Germans.

Once the war started, however, the complex logic of the risk fleet proved illusory, and the superior British fleet quickly immobilized the

German fleet. The so-called risk fleet thus worked in reverse. "The Germans' naval effort and expenditure had been largely concentrated on building battleships for a battle that they would not risk."[4] Other German naval efforts—using fast surface ships to raid British merchant vessels and cruisers to inflict damage on Great Britain's colonies—also failed.[5]

Before the war both British and German doctrine called for submarines to support the fleet. With one notable exception, no German or British military or political leader anticipated using U-boats as commerce raiders. "The use of the submarine in this way had not been foreseen by any major naval figure except Admiral Fisher, and he had failed to convince British politicians that he was right. It was thought that no civilized power would risk the obloquy from the deaths of passengers and crews that would ensue. German naval opinion itself had not seriously considered the option before the war."[6]

In the fall of 1914, however, the German surface vessels were largely immobilized by the British blockade. As an experiment, a few U-boats were ordered to attack British naval ships. This proved to be successful; the Germans sank a number of ships, including three old cruisers off the coast of Holland and the super-dreadnought *Audacious.*

These results were revolutionary. Sir Julian Corbett, the official naval historian of the war, noted that "nothing that had yet occurred had so emphatically proclaimed the change that had come over naval warfare."[7] Both the Germans and British responded quickly.

As the rate at which the Germans sank British naval ships increased, the British navy altered its strategy. British naval ships began to travel in large groups and were stationed at Scapa Flow and other remote Scottish ports, far from the U-boats' limited range. Although this change in strategy came too quickly to be suitable for the dominant indicator approach, it does show that the British were capable of adapting and altering their strategies. This is also the only time that the admirals clearly acted because of their concern about losing their own ships, perhaps because this loss affected their ability to impose the blockade on Germany, as well as to fight the U-boats. This situation also captures the interactive nature of strategy. Because the British successfully placed their naval ships out of easy reach of the U-boats, if the Germans wanted to continue to use U-boats to sink British ships they would have to find new, closer, and less protected targets. Merchant ships, whose routes put them within easier reach of the U-boats, seemed ideal targets; they traveled alone, sailed close to German-controlled ports, and lacked weapons to defend themselves.

Following the events of autumn 1914, the Germans not only used U-boats to attack merchant ships but largely reoriented the focus of the navy. Germany rapidly built up its U-boat resources. "The Germans started the war with 18 submarines (most of which operated on paraffin), and finished with 344 oil burning U-boats, with an additional 226 under construction and 212 planned."[8] Success also affected the desirability of U-boat commands. Serving on a U-boat, which had previously been detrimental to a naval officer's career, became the best way to advance. Surface vessels were increasingly relegated to a support role for U-boat operations.

In the fall of 1914, the Germans also began to sink merchant vessels under "prize rules." Under prize rules, the German submarine (or naval ship) fired a shot across the merchant ship's bow, and demanded its surrender. If the ship surrendered, the merchantmen were provided with sufficient time to man their lifeboats or, if none were available, were taken prisoner aboard the U-boat. The U-boat then put its own crew on the merchant ship or, as frequently occurred (given the effective British naval blockade), sank it. Prize rules were designed to limit the loss of life, and as a rule of war, they represented restrictions on German U-boat actions. As long as these restrictions did not seriously affect the Germans' ability to sink merchant ships, they largely abided by them.

But the British could not afford to lose merchant ships or crews to the Germans, and by 1915 they began to arm the merchant ships with guns large enough to sink a U-boat. The U-boats risked their own survival if they surfaced and tried to take the merchant ships according to prize rules. The U-boats, therefore, increasingly began to use their greatest asset—stealth. The U-boats began to sink merchant ships without warning, using both their deck guns and torpedoes. The lack of warning is the "unrestricted" element in unrestricted warfare.

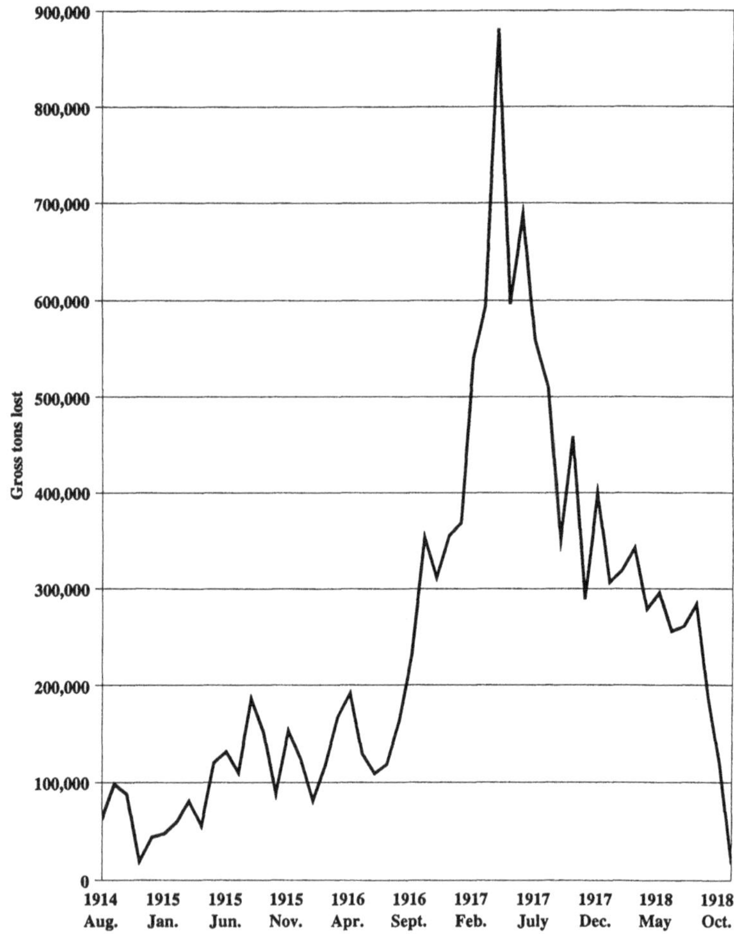

Figure 3.1 World Monthly Shipping Losses During World War I

The Germans conducted an unrestricted campaign against shipping in the area around the British Isles between February and August 1915 (during which time they sunk the *Lusitania,* on May 7). They ceased unrestricted submarine warfare in August, largely because of U.S. pressure, but they began again in late January 1917 (owing, arguably, to setbacks in the war on the continent). After the reintroduction of unrestricted U-boat attacks, the British shipping situation dramatically worsened; 25 percent of all ships leaving Great Britain failed to reach their destinations.[9] Shipping losses came to a climax in April 1917, when more ships were lost than in any other month in *either* world war. This peak can be seen in figure 3.1.[10]

The British had not anticipated and were not immediately prepared to deal with the German strategic shift. Before the war, the British had given virtually no thought to the problem of antisubmarine warfare and lacked resources, men, and administrative capability. Admiral John Jellicoe writes: "British antisubmarine measures were almost non-existent at the commencement of the war."[11] One reason for the British lack of preparation is that they had planned to blockade German ships. This meant that they too were conducting commerce raiding; only the manner in which the ships were taken fundamentally differed—by surface ships rather than submarines. The British assumed that if their blockade was successful, German ships would be no threat. And they were largely correct. Their blockade was successful, and the threat posed by the German ships largely neutralized. The U-boats, however, were another matter and had not been considered in the blockade plan. The German choice of U-boats as a weapon against the British was thus completely unanticipated and, as we shall see, proved to be extremely effective.[12]

THE STANDARD STORY

Historians like A. J. P. Taylor have presented what Arthur Marder calls the "standard story" of British naval strategy in World War I.[13] The standard story states that when the Germans began to use U-boats to sink British merchant ships, the British admirals, wedded to a strategy of sea patrol by their love of offense, were unable to adapt. Everyone but the admirals realized that the solution was to return to the historic British naval strategy of convoy. As the war continued, shipping losses became enormous. "By December 1916 Britain had lost 738 ships of more than 2,300,000 tons, one-fifth of the world's largest merchant fleet, most of it to submarines, with mines and surface raiders accounting for the rest."[14]

The standard explanation further states that the admiralty claimed to realize the extent of the danger but refused to alter its preferred strategy. One of the admiralty's objections to convoys was that the number of ship movements—which it claimed approached 2,500 per week—made convoys a logistical impossibility. But civilian analysis showed that this figure overstated the real number by a factor of more than seventeen: "Lloyd George inquired at the Ministry of Shipping and found that the correct figure was less than 140—the rest was coastal trade."[15]

Lloyd George had hoped to avoid the internal political costs associated with forcing a strategic change upon the admirals—the men who were supposed to be the naval experts. But the admirals failed to see the dramatically deteriorating situation. Finally, the standard explanation states that on April 26, 1917, Lloyd George went to the Admiralty Board, where he "gave the formal order that convoys must be instituted. The admirals belatedly discovered that they had been in favor of convoys all along. The first convoys sailed on 10 May. After further orders from Lloyd George, the system became regular for all shipping across the Atlantic. *It was an immediate success.*"[16] Lloyd George and the civilians were thus responsible for the switch from sea patrol to convoys, and the convoy strategy was seen as a universal and immediate success. Success was further ensured by the American entry into the war in April 1917.

This story, however, raises a number of critical, substantive questions that have theoretical import. Four of the key unanswered questions, and their answers, fundamentally influence the application of the alternative models to this World War I case.

First, why did British civilians wait so long to intervene? As we can see in figure 3.2, by February 1917 the British had lost 5 million tons of gross shipping (almost 40 percent of what they eventually lost in the entire war). Why did the civilians not act at the end of 1914, when 312,672 tons were lost in just five months, or in 1915, which ended

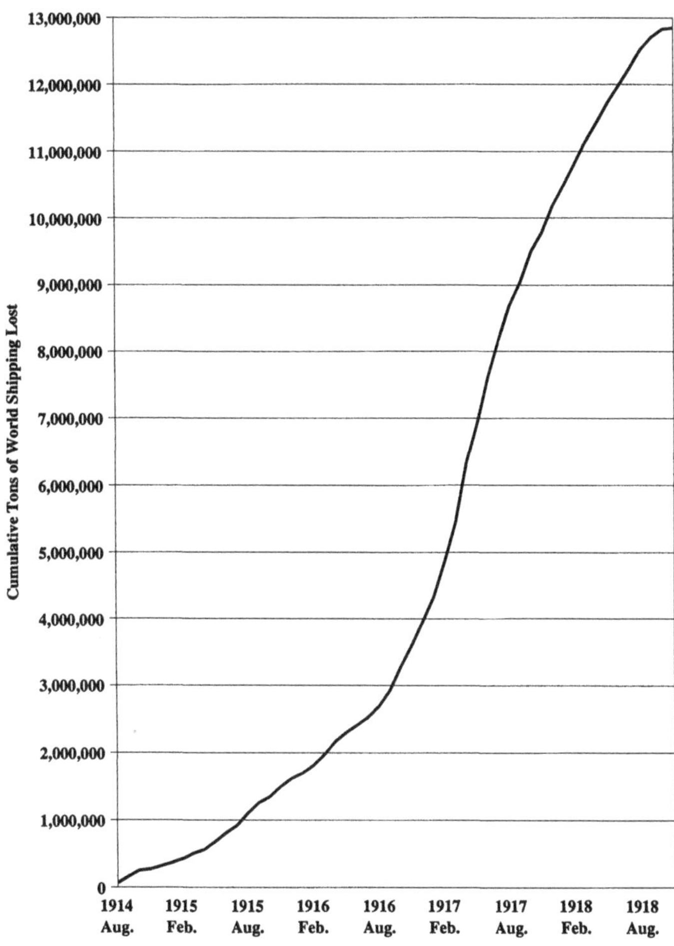

Figure 3.2 Cumulative World Shipping Losses During World War I

with 1.62 million tons sunk? In 1916 British and Allied merchant shipping losses totaled 3.95 million gross tons; what occurred in April 1917 that convinced civilian leaders that shipping losses were *now* a significant problem? It is important to remember that in January 1917 unrestricted warfare, which had ended in 1915, was reintroduced. It was in this earlier employment of unrestricted warfare that the most notorious German sinkings, the *Lusitania* and *Arabic,* for example, occurred. If civilians believed that lost ships had always been a problem, why did they wait until April 1917 to change policies?

Second, why did whatever convinced civilian leaders that there was a problem not convince the admiralty? Why did the admirals fail to see that the situation was as desperate as the civilians portrayed? In addition, why did the admirals not see convoys, whose value was apparently obvious to everyone else, as a better strategy?

Third, what does it mean to say (as many actors stated at the time and as many scholars wrote later) that the introduction of convoys was an "immediate success"? As we can see in figure 3.2, almost 60 percent of the total British gross tonnage merchant shipping losses occurred *after* the introduction of convoys, during a time period that represents only 36.5 percent of the war's duration. That is, on average, more shipping was lost per month after the introduction of convoys than before. Does that represent a success? If so, did everybody see it as equally successful?

Finally, what did either civilian or military organizations learn from the experience? Did they alter their beliefs about the relation between actions and outcomes for future decision making? An analysis of the dominant indicators employed by both civilian and naval leaders helps to answer these questions. I begin by looking at how civilian leaders evaluated the antisubmarine situation in the first half of the war.

THE EVALUATIONS

The timing of Lloyd George's implementation of convoys represents an interesting historical puzzle. Why did the prime minister intervene when he did? The standard explanation states that the timing was determined by three events. The United States entered the war, making convoys a more workable strategy by supplying greater numbers of escorts. Second, the civilian and army staffs examined the admirals' claim that the number of weekly ship movements was 5,000 (2,500 departures and 2,500 returns) and found that the effective number of ocean-going ships departing or returning to the British Isles was fewer than 300. The third reason was the enormous losses inflicted by the U-boats in April

1917. During that month Great Britain and her allies lost 881,027 gross shipping tons, the most ever lost in one month. Each of these reasons has problems, however, for explaining the timing of the prime minister's intervention.

Using both the American entry into the war and the discovery of the actual number of ship movements that required convoys to explain why Lloyd George acted begs the question of intervention. We would still like to know both what triggered him to act then and why the Americans chose to intervene in April 1917 and not at another time. These interventions, foreign and domestic, thus become part of the behavior to be explained, rather than a causal argument for what we observed.

Second, although 881,027 gross tons of shipping lost in a month was unprecedented, so were the 353,660 gross tons lost in September 1916 and the 185,866 gross tons lost in August 1915. In fact, although the losses of April 1917 established a record high, it was the *twelfth* record high since the beginning of the war, and it was only known to be a record high after the war ended. Simply stating that April contained the largest number of losses in a month does not provide a convincing argument of the conditions necessary to change civilian preferences. Furthermore, why the previous inaction in the face of record losses? Not all the behavior we want to explain occurred in April 1917. Why were the earlier record losses insufficiently bad to trigger action? In order to understand the timing of Lloyd George's naval strategy intervention, we need to examine the context in which British military decisions were made.

Both secondary historical accounts like Aaron Friedberg's *The Weary Titan* and primary sources like War Cabinet documents suggest that although the prime minister presided over the government, the service heads had great autonomy in their operations. The prime minister could dismiss the First Sea Lord or call for a change of strategy, but such actions had strong political repercussions and could not be taken lightly. Discussing whether he should have dismissed British Continental Army commander General Sir Douglas Haig, Lloyd George said that in "considering whether we should have gone further and taken more drastic action by replacing Haig and Robertson, I had always to bear in mind the possibility that such a step would inevitably have given rise to political complications. Both had considerable backing in the Press and the House of Commons and inside the Government."[17] The prime minister could not act on military matters without incurring domestic political costs. At the same time, inaction had its own costs.

In December 1916 Lloyd George became prime minister and head of the newly organized British War Cabinet. The War Cabinet contained representatives from the key political parties (Liberal, Labour, Conservative) and key civilian government organizations (like the Exchequer). No military leader or civilian head of a military organization was represented on the regular board (they were occasionally called in to provide evidence or thoughts on particular subjects).

The War Cabinet had responsibility for planning and executing Britain's wartime actions at home and abroad. It was particularly interested in maintaining supplies to Great Britain. There were four ways to maximize supplies: 1) increase food production and decrease consumption; 2) increase the merchant ship supply; 3) decrease the multiple demands on shipping (mainly, cut the supply of goods and military protection to other parts of the British Empire); and 4) decrease the U-boat threat.[18]

By the end of 1916 significant efforts were under way on all four solutions. But the supply and demand for food stuffs were constrained, as was the supply of ships (although, by the end of spring 1917 the latter began to increase). Cuts were made to Empire commitments, and new plans (such as the invasion of Greece) were put off in order to keep ships free. The remaining solution was to decrease the U-boat threat. Given their interests, civilian leaders relied on the indicator tons of merchant shipping lost when assessing British success against the U-boat.

Civilians wanted to decrease the amount of merchant shipping tonnage sunk by German U-boats. Although some supplies were more important than others, the key concern was the availability of gross shipping tons capable of transporting food and war materials from the Empire and allies to the United Kingdom. Shipping tons not only provided an indicator for how many supplies were getting through to Great

Britain at a particular moment, but they also provided an indicator of future shipping capability, because a sunk ship lost both the cargo and the ship itself.

The other critical indicator that concerned civilians was the monthly production of new merchant ships. British production remained largely constant at about 50,000 tons per month until mid-1917, when the number began to rise slowly.[19] The unchanging nature of new ship construction means that the indicator did not play an important role in the decision making process until after April 1917. The mid-1917 rise in ship construction further supported civilian assessments, made on the basis of other information, that the antisubmarine war was proceeding well.

Together, ship building per month and ships sunk per month represented the civilian's dominant indicator set. The accounts of British decision makers show that they assessed success largely in terms of calendar months. Furthermore, decision makers reacted quickly to changes in their indicators. Not only was the lag time small, so that we would expect decision makers to react to information shortly after they received the monthly data, but there were anticipation and projection of monthly figures. Thus, most decisions occurred in either the last week of a key month or the first week in the month following.

Looking at monthly shipping losses after the fact, we can see that April 1917 stands out. It was the worst month of the war. But despite the implicit assertion by a number of scholars, British civilians had no way of knowing that the April losses would be the largest in the war (let alone the largest in both world wars). The British had no way of distinguishing this record from the previous eleven record bad months and could not determine that it would be the last month of record shipping losses and the worst of the war.

The record absolute values by themselves are insufficient to explain what was special about spring 1917. April losses were enormous, resulting in the loss of 10 percent of the British shipping stock. But March and February each cost the British 7 percent of their shipping stock. No scholar argues that 7 percent is acceptable but 10 percent represents a crisis. In fact, Lord Curzon argued in January 1917 that there was no cause for alarm because the Germans had "succeeded in diminishing the British mercantile tonnage a *mere* 5 or 6 percent of the gross tonnage."[20] Therefore, it is difficult to say that 10 percent acted as an aspiration level, which, when exceeded, led to dissatisfaction.

Civilian discontent with the shipping situation manifested itself four times. In August 1915 civilians began to discuss the need for change, but before any positive action was taken, the Americans intervened and forced the Germans to discontinue unrestricted U-boat warfare.[21] In December 1916 the Asquith government fell, to be replaced by the government of the former minister of munitions, Lloyd George.[22] Third, Lloyd George, acting as head of the civilian War Cabinet, claimed in late February 1917 that the current strategy was not working.[23] Finally, On April 26, 1917, he intervened and altered the strategy—incurring the political wrath of the powerful admiralty.[24]

We can see each of these changes as an increase in civilian conviction that the sea patrol was not working and needed to be replaced. Each step thus represents an ordinal increase in the certainty that the current policy was failing. Ideally, we would like to have a general model that would provide an explanation for each change. By looking at the rate of change of the civilian dominant indicator of ships sunk we can explain this behavior.

Let us look at the crisis of August 1915.[25] An analysis of the change in dominant indicators employed by the civilians captures their concern. The August total of 185,866 tons sunk represented a record jump in both the acceleration of shipping lost, 76,226 tons, and the rate of change in the acceleration of shipping loss, 98,014 tons. August 1915 was the first month where such actors as Lloyd George and scholars like Dan Van der Vat and Arthur Marder agree that civilians first assessed sea patrol as failing. It was the fifth absolute record but the first month that experienced record increases in the acceleration and change in acceleration of ships sunk. Thus the dominant indicator approach helps to explain why decision makers were concerned in August but not in earlier months.

Before the civilians' new strategic assessment could result in a strategy change, however, America acted decisively. Threatening to enter the war, the United States forced Germany to back down from unrestricted submarine warfare. Lloyd George wrote that in August 1915, after the sinking of the *Arabic,* "the German Government promised to instruct their submarine commanders not to sink further liners without warning, and after very strong pressure even went so far as to proffer a tentative disavowal of the action of the submarine commander who sank the *Arabic.*"[26] This was an unprecedented retreat for the Germans, who had successfully held against similar demands by the Americans after the sinking of the *Lusitania* in spring of that year. This decisive action seems to have satisfied British civilian concerns raised by the August figures. The civilians then focused on non-naval concerns until the fall of 1916. This represents a good example of a change in assessment without a corresponding change in policy; the rate at which things were changing for the worse was slacking off.

British civilians once again became concerned that the navy's strategy of sea patrol was failing in the fall 1916, when there was a sudden increase in losses. In the four months before November, shipping losses began to increase. In October, losses occurred at record rates of acceleration, suggesting that the situation was extremely bad. Shortly after this, the Asquith government fell and Lloyd George became prime minister.[27]

Shipping losses in January 1917 were 368,000 tons per month, a new high. Despite the record-setting losses, however, Lloyd George kept relatively silent. The standard story contains no explanation of why the new prime minister failed to act. But a close analysis of the data shows that the increase in the loss rates was slowing. In January the acceleration of losses was 13,382 tons—about 30 percent of what it had been in December and only 12 percent of the October high. More important, the January change in acceleration, −30,249 tons, was a serious drop, suggesting that the rate at which the situation was deteriorating was slowing. This situation changed dramatically in February.

On January 31 the Germans declared the area around the British Isles, parts of France, and the Mediterranean an unrestricted war zone. The Germans had sent peace overtures to Great Britain that were rejected on December 19, 1916, by Lloyd George.[28] This enabled the more militant factions in Germany, who had been arguing for a more aggressive approach to war on land and sea, to convince the chancellor that unrestricted submarine warfare represented one of the few remaining mechanisms available for changing the status quo.

Since their previous implementation of unrestricted submarine warfare in 1915, German U-boats had improved in quality and quantity. As a result of the increased effectiveness of unrestricted submarine warfare, British mercantile losses skyrocketed. Not only did the Germans sink a record 540,000 tons of world shipping in February, but the rate of loss accelerated at an increasing rate. Shipping losses accelerated in this month by 171,485 tons (more than thirteen times December's rate), and the increase in acceleration was a record 158,103 tons (compared with −30,249 tons in January). February represents only the second time that both the acceleration of losses and the change in the rate of that acceleration set records. The situation was going badly and deteriorating at an increasing pace.

These figures profoundly affected the civilian estimate of the situation. Lloyd George declared toward the end of February: "The ultimate success of the Allied cause depends, in my judgement, on our solving the tonnage difficulties with which we are confronted."[29] He evaluated the current situation by saying: "There was disaster in front of us."[30]

In the middle of February, as the acceleration and change in acceleration of losses were climbing, the prime minister had breakfast with First Sea Lord (Admiral) Jellicoe, First Lord of the Seas Sir Edward Carson, and Admiral Alexander Duff, who was head of the antisubmarine division. Lloyd George presented these naval leaders with a strongly worded memo advocating the use of convoys. The navy refused. This put the prime minister in an awkward position; How could he refute the admirals' opinion when they were supposed to be the naval experts? "But what ought the War Cabinet to have done in the face of this official refractoriness? When it is a matter of life and death, it is a serious matter for amateurs to interfere and recklessly exercise their authority by over-riding the opinion of the most famous specialists that are available in the Kingdom. How much greater an act of temerity would it be were it a question of the life and death of a whole nation! You could, of course, call in another specialist. But who was there whose reputation stood as high in naval councils as Admiral Jellicoe?"[31] But Lloyd George knew that Great Britain could not wait long: "We could not take too long over the process, for *our ships were being destroyed at an alarming rate.*"[32] Lloyd George publicly suggested three actions: building more ships, conserving resources at home, and new action "by the Navy to grapple with the menace."[33]

In March shipping losses hit another record high of 593,841 tons. But the rate of losses was accelerating at only 53,835 tons, and the change in the rate of acceleration decreased to −117,650 tons, suggesting that the situation was bad but improving. This represents a good example of how a record high loss can be good news. Consequently, no actions were taken by civilians in this record-setting month. In fact, March seems to disappear from most narratives, with February leading directly to April in descriptions of the naval war. No author attempts to explain the *inaction* of civilian leaders during this month of unprecedented losses. The loss rate was 400,000 tons more than it had been a year earlier, yet the civilians failed to evaluate the situation as desperate enough to require action. By looking at the acceleration and change in the rate of acceleration of the civilians' dominant indicator, we have a parsimonious explanation for this inaction; the civilians failed to intervene because the figures, despite their record-setting absolute value, showed that the situation was improving.

In April, Great Britain and her allies lost a record 881,027 tons of shipping, and the rate at which these losses were occurring was dramatically increasing. Compared to a year earlier these figures were staggering. Great Britain in April 1916 had experienced what was then an unprecedented high of 191,667 tons lost.

The admirals had predicted before April 1917 that during that month Great Britain and her allies would lose 600,000 tons of shipping.[34] This prediction alone was not enough to trigger Lloyd George to intervene in naval affairs. But the actual figure was a dramatically larger jump in losses than anything previously experienced or predicted. Like February, April was one of only three months to experience record highs in both acceleration (287,186 tons, more than 100,000 tons greater than the previous record) and the change in acceleration (233,351 tons, about 75,000 tons more than the previous record). The situation was accelerating in the wrong direction at an increasing record rate, and civilians reacted.

Lloyd George noted that "if Allied shipping continued steadily to disappear at this accelerating rate, the end was not distant."[35] Lloyd George and the civilians saw the situation as desperate.

Given the substantive increase in the rate of ships lost, and the update on the effectiveness of the strategy, it is not surprising that Lloyd George considered this a crisis that required immediate action, even if the action had high political costs. There were only three months in the war that had record acceleration and changes in acceleration of losses. April's records, however, led to further reconsideration of the likelihood of sea patrol being the right strategy. As a result, the civilians perceived that a crisis had developed that needed immediate attention—even if that attention required political intervention in military matters. Analysis of these changes thus provides us with the missing *ex ante* triggers for updating beliefs about the need to incur costs that previous historical accounts, which focus solely on the magnitude of the loss, have been unable to provide.

From December 1916 through the spring of 1917, Admiral Jellicoe headed the British navy. Beneath him in the hierarchy were two key posts. Admiral of the Fleet David Beatty was solely concerned with running the Grand Fleet, which comprised the huge blue-water ships like dreadnoughts, battleships, and cruisers. The second position was new. Jellicoe created an Antisubmarine Division shortly after assuming his position. He appointed Admiral Duff to head the division, which pursued technological and tactical means of dealing with U-boats. Jellicoe had responsibility for all naval activities, which included preparing for battle with the German fleet, running the British blockade, transporting troops, launching amphibious attacks, and protecting shipping.

Admirals Jellicoe and Duff, along with their staffs, maintained strict agreement on their views of convoy.[36] These are the men to whom I refer when discussing the "admirals."[37] The admiralty was in charge of defeating the German naval threat. It primarily interpreted this mission as the destruction of German ships and boats. Jellicoe describes what he sees as the objectives imposed on the navy and the mission the navy created to meet those objectives. In a briefing to U.S. Admiral Mayo in August 1917 (after the switch to convoy), Jellicoe told Mayo that the navy had to meet three "duties":

1. The protection of the sea communications of the Allied armies and the protection of British and Allied trade.
2. The prevention of enemy trade in order to interfere with its military operations and to exert economic pressure.
3. Resistance to invasion and raids.

Jellicoe then told Mayo that it "was pointed out that the question at issue in each case was the control of sea communications, and in order to attain that control permanently and completely, the enemy's naval forces both above and below water had to be destroyed or effectually masked."[38] The British navy saw its mission as the destruction of German naval forces.

The admirals transformed the shipping problem into a U-boat problem and wanted a strategy that would maximize the number of U-boats sunk. Jellicoe wrote: "Our object was to destroy submarines at a greater rate than the output of the German shipyards. This was the surest way of counteracting their activities." He added: "It was mainly for the purpose of attack on the submarines that I had formed the Anti-Submarine Division of the Naval Staff."[39] The admiralty relied upon the number of U-boats sunk as its dominant indicator for evaluating policy performance.[40]

Many historians have since disagreed with the admirals' choice of assessment criteria. Patrick Beesly states that "the defeat of the unrestricted U-boat campaign did not depend on the number of U-boats sunk." Marder writes: "Sinking submarines is a bonus, not a necessity."[41] But although there are debates about the appropriateness of the navy's criteria of success, scholars agree that the admirals primarily relied upon U-boats sunk when measuring the performance of their anti-submarine strategies.[42]

Jellicoe was not indifferent to the problem of shipping losses, but he thought that sinking U-boats was the best way to minimize losses in the long run. He wrote that "the sinking of one enemy submarine meant the possible saving of a considerable number of merchant ships."[43] Jellicoe and the admiralty thought that the only long-term solution to the shipping problem was the removal of the threat—destruction of the submarines. "But the convoy system, by itself, did not, in 1917, cause the destruction of German submarines, and the only sure way of meeting the danger was to destroy submarines at a greater rate than they were being produced."[44]

The admiralty was originally firmly against a convoy. It believed that convoys would decrease its ability to destroy U-boats and lead to increased merchant sinkings. In January 1917 it released a memo that stated: "The system of several ships sailing company, as a convoy, is not recommended in any area where submarine attack is a possibility. It is evident that the larger the number of ships forming the convoy, the greater is the chance of a submarine being enabled to attack successfully, and the greater the difficulty of the escort in preventing such an attack."[45] The admiralty not only believed that convoy would be an ineffective strategy for destroying U-boats, it was unconvinced that the sea patrol strategy was performing poorly.

Looking at figure 3.3 and the graph of monthly U-boat losses, we can see that the monthly number of U-boats destroyed rapidly increased after November 1916. November and February 1916 were good months for the admirals; during both months, the acceleration and change in acceleration in U-boats sunk was positive (unlike the civilians, the admirals want to maximize this indicator, so *good* means that the acceleration and change in acceleration of U-boat losses is positive, and *bad* that they are both negative).

These data also suggest a reason no change occurred in late February 1917, when Lloyd George sent the admiralty his strongly worded memo encouraging a change to convoy. The admirals did not respond because, through their lens, February was an extremely successful month: the British navy sank five U-boats (an absolute record) and were sinking U-boats at an accelerating rate. In other words, the situa-

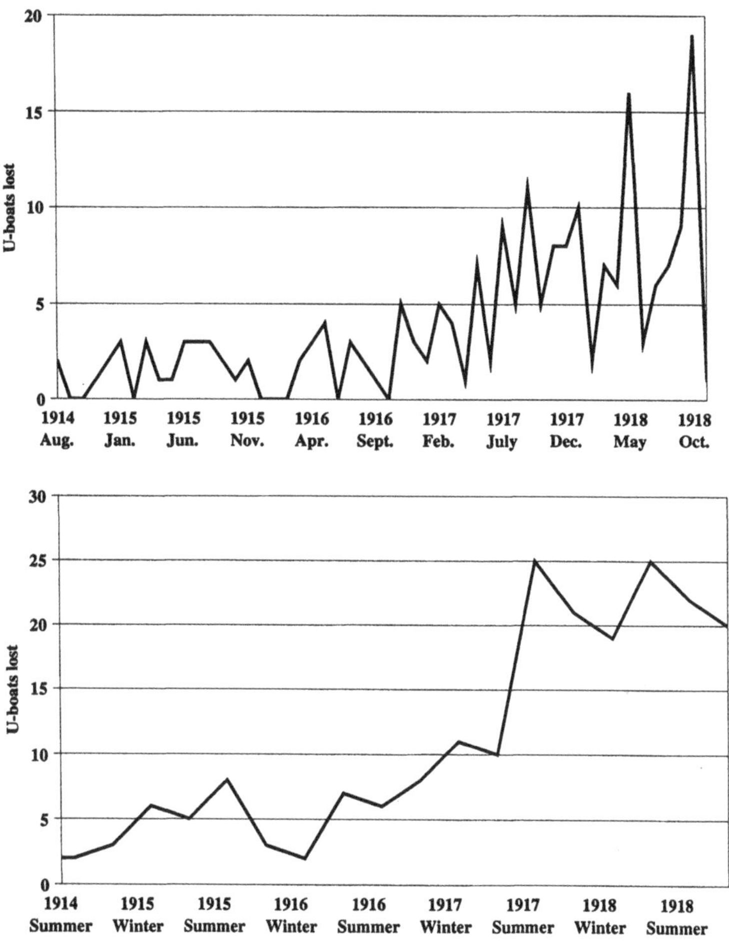

Figure 3.3 Monthly and Quarterly U-Boat Losses During World War I

tion was going well and improving at an increasing rate—clearly not the time to change strategies.

This situation rapidly changed, however, in March and April, when the British sank an increasingly small number of U-boats (just one in April). In these months the rate of U-boat losses was decelerating at a steeper rate, and the admiralty became increasingly worried and open to civilian suggestions.

Quarterly data are helpful for getting a sense of the larger picture the admirals viewed. These data, also shown in figure 3.3, suggest that fall 1916 and winter 1917 were largely good quarters for the admirals. In fact, since the winter of 1916 the British had almost continuously improved their ability to sink U-boats. This increase, however, dropped off in the spring of 1917.

The admirals' attachment to U-boat kills as a means of policy evaluation explains why they were unaffected by the shipping-loss statistics that so impressed the civilians. The admirals were aware of the shipping-loss figures. But Jellicoe and the admirals thought that increased antisubmarine efforts were the only viable long-term solution to the problem. The admirals' reliance on the number of U-boats sunk to assess strategy becomes even clearer when we look at military and civilian assessments of convoy.

There is general agreement that civilians saw the introduction of convoys as extremely successful. And yet, as we saw in figure 3.2, more than half of both world shipping and British shipping losses occurred after April 1917. In the eighteen months previous, 4,986,905 tons of ships were lost, compared with the 6,463,102 tons lost in the eighteen months between April 1917 and the end of the war. Furthermore, unlike what happened in World War II, the Americans immediately supported the British convoy strategy, and there was not a disproportionate number of sinkings off the American coast.[46] Furthermore, during the five months from April to August 1917 all the monthly losses were above 500,000 tons. The absolute value of ships lost thus does not suggest a successful situation. With what criteria, then, did civilians see convoy as "immediately successful"?

Civilian leaders saw the implementation of convoys as successful because the rate of losses decelerated dramatically. As one can see by looking at the graph of cumulative losses in figure 3.2, April represents an inflection point (the middle of an S-curve), the point at which the rate of increase begins to consistently decrease. Before April 1917 the acceleration and change in acceleration of losses were both increasing, while after April the loss rate began to drop. Civilian decision makers did not know that April would represent the month of largest losses, but they could detect that the marginal rate at which losses were increasing was decreasing. No month after April registered both record acceleration and change in acceleration of shipping losses. In fact, monthly shipping lost after April 1917 never grew faster than the rate experienced in October 1916 (let alone the dramatic jumps experienced in February and April 1917).

Monthly absolute values of losses, however, did exceed all previous values except for April 1917. Both May and June set records for the second highest months, with losses of 596,629 and 687,507 tons, respectively. Thus the absolute values continued to remain high, while the rate of increase (the acceleration and change in acceleration) of monthly losses dropped dramatically.

Quarterly data again help us get a better sense of the larger picture. April, May, and June 1917 represent a record high quarter, at 2,165,163 tons of ships lost. Furthermore, both the third and fourth quarters of 1917 greatly exceeded any quarter of 1916 or 1917—including the autumn of 1916, when the Asquith government fell. But as bad as things were on an absolute level, the rate at which they were bad and getting worse was decreasing. This is especially clear if we look at the rate of change of losses during the year from October 1916 to October 1917. No quarter after spring 1917 experienced an increasing acceleration of losses. In every quarter the situation was getting better at the same or an increasing rate.

These changes in the rate of ships lost were recognized by civilian leaders. Lloyd George said that "up to the date of the initiation of the convoy, the sinkings mounted upwards month by month," but "the rate at which British vessels were sunk by enemy action showed a steady decline in 1918 from the appalling height which it had reached in the spring of 1917."[47]

Most historical narratives that attempt to explain why the situation was a success point to the fact that April 1917 showed the all-time high in shipping loss. But it was impossible for civilian leaders to know that April would be the last in a series of repeated record high absolute values. Looking at record values of the rate of change provides a more discreet mechanism for explaining the conditions under which decision makers updated their beliefs.

Some historians do argue that the success was due to changes in the rate of increase. C. R. M. F. Cruttwell writes: "But for the last quarter of 1917 the destruction of tonnage was little more than half that of April–June, and throughout 1918 the curve of decline though slow was steady."[48] Marder notes: "The crux of the matter was the sharply rising curve of shipping losses."[49] None of these historical treatments, however, analyzes the actual rate of change or attempts to explain why some months, such as March, failed to generate civilian intervention.

Analysis of the dominant indicators helps explain why the civilians saw convoy as a success. Perhaps even more noteworthy, however, this approach can help us understand a question almost entirely ignored in the analysis of the war: Why did the British admiralty also see convoy as a success?

After April 1917 two changes occurred in admiralty evaluations of the antisubmarine strategy. First, although previously the rate of U-boats sunk had in general suggested that the sea patrol was performing satisfactorily, the admiralty now had strong reasons to disregard this and to evaluate the performance of convoys as excellent and improving at an increasing rate. Second, and linked to the first, the admirals came to believe that convoys were the best strategy for sinking U-boats.

In February 1917 U-boat losses suggest that the strategy of sea patrol was performing well and getting increasingly better. Although losses were not accelerating at record levels, by performing categorically as well as possible, these figures suggest that the admirals were likely to be satisfied with the current policy and would thus fight attempts to substitute an alternative policy of unknown performance potential. Thus, the admirals were not receptive to Lloyd George's February attempts to implement convoy strategy. But in April, when Lloyd George made his most strenuous insistence on policy innovation, the admirals were significantly less enthusiastic about sea patrol. The April figures show a substantial reversal. Sea patrol was now performing as poorly as categorically possible—the situation was bad and getting increasingly worse. Although the month's figures were not a record (so the admirals were not dissatisficed), the admirals were likely to be more receptive to another policy when their current policy was performing poorly than when it was performing well.

When measured by the number of U-boats destroyed, the naval situation dramatically improved after April 1917, as seen in the analysis of aggregate U-boat losses in figure 3.4. In May, the first month that the admirals began convoying merchant ships, the British sank seven U-boats (an absolute record). Because they had only sunk one the previous month and four in March, this resulted in both record acceleration and change in acceleration of monthly U-boat sinkings. Through the lens of U-boats destroyed, the admirals saw convoy as a dramatic success; the situation was going well and improving at increasing, record rates.

Further analysis of these numbers demonstrates that although there were still bad months, in general, convoy proved to be even more successful when judged by the admirals' dominant indicators than by those of the civilians. Seventy percent of all U-boat losses occurred after April 1917 (compared with 50 percent of the world shipping losses). The admirals were successfully pursuing their mission. Jellicoe wrote that "our success in sinking submarines increased quarter by quarter in spite of the great difficulty of dealing with an enemy who could only be seen on the rarest occasions."[50]

By the fall of 1917 virtually every British, Allied, and neutral ship was under convoy, and the admirals made an astonishing discovery: convoy was a better strategy for sinking U-boats than offensive patrolling.[51] The admirals became increasingly supportive of convoy as

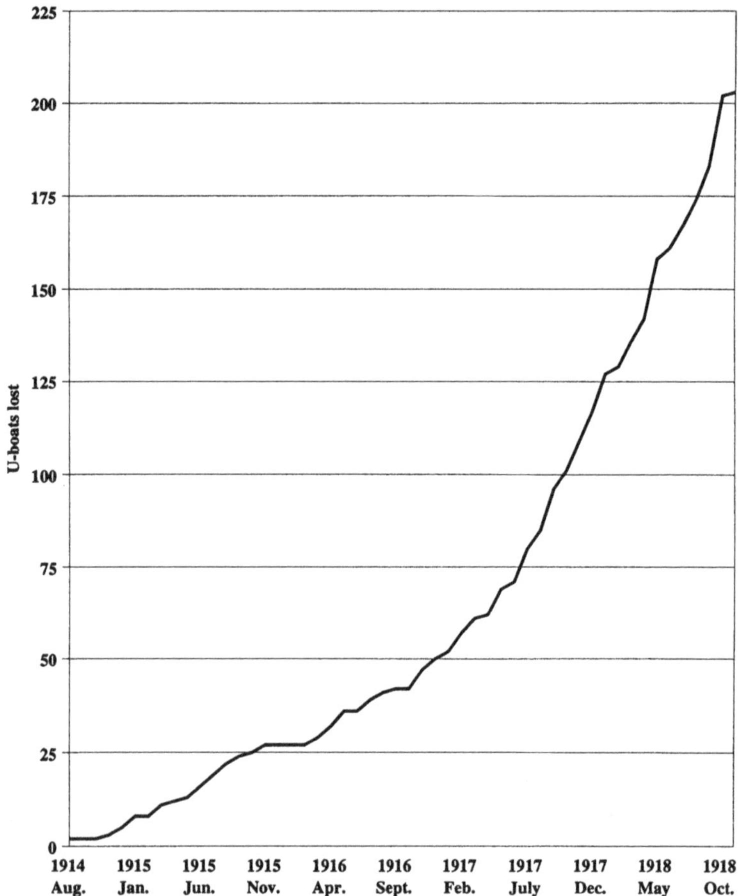

Figure 3.4 Cumulative Number of U-Boats Lost During World War I

an effective strategy. Holger Herwig notes: "The mounting losses of U-boats—up from nineteen in 1915 to sixty-nine in 1918—attest to the tactical ineffectiveness of the submarines against convoys as well as to the adversary's efficacy in anti-submarine warfare."[52] Thus, the admirals determined during World War I that convoys were an effective means of sinking U-boats. They changed their beliefs about the utility of convoy.

Although few scholars specifically address why the British naval leadership saw convoy as a success, those that do tend to suggest that the British admirals also appreciated the decrease in the rate of merchant ships sunk. The admirals were in favor of decreased shipping losses, but they saw the success of the convoy strategy almost solely in terms of its increasing ability to sink U-boats. Jellicoe noted that convoys allowed the more efficient use of weapons to attack submarines.[53] The admirals' belief that convoys were the best way to destroy U-boats will become especially clear in the next chapter, on World War II, when we look at the lessons that the British navy drew from World War I.

OFFENSE VERSUS DEFENSE

The concepts of offense and defense are critical to the Cult of the Offensive arguments, which declare that militaries always favor the offense. The case I have just discussed demonstrates the difficulty and limited utility of dividing strategy into offense and defense, as well as the complexity of organizational preferences.

Convoy is seen as both an offensive and a defensive strategy. Traditionally, analysts have seen it as a defensive strategy because it is less oriented toward the finding and destroying of enemy forces than is the strategy of sea patrol. But this view does not clearly represent the view of policy makers at the time. In his August 1917 discussion with U.S. Admiral Mayo, Jellicoe noted that "finally Admiral Mayo was informed that the convoy system itself was looked upon as an offensive measure since the German submarines would, in order to attack vessels under convoy, be forced into contact with the fast craft engaged in the work of escort and thus place themselves in positions in which they could themselves be successfully attacked."[54] A number of the historians and analysts who see the navy's strategy of sea patrol as offensive describe naval behavior in a Cult of the Offensive-like manner. For example, John Terraine writes: "For the Royal Navy, 'attack' was the key word; all naval tradition, and the training based upon it, was founded upon the principle of carrying the war (or the battle) immediately to the enemy."[55] Although

I agree that the navy wanted to attack U-boats, I think that claiming that they sought only offensive strategies is empirically incorrect.

Ironically, most of the criticism of the navy at the time argued that it was not aggressive enough. Admiral Doveton Sturdee wrote in 1916 that there "still exists . . . a feeling that there is a lack of offensive energy on the part of the Admiralty and the Fleet in general."[56] In May 1917 papers like the *Daily Mail* and *Land and Water* claimed that "the Admiralty were slow in appreciating the position, it was said; they were conducting a defensive war: 'passive resistance' would never defeat the U-boat; they would solve the problem only by finding out the wasps' nests and destroying them."[57] Prime Minister Lloyd George was unable to convince Admiral Jellicoe to create an Offensive Operations division. Lloyd George claimed that "at a meeting of the Cabinet War Committee on June 20th, 1917, I asked the First Sea Lord whether the Admiralty were making any progress in the organization of an Offensive Section of the Operations Division. Admiral Jellicoe said . . . that this section would very likely only waste his time."[58]

The prime minister believed that the navy was stuck on defensive strategies. He noted that it "is also interesting to record Admiral Jellicoe's opinion as to the offensive value of an overwhelming fleet. I was dissatisfied that our Navy with all its tremendous power could do so little against the Belgian harbors, which were needed as bases for the German submarine and torpedo flotillas, and I asked Jellicoe whether, if the German Fleet had the same preponderance over ours as we and the Americans together now enjoyed over theirs, they could not make Dover or Harwich untenable for our fleets. He denied we had an overwhelming preponderance."[59]

The British admirals continued to refuse to operate in the offensive manner that Lloyd George advocated, despite their jointly recognized success at dealing with the U-boat problem. This was a major reason for Jellicoe's dismissal at the end of 1917. Marder notes that "parallel to the growing restiveness over the failure of the Admiralty to solve the U-boat problem was that over the seeming lack of an offensive naval strategy. . . . Two schools of thought were again revealed, each with its naval and civilian spokesman."[60] From the beginning of the war, civilian leaders like Lloyd George and Winston Churchill wanted to use the Grand Fleet actively in attacking the shores of the enemy. This was a motivation for Churchill's attack on Turkey in the Dardanelles and his interests in Salonika and the Baltics. The navy was against these plans because it was convinced that it would lose its battleships without sinking German battleships in exchange. Historians have shared this view. Marder claims: "Forcing the Dardanelles would have been child's play in comparison to an attack on such fortified places as Wilhelmshaven and Kiel."[61] The offenses promoted by the civilians were serious undertakings with potentially disastrous results.

Civilian discontent manifested itself in the summer of 1915 and again in February and April 1917. Civilians were largely pleased with the situation after April 1917. Naval decision makers were somewhat pleased with the situation before April and more excited about their prospects for winning after the implementation of convoy. The alternative action-reaction model helps to explain a great deal of the strategic naval changes observed in World War I. In response to the British blockade, the Germans altered their strategy and switched to U-boat attacks on commerce. The British responded by arming merchant ships, and the Germans switched from following prize rules to unrestricted warfare. In response, the British changed to convoys. The action-reaction model, however, fails to help us understand the answers to the four critical questions with which we began the chapter: (1) Why did civilians wait until April 1917 to act? (2) Why did the civilians and naval leaders disagree about the success of sea patrol? (3) Why did both civilians and naval leaders see convoy as a success? and (4) What lessons about strategy were learned from the experience? In order to answer these questions, we need to move beyond the action-reaction model and look at the dominant indicator approach.

The largely single-peaked nature of world shipping losses, and the occurrence of the switch to convoys at the global maximum, enables us to compare the dominant indicator and absolute-value models. The problem with the absolute-value model is not that it missed the April 1917 climax but rather that this was the twelfth record of the war. Thus the model is not discriminate; it made many incorrect predictions of civilian behavior. The dominant indicator approach was more selective, making fewer incorrect predictions and also capturing the key events that triggered civilian action. In terms of naval assessments, the dominant indicator approach helped explain why the admirals fought the civilians' proposed change to convoy and also why the admirals saw convoys as successful.

Finally, this case does not support the Cult of the Offensive approach. First, it is not clear how the concepts of offense and defense apply to naval strategy; to the extent that they do, the military appears to advocate a number of defensive positions. Second, while the navy did promote sea patrol, it was also a strong supporter of convoy. This establishes World War II as a test; if the admirals try to use sea patrol to meet the U-boat threat, then arguments on evaluation offered by Van Evera and Snyder (assuming that sea patrol is more offensive than convoy) are supported. If, however, admirals switch to convoys because they maximize the number of U-boats sunk, then we need to look at the evaluation process and the role of dominant indicators.

Chapter 4

British Antisubmarine Decision Making in World War II

How willingly would I have exchanged a full-scale attempt at invasion for the shapeless, measureless peril, expressed in charts, curves, and statistics!

—Winston Churchill, *The Grand Alliance*

Unlike World War I, in which the British were never forced off the European continent, the British lacked both a presence on the continent and a major European ally during much of World War II. Without supplies from the United States and the Western Hemisphere, the British were unable to feed themselves, let alone beat off the planned German invasion of their islands (code-named Operation Sea Lion).[1] The transportation of supplies by sea was thus even more critical to Great Britain during World War II than during World War I. Recognizing the country's dependence on merchant shipping, the Nazis directed enormous resources into their U-boat attacks on British shipping.

The outcome of the battle between U-boats and British naval and merchant ships, called the Battle of the Atlantic by Winston Churchill, is seen by many historians as critical to the Allied victory. Dan Van der Vat claims that a British naval defeat would have led to "the collapse of the United Kingdom."[2] John Keegan says that the British naval escorts and merchant ships stood "between the Wehrmacht and domination of the world," and that "had those 'statistics, diagrams and curves' which blighted Winston Churchill's days and nights in 1940–2 turned wrong, had each U-boat on its patrol line succeeded in sinking only one more merchant ship in the summer of 1942, when losses already exceed launchings by 10 per cent, the course, perhaps even the outcome, of the Second World War would have been entirely otherwise."[3] Allied leaders at the time also recognized the critical threat posed by the U-boats. Churchill issued a directive on March 6, 1941, that identified the anti-submarine fight as the top British priority.[4] His intense concern about the Battle of the Atlantic was perhaps best demonstrated when he wrote that "the only thing that ever really frightened me during the war was the U-boat peril."[5]

During the war, 2,838 British ships massing 14,687,231 tons were sunk, resulting in the deaths of 30,248 British merchant marines.[6] Official British naval historian S. W. Roskill wrote: "In all the long history of sea warfare there has been no parallel to this battle, whose field was thousands of square miles of ocean, and to which no limits in time or space could be set. In its intensity, and in the certainty that its outcome would decide the issue of the war, the battle may be compared to the Battle of Britain of 1940."[7] By all accounts, the British were victorious in the Battle of the Atlantic.

But even though there is agreement that the British defeated the U-boat threat, there is less agreement as to why. Analysts have provided a long list of reasons why the Allies won the Battle of the Atlantic. Rear Admiral John D. Hayes writes that the "success can be attributed to radar; sonar . . . high-frequency direction-finding; the escort carrier; antisubmarine support groups of destroyers, which reinforced the escorts of convoys under attack; and the extension of land-based air power across the Atlantic by the employment of B-24 Liberators."[8] The British implementation of a strategy of convoy was seen by many World War II participants and historians as a critical factor in the German defeat.

Lists like Hayes's, however, do not address questions central to strategic assessment. Were the British civilian and naval leaders satisfied with convoy? Were alternative strategies considered? More generally, we would like to develop an explanation for British strategic assessments in the war against the U-boats. Although there are many fine descriptions of the Battle of the Atlantic, few analysts have attempted to apply general approaches to British naval strategic assessment. This is probably because, unlike World War I, there were no critical British (and few German) strategic changes in the U-boat war. But there *were* a number of changes in organizational assessments of success. Thus, an approach that explains organizational strategic assessment can be applied to this case, even though there was little actual strategic change.

Assessments of the outcome of the Battle of the Atlantic in World War II shifted dramatically and rapidly throughout the war. Unlike World War I, where monthly sinkings of merchant ships rose and dropped smoothly in a single-peaked, monotonic trend, all indicators in World War II varied dramatically over time. In World War I, both admirals and civilians agreed after spring of 1917 that the situation was good and getting increasingly better. Positive assessments of the situation were less unified in World War II. Finally, the two wars can act as a test of whether actors, particularly the British navy, updated their beliefs about the importance of convoy to their dominant indicators.

THE ADMIRALTY'S VIEW OF CONVOYS

The British admirals began World War II where they left off in World War I, employing a convoy strategy.[9] On August 26, 1939, the admiralty took control of all British shipping, and on September 2, one day after the Germans attacked Poland, the British escorted their first convoy.[10] "The British Admiralty did not after all ignore the greatest naval lesson of the First World War, the need for mercantile convoys. The first was formed in anticipation of war with Italy as well as Germany, which would make the Mediterranean unsafe."[11] British admirals employed convoy even before the British declared war on Germany.[12] This was not an isolated phenomenon; the admirals began the war by convoying 2,500 ships per month.[13] Various accounts show that the admirals were committed to, and planned to implement, a convoy strategy well before the invasion of Poland.[14] Given the admiralty's hostility toward convoy before World War I, one might wonder why the admirals developed and deployed convoys in World War II. Put differently, it is clear that the admirals learned a lesson in World War I, but it is less obvious what that lesson was.

The British admirals did not support convoy because they believed that it provided the best protection for merchant shipping. Rather, they supported convoys because they now believed that convoys presented the best opportunity to destroy U-boats. British admirals learned in World War I that the most difficult problem in hunting U-boats was finding them. The admirals now knew where the U-boats were likely to be—near the convoy. In retrospect, this may seem obvious, but the conclusion was profound at the time. "Convoying naturally enhanced the power of escorts, by multiplying the number of naval ships keeping company with merchantmen; and it also improved the escorts' chances of finding a U-boat target in a variety of ways. Convoying drew the U-boats to warships, instead of forcing the latter to embark on almost always fruitless searches; and it directed an escort toward a U-boat, at a range close enough to lend counter-attack the chance of success once a torpedo was fired."[15] Thus, convoys proved to be an effective way to surmount the most difficult barrier in destroying U-boats.

British naval strategists argued that the use of convoys was an effective strategy for finding and sinking U-boats. As we saw in the analysis of antisubmarine warfare in World War I, one of the lessons that the admirals recognized after 1917 was that convoys facilitated the destruction of U-boats.[16] As it acquired more escorts, the British navy became increasingly effective at sinking U-boats. Charles Sternhell and Alan Thorndike write: "In September 1940 the U-boats were attacking convoys with impunity. . . . in September 1941 it was a matter of keen disappointment if a convoy were attacked and the enemy escaped unpunished."[17] The navy's improved results from convoy made it an even stronger supporter of the convoy strategy.

By the time of the American entry into the war in December 1941, the British admirals had become adamant proponents of convoy.[18] The Americans, who had largely favored convoys in World War I and who were experiencing disastrous rates of loss of merchant ships right off their own coast, fought the imposition of convoys and were slow to adopt such basic defensive measures as blacking out the lights of coastal cities. (Coastal city lights backlit the ocean-going merchant ships, creating clear silhouettes that made it easy for the German U-boats to locate, identify, and destroy them.) The British admirals incurred high political costs by strenuously pushing Admiral Ernest J. King, the U.S.

chief of naval operations (an admitted Anglophobe), to adopt convoys: "On the 19th of March the First Sea Lord told Admiral King that he 'regarded the introduction of convoy as a matter of urgency,' and that convoys with weak escorts were preferable to no convoys."[19] The admiralty continued to demand that America implement a convoy system; the American navy did so in the summer of 1942.

Critics, although recognizing the navy's commitment to convoys, claimed that early naval construction priorities were not sufficiently focused on building convoy escorts: "It is true that convoy was accepted, but how best it could be applied remained unanalyzed, and the building of relatively cheap escort vessels did not absorb as high a proportion of the Naval Estimates as events of the First World War seemed to warrant."[20] But as the war continued the admirals directed an increasing amount of their resources to convoy escorts. As in the earlier war, the admirals assessed the value of convoys by their ability to sink enemy submarines. Roskill writes that a May 6, 1941, naval report argued that concerning "the long-disputed question whether the destruction of U-boats would be more effectively accomplished by hunting for them or by escorting convoys as strongly as possible, the Committee expressed its conviction that 'we cannot afford to weaken our convoy escorts to provide the ships required for searching forces until far greater strength is available than is at present in prospect.'"[21] As the war progressed, this lesson became increasingly clear to the British. The First Sea Lord stated that "this is one of the hardest lessons of the war to swallow. To go to sea to hunt down and destroy the enemy makes a strong appeal to every naval officer. It gives a sense . . . of the offensive that is lacking in the more humdrum business of convoy protection. But in this U-boat war . . . the limitations of hunting forces have made themselves very clear."[22] These statements seem to support views that offensive strategies are a military's first response. But they also call into question the Cult of the Offensive arguments, such as those made by Van Evera and Posen, that militaries cannot learn to prefer other strategies and always favor the offense. Instead, this example suggests a more complex pattern of behavior, as noted by Deborah Avant and Kimberly Marten Zisk and as represented by the dominant indicator approach.

Stephen Peter Rosen has argued that even though the admirals in World War I did learn to appreciate convoy, they were convinced by information provided to them from a new indicator. "For the resistance to be overcome the Royal Navy had to learn to look at different categories of information. Instead of focusing on enemy submarines sunk by patrols, it had to focus on the number of merchant ships at risk to submarines. The new strategic measure of effectiveness was the proportion of transatlantic sailings that survived, a proportion the Navy could not determine before the spring of 1917 because its statistical measures were oriented towards other goals."[23] I disagree with Rosen's view. As we saw in the study of World War I, the admirals retained their reliance on the number of enemy submarines sunk as a critical indicator of success. It is through this lens that they assessed their antisubmarine strategy and through this lens that they embraced convoy as an effective strategy for sinking U-boats.

THE CIVILIAN VIEW OF CONVOYS

Civilian naval evaluations focused on a number of critical time periods early in the war. As in World War I, the tons of merchant shipping built and lost was the primary concern of civilian decision makers. Churchill wrote in December 1940 to President Franklin Roosevelt that "the prime need is to check or limit the loss of tonnage on the Atlantic approaches to our island. This may be achieved both by increasing the naval forces which cope with the attacks and by adding to the number of merchant ships on which we depend."[24] Churchill and other civilian leaders repeatedly discussed the need to contain merchant shipping losses and expand new boat construction. But unlike World War I, the crisis for civilians came early in the war.

In figure 4.1 we can see both the monthly and cumulative merchant losses experienced by the British and the Allies.[25] The graph of monthly losses is not single-peaked, like that of World War I shipping losses. From both graphs we can see that losses appear to go through two cycles of increase and decrease, after which they drop off dramatically. The cumulative curve also looks different from that of World War I. There is no obvious inflection point at which the trend begins to

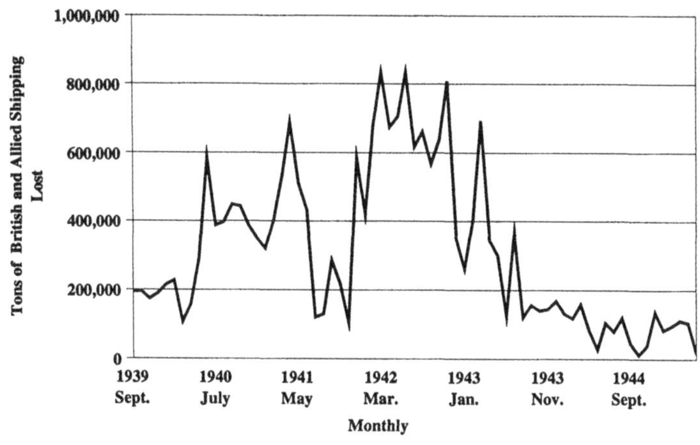

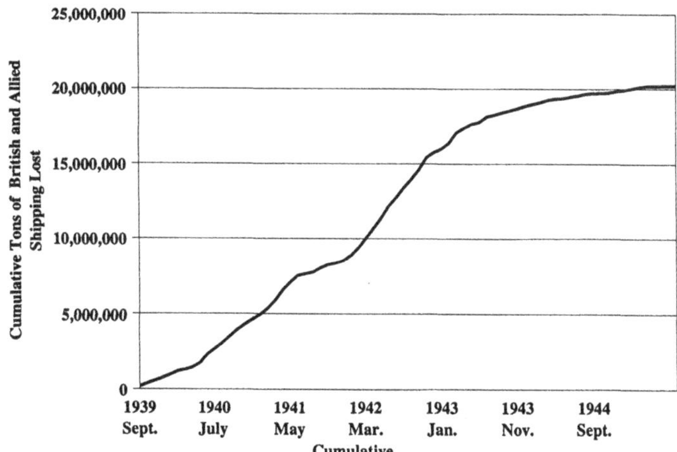

Figure 4.1 Monthly and Cumulative British and Allied Shipping Losses During World War II

decrease marginally. Instead, losses largely increase until the spring of 1943, when the curve begins to flatten. These data, along with the acceleration and change in acceleration derived from them, correspond well to the critical assessments made by British civilians. If we examine the events of spring 1940, we can see how these data help explain British antisubmarine strategic assessment.

Two important events occurred in May 1940 which suggest that civilian leaders were dissatisfied with the naval situation. In a politically costly move that German submarine commander Karl Dönitz labeled drastic and that was not popular with the British people, Great Britain occupied Iceland on May 8 in order to develop new bases for its convoy escort planes.[26] And on May 15, in his first telegram to President Roosevelt as prime minister, Churchill requested "the loan of forty or fifty of your older destroyers to bridge the gap between what we have now and the large new construction we put in hand at the beginning of the war."[27] This request, when finally implemented, had both domestic and international costs.

The American destroyers represented a critical element in British defense hopes for the Battle of the Atlantic. At the time, the United States was still legally enjoined from supporting the British, and Churchill realized that his request would be unpopular with the American Congress and public. Churchill wrote again in June to Roosevelt, stating that "nothing is so important as for us to have the thirty or forty old destroyers you have already had reconditioned."[28] In July, Churchill wrote yet again, asserting: "We could not sustain the present rate of casualties for long, and if we cannot get a substantial reinforcement the whole fate of the war may be decided by this minor and easily remediable factor."[29]

On August 13, Roosevelt offered Churchill the American ships if the British would provide the United States with military bases on Newfoundland and in the West Indies.[30] The United States' neutrality laws precluded Roosevelt from giving the British the destroyers, but he could trade them. The additional destroyers dramatically improved the British situation. "The Royal Navy's destroyer-strength was thereby increased, in due course but much faster than by any other available means, by one third at the stroke of a pen."[31] Thus, the strategy did not change, but the new resources helped make convoy more effective.

More important than the actual effect of the American aid (which has since been debated) is the assessment that the request represents. The neutrality laws were popular in the United States, and Churchill's request was likely to be politically costly for Roosevelt. As a sign of the strength of isolationism, lend-lease would not pass Congress until March 1941, and then by only one vote.[32] American opinion was still strongly pro-neutrality. Similarly, the occupation of nonbelligerent Iceland and the ceding of sovereign territory in Newfoundland and the West Indies were likely to have domestic political costs for Churchill. Churchill recognized the costly nature of his request.[33] He and the other civilian leaders were willing to incur these costs because they were extremely concerned and dissatisfied with the naval situation. This pessimistic view of the Battle of the Atlantic contrasts with the much rosier outlook just previous to Churchill's assumption of power.

Just a month earlier, civilians had seemed to think that the naval war was going well. Prime Minister Neville Chamberlain, in a speech on April 4, summed up the naval situation by saying that "Hitler missed the bus."[34] Less than five weeks later, on May 10, largely because of the defeat in Norway, Chamberlain's government fell.[35] At the same time, British civilians altered their assessment of the naval situation from very good to extremely bad.

Previous accounts have not explained what changed in the evaluation of the naval battle. Shipping losses, which had set absolute records in the months of October 1939 and January and February 1940, did not set an absolute record in April 1940. With only 158,218 tons of gross shipping sunk, April represented the second-least-damaging month since the war started. Even in September 1939 the British had lost more shipping. Thus, the absolute figures do not help explain the civilian concern at the beginning of May.

The rate of change of shipping losses helps explain the rapid turnaround. In March shipping losses decelerated at a record rate, −119,911 tons, and the rate of acceleration was itself shrinking at record rates, −132,325 tons. Thus, the situation was going extremely well and improving at an increasing rate. But this positive situation dramatically changed in April, when the acceleration, 51,209 tons, and change in acceleration, 171,120 tons, of shipping losses increased at record rates. Thus, in a short time, the civilian assessment changed to one of going extremely badly and getting worse at an accelerating rate.

In April the U-boat situation was bad and getting worse at an unprecedentedly fast rate, but, with only 158,218 tons sunk, it did not represent an absolute monthly record. Thus, although the deteriorating situation for the British Expeditionary Force against the Germans probably had more to do with the fall of the government than the naval war, the record changes in the rate at which shipping was sunk help explain the civilians' costly actions to improve the antisubmarine war.

In the summer of 1940 the Germans began to employ Wolf Packs—groups of U-boats that acted together and allowed the Germans to use signal-intercept intelligence and ship spottings more effectively. Like the gain from grouping merchant ships in convoys, grouping U-boats into Wolf Packs increased each submarine's individual effectiveness. When one submarine found a convoy, the other members of the pack would converge on it. The Germans had developed the Wolf Pack idea before the war but had to wait until the defeat of France to obtain the French Atlantic ports they required for the implementation of this new strategy. (Controlling the French ports reduced the number of submarines necessary to implement the strategy because it enabled them to reach the Atlantic more quickly, which meant that they could spend more time on station, hunting merchant convoys. The Germans were thus able to employ the strategy more quickly than they could have had they needed to wait for production to meet the necessary numbers.)[36]

At the end of the summer of 1941, civilian assessment of the naval war radically changed again. By the end of summer, many British civilian leaders believed that they had conquered the U-boat threat. "In certain quarters in London the reduction in losses in the summer months led to a surge of optimism and to some premature conclusions that the corner had been turned in the Battle of the Atlantic. One result was a proposal to divert Coastal Command's few long-range bombers to the offensive against German shore targets."[37] A number of powerful civilians, interested in building more strategic bombers, tried to divert resources from the construction of convoy escorts. This despite the loss of 432,025 tons of shipping in June. An analysis of the quarterly rates of change of shipping lost captures this seasonal assessment. During the summer, Allied shipping losses dropped at their fastest rate yet, with record rates of change. This quarter set the tone for the civilian assessment of the Battle of the Atlantic for the rest of the war. Churchill wrote: "The losses inflicted on our merchant shipping became most grave during the twelve months from July '40 to July '41, when we could claim that the British Battle of the Atlantic was won."[38]

Previous studies have been unable to explain in a systematic way why Churchill thought July 1941 represented victory in the Battle of the Atlantic. Looking at the movement of his dominant indicators, however, we see that July set records for its rapid rate of decrease. Both the acceleration of shipping losses (−311,050) and the change in acceleration (−495,618) suggested that the situation was going extremely well and improving at increasing, unprecedented rates. After this time, British civilians were never again either extremely satisfied or dissatisfied with the naval war. Even though they put pressure on the Americans in the winter of 1942 to implement convoy as soon as possible, there was no "crisis" in the U-boat war, as there was in 1940 or 1917. Although there were three absolute-value records, no month in the rest of the war had a positive record increase in the acceleration and change in acceleration of shipping losses. Indeed, December 1942 set records for deceleration and change in deceleration, suggesting that the situation was improving rapidly.

The civilian ambivalence contrasts sharply with the attitude of the admiralty, which shared some of the civilian concerns about the naval war in the first half of the war but which was extreme in its assessment of the situation in the second half of the conflict.

ADMIRALTY EVALUATION

As we saw during the discussion of convoys in World War I, the British navy relied on the number of enemy U-boats sunk and number of new U-boats created as its dominant indicators. It was concerned when "new U-boats were entering service much faster than we were sinking them."[39] But the navy worked within a convoy strategy. As Admiral Sir Max Horton, First Sea Lord during World War II, noted, British naval ships would escort convoys and come to their rescue when attacked, but in doing so their mission was to find U-boats and "hunt them to the death."[40] Thus, the destruction of U-boats took place within the convoy system, as opposed to within the strategy of sea patrol.

Employment of the dominant indicator approach does not require that decision makers have accurate information (compared with *ex post* accounts), only that they rely on the indicators when making their decisions. But British navy figures on German U-boat losses and construction were generally quite accurate. Roskill writes that the "Admiralty's assessments of the losses inflicted on the enemy and also of his total submarine strength were, in fact, nearly correct throughout this period. For example, by the end of April, 1940 the Assessment Committee considered that nineteen U-boats had been destroyed and that forty-three were in service. The actual figures we now know, were twenty-two and fifty-two."[41]

Unlike in World War I, the Germans radically increased their U-boat production, from between five and ten per quarter at the beginning of the war to between sixty and seventy from mid-1942 until the end of the war. By examining the rates of change of U-boat losses and construction, we can predict naval strategic assessments. That is, like jumps in U-boat losses, sudden changes in the number of U-boats built correspond to the British admirals' assessments of success in their war against the German submarines.

Also unlike World War I, the Allied navies did not act alone against the German threat; Allied air forces, in particular the Royal Air Force's Coastal Command, played a major role in the defeat of the U-boat. An important means by which the RAF contributed to this defeat was through its three air offenses against U-boats in the Bay of Biscay. These offenses, spread throughout the war, had two effects. First, they sank a number of U-boats. Second, they forced the U-boats to traverse the Bay of Biscay submerged, which increased the time required for the

U-boats to get on station to intercept convoys and reduced the length of their patrol.[42] The Coastal Command reluctantly provided the air craft to patrol the Bay of Biscay, preferring to attack basic manufacturing plants and cities in Europe.[43] But requests by the navy to attack patrolling U-boats, or U-boat pens, demonstrate naval concern about the outcome of the U-boat war. As Terraine writes, appeals to the RAF for the bombing of U-boat bases were "only further evidence of the Admiralty's shaken nerves."[44] Thus, the RAF's involvement in the U-boat war affects the analysis in two ways. First, not all U-boat sinkings could be seen as resulting from naval actions, although all are seen as contributing to the perception of victory in the U-boat war. Second, admiralty requests for additional RAF bombing represent signals of concern regarding the naval war.

Like their fellow civilian leaders, British naval leaders rapidly altered their assessments of their battle against the U-boat threat between success and failure. Unlike World War I, however, where both British civilians and admirals agreed in their evaluation of convoy effectiveness after its implementation, civilian and admiralty views in World War II also alternated between strict agreement and fundamental opposition. Analyzing these periods of reassessment, we see that the dominant indicators do a good job at capturing the environmental factors that influenced the admiralty's strategic assessments. The critical periods of British naval assessment in the Battle of the Atlantic came in the spring and summer of 1940, the winter, spring, and fall of 1941, the winter of 1942, and the spring and summer of 1943.

1940

The admirals, like the civilians, believed that the situation in early 1940 was progressing well. Unlike the civilians, however, they saw the situation as remaining positive throughout spring. While the government fell, England established bases on Iceland, and Churchill urgently telegrammed Roosevelt for additional resources, the admirals evaluated the situation as stable. In an official naval assessment in May, the admirals wrote that "the state of the sea war, and in particular the war against

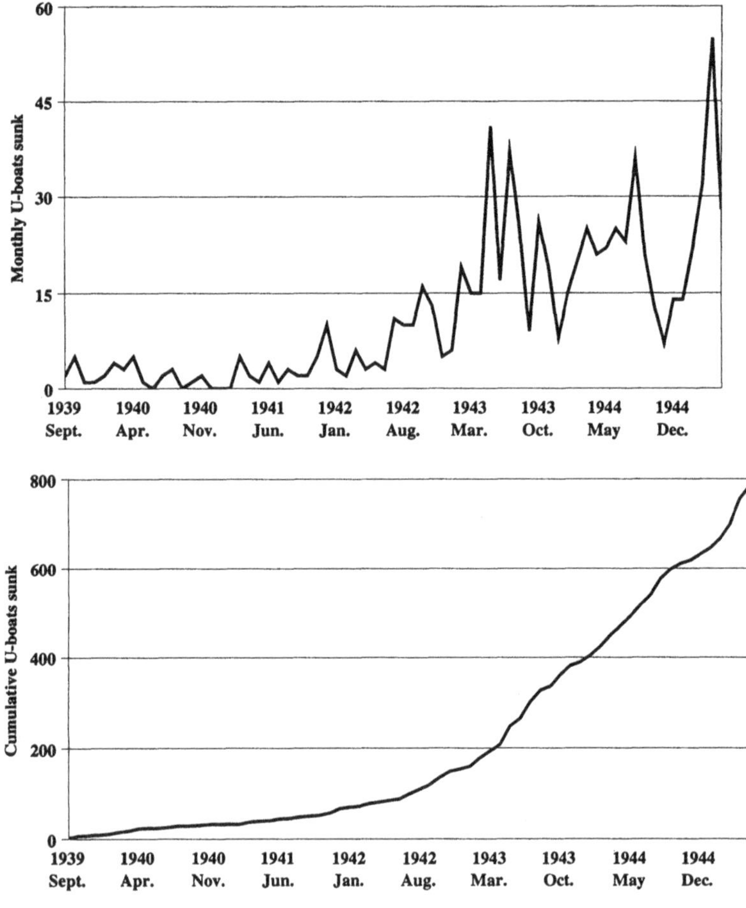

Figure 4.2 Monthly and Cumulative German U-Boat Losses During World War II

U-boats, was not considered unsatisfactory."[45] Why did the British navy choose not to alter its position on its success in the antisubmarine war after April, as the civilian leadership had?

Figure 4.2 shows monthly and cumulative U-boat losses. Figure 4.3 displays quarterly records of U-boats built and sunk as well as total

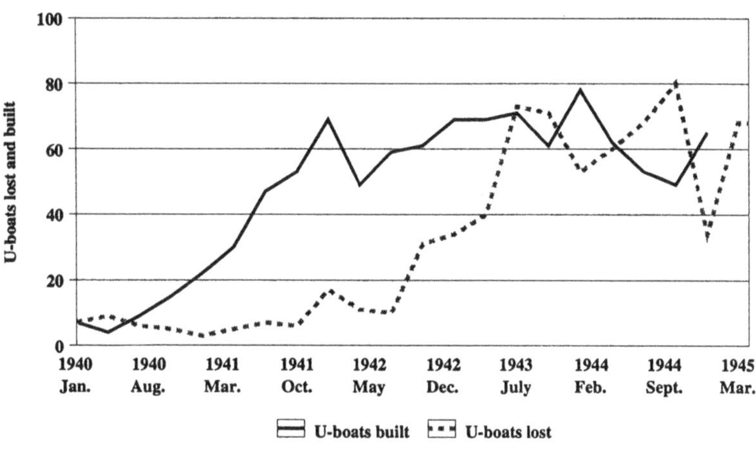

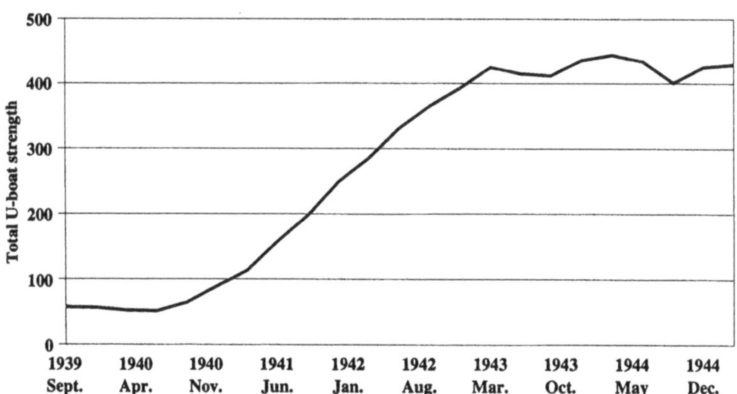

Figure 4.3 U-Boats Built and Sunk and Total U-Boat Strength During World War II

U-boat strength. The dominant indicators represented in these graphs help explain why the British admirals continued to see the situation as "not unsatisfactory" while the civilian leadership viewed it as extremely unsatisfactory.

Viewed through the lenses of the British navy, the situation was going well. The rate at which U-boats were being sunk increased, and the rate of new U-boat construction sharply decreased. In April five U-boats were lost, up from three in March, resulting in positive increases in both the acceleration and change in acceleration of U-boat losses. At the same time, U-boat construction dropped from seven in fall 1939 to four in winter.[46] The admirals' indicators suggested that the situation was going well and improving. They were sinking U-boats faster than the Germans could build them. These figures suggest that the situation was progressing well for the admirals and help explain why the admirals' and civilians' evaluations differed so sharply.

The Royal Navy's positive assessment changed at the end of spring, however. During May and June the British sank only one U-boat. In the spring and summer, U-boat construction per quarter rapidly increased to nine and fifteen boats, respectively. The dramatic impact of these changes can be seen by looking at the total U-boat figures. Thus, by the measures employed by the admirals, the situation was deteriorating at an increasing rate. Unlike their temperate stance earlier, in summer the admirals applied significant pressure on Churchill to obtain the destroyers from the Americans.[47] Their concerns further intensified as the situation increasingly deteriorated.

1941

By the winter of 1941, the British battle against the U-boats, as measured by the admiralty's dominant indicators, rapidly deteriorated. In December 1940 and January and February 1941, the navy failed to sink a single U-boat. Construction of U-boats also increased, from twenty-two in the fall of 1940 to thirty in the winter of 1941. And in the spring of 1941, U-boat construction shot up from thirty to forty-seven, which created the only quarter with both record-setting acceleration and change in acceleration of new boat construction. The rate of change of the dominant indicators thus captures the changes that concerned the admirals. The admirals put tremendous pressure on Churchill to dedicate additional resources to the problem. The Battle of the Atlantic Committee and Directive proposed by Churchill in the first week of March addressed demands made by the admiralty, which had grown "thoroughly alarmed" at the situation.[48]

These efforts had a significant impact on the situation, leading to a rapid change in naval assessment. The navy's effectiveness at sinking U-boats contributed to the general belief that naval victory was at hand, a belief, as we saw earlier, that pervaded the British leadership throughout the summer. Thus, in June both the civilians and admirals thought that their war against the U-boats was progressing well.

Unlike the civilian leadership, however, the admirals' evaluations of naval success did not extend into the rest of the summer. In the remaining months of the summer, the navy was not as optimistic as the civilians were; the navy believed that positive assessments of the U-boat situation made by civilians were premature at best and inaccurate at worst. Roskill, the official naval historian, wrote that by September it "was clear to the Admiralty that new U-boats were entering service much faster than we were sinking them."

In the Bay of Biscay, Coastal Command patrols were successfully limiting the German exploitation of French ports. One of the reasons for the RAF's success in this effort was that so many of the Luftwaffe's planes were pulled out of Western Europe for use on the Eastern Front.[49] But the RAF, like the civilians, saw the U-boat threat as diminishing during the summer and wanted to shift bombers from Coastal Command to the strategic bombing effort. The admiralty fought this move, with board members claiming that the navy needed "every single surface ship and every long-range aircraft we can possibly muster. Any suggestion that the corner has been turned is not supported by the facts."[50]

This leads to an obvious question: Why did the naval and the civilian/air force leadership reach such divergent views of their success against the U-boat threat? The different movement of indicators in each organization's dominant indicator set helps explain the factors that led the civilians and the navy to reach contradictory evaluations.

During the summer the navy sank six U-boats, fewer than it had the previous quarter, resulting in a negative acceleration and change in acceleration of U-boat losses (although not at record rates). From their view the situation was bad and getting increasingly worse. In addition, U-boat production continued to increase, reaching fifty-three boats per quarter. Thus, both of the admirals' indicators suggested that the situation was bad and deteriorating at an increasing rate. These figures suggest a much more pessimistic picture than the civilian assessment discussed earlier. The RAF, which wanted to use its bombers exclusively for strategic bombing, was unwilling to increase resources for Coastal Command to pursue a mission that was not only the job of the navy but was believed by the civilians to have been successfully completed. This helps explain why the civilian and naval leadership reached divergent assessments of British success against the U-boats, and why the navy had to fight to retain its resources.

1942

In the winter of 1942, the navy was torn in its assessment of the antisubmarine situation. The British began the year badly, sinking only three U-boats in January (down from ten the month before, a record-setting drop in both acceleration and change in acceleration). Quarterly data (helpful because of the small monthly U-boat loss figures) also show the negative situation. During the winter, eleven U-boats were sunk, down from seventeen the previous quarter and resulting in record drops in the acceleration and change in acceleration of U-boat losses. But at the same time U-boat construction dropped dramatically, falling from sixty-nine to fifty-three boats after seven quarters of continuous growth.[51] This sudden drop resulted in the only record decrease in both the acceleration and change in acceleration of U-boat construction in the entire war. These mixed signals created organizational gridlock and facilitated the navy's silence on the issue. In other words, during the first quarter, the navy's indicators suggested that the situation was going both as well as it could and as badly as it could. These conflicting signals helped create a largely conflicted organization. Thus, as we saw earlier, the British admirals strongly encouraged the Americans to adopt convoy, while at the same time they grew increasingly concerned about its effectiveness.[52] Similarly, the admirals requested that the RAF renew its patrols of the Bay of Biscay. Coastal Command planes sank two submarines in July, and an RAF squadron leader invented the Leigh Spotlight, which helped aircraft sink U-boats.[53]

This gridlock ended. An increasingly large number of U-boats was destroyed during the second half of the year, with losses of thirty-one and thirty-four U-boats, respectively, in the two last quarters of 1942. And although U-boat construction increased to 1941 levels, the rate of increase was not dramatic. Thus, through the lens of the navy, the situation, which had been ambiguous earlier in the year, resolved into an increasingly positive one in the second half of 1942.

1943

Many historians and analysts believe that the critical turning point in the antisubmarine war occurred during the late spring and summer of 1943.[54] The admiralty's view was extraordinarily volatile during this period, shifting rapidly from declarations of defeat to boasts of victory.

Spring began with "the crisis of the Atlantic battle."[55] The navy assessed the war against the U-boats as terrible and becoming worse at an increasing rate. The situation was so bad that the navy questioned its choice of strategy. As Admiral Arthur Hezlet wrote in March, the "U-boats were now achieving results nearly as great as in April 1917 but against convoys, not independent ships. . . . German hopes rose and it seemed as though numbers might yet master the convoy system. The Allies' anxiety was such that convoy itself was challenged as a principle."[56] An official admiralty assessment of the U-boat war, written at the end of 1943, stated that in the spring, "It appeared possible that we should not be able to continue [to regard] convoy as an effective system of defence."[57] The admirals feared that the convoy system was failing. But their assessments during this period changed several times.

Almost as soon as the crisis arose, "the pendulum had swung back central again," and the British situation improved.[58] Following this the British declared victory in the war against the U-boats, and the Germans acknowledged defeat. At the end of May, Admiral Horton, the former submariner in charge of the Western Approaches Command and the new First Sea Lord, sent this communiqué to all units: "In the last two months the Battle of the Atlantic has undergone a decisive change in our favour. . . . All escort-groups, support-groups, escort-carriers and their machines as well as the aircraft from the various air-commands have contributed to this great success. . . . The climax of the battle has been surmounted."[59] At the same time, German naval commander Dönitz wrote in his diary on May 24: "We had lost the Battle of the Atlantic."[60] Thus both the German and the British navies proclaimed Britain the victor of the Battle of the Atlantic at the same time.

Virtually every naval analyst who studies the war has a list of factors that contributed to the victory.[61] But although there is frequent disagreement about the relative importance of such factors as air cover versus radar capabilities, there have been few attempts to use a general approach to explain the assessments. Given the extreme change of beliefs from defeat to victory, this is not surprising; rapid change is extremely difficult to capture. But the dominant indicator approach can help us understand the sudden change in conditions that led to these dramatic assessments.

There is agreement that the increase in the number of U-boats sunk greatly affected the admiralty's evaluations *at the time*.[62] Admiral Hezlet wrote that the "crisis for the U-boats came in May. . . . The most significant fact was the very rapid rise in the total U-boat losses for the month. Forty-one U-boats were lost, six in a new offensive by aircraft in the Bay of Biscay. These casualties were at nearly double the rate at which U-boats were being built; Admiral Dönitz therefore ordered the withdrawal of U-boats from the North Atlantic and the campaign against shipping collapsed."[63]

Between March and May the admiralty's assessments swung between perceptions of defeat and victory. In both March and April the Germans lost fifteen U-boats. This was the third highest figure ever for monthly U-boat losses. Thus, the absolute approach does not explain what triggered such rapid despair in the British. In May the Germans lost forty-one U-boats, a record by all measures. This swing in assessments can thus be explained by looking at the rate of change of the admirals' dominant indicators.

We can see by figure 4.2 that the rates at which U-boats were sunk shifted radically between March and July. In February, a record nineteen U-boats were sunk, up from six in January. But this increase stopped in March, with a sudden drop to only fifteen U-boats sunk. The navy's performance, however, improved in May, when forty-one U-boats were sunk, setting records for both the acceleration and change in acceleration of U-boat sinkings. In May the situation was going well and improving at an increasing rate. Also in May, Admiral Dönitz withdrew the U-boats from the Atlantic, moving them into the Mediterranean Sea, and the Allies declared victory in the Battle of the Atlantic. With victory came expectations of lower U-boat sinkings because, with fewer U-boats in the Atlantic, they were harder to find and sink (particularly with a strategy of convoy).

The British admirals shifted dramatically from an assessment of imminent failure to one of complete victory. These changes are accurately captured by the changes in the dominant indicators employed by the admiralty. Looking at the U-boat data displayed in figure 4.3, we see the net effect of British efforts to sink U-boats and German efforts to build them. The indicator of total German U-boat strength, which had been continually increasing since the summer of 1940, largely flattened out in the winter and spring of 1943. Thus, although it remained close to its absolute record value, German U-boat strength did continue its upward trend. It is the end of this trend, and not the four hundred U-boats still available to Dönitz, that so pleased the British admirals.

This assessment of Allied success in May was not unique to the British. Keith Tidman writes that the Americans also realized that the Allies had gained the upper hand through their destruction of U-boats.[64] Furthermore, the Germans also explicitly recognized the Allied victory, both in statements made at the time and through their decision to pull the U-boats out of the Atlantic. This assessment, as with most of the German U-boat decision making, was based on assessments derived from quantitative indicators.

GERMAN NAVAL EVALUATIONS

From the beginning of the war, the Germans attempted to assess the situation and make changes to improve their performance.[65] The German navy, led by Admiral Dönitz, measured success through the number of merchant ships sunk per U-boat. Dönitz wrote: "Our primary aim was to sink as much shipping as possible in the most economical manner. In other words, the sinkings per U-boat per day-at-sea had to be maintained at the highest possible level."[66] Dönitz was adamant about focusing on sinking enemy ships and not using the navy for activities that would not contribute to this measure of success. "The strategic task of the German Navy was to wage war on trade; its objective was therefore to sink as many enemy merchant ships as it could. The *sinking of ships* was the only thing that counted. In theory then, any diversion, however attractive, which resulted in a reduction of the number of ships being sunk was inadmissible."[67] Other sources verify Dönitz's assertion that the Germans measured success through the amount of shipping destroyed by each boat.[68]

Perhaps more than most military organizations, the German U-boat forces relied on quantitative information to evaluate their progress. The Germans measured U-boat capability by the "effective U-boat quotient."[69] As Dönitz stated in 1940: "The effective U-boat quotient, by which I mean the average sinkings per U-boat per day for all U-boats at sea, had to be kept as high as possible."[70] This figure measured the success of the Germans' naval policy and the health (returning to Zisk's phrase) of the organization. Referring to a graph of the U-boat quotient, Dönitz declared that "as a temperature chart reveals to a doctor the condition of his patient, so this graph showed U-boat Command the incidence of any changes taking place, for better or worse, in the various operational areas, which might otherwise have been obscured by some transitory success or failure, or might never have come to light at all through lack of any clear indication."[71] The Germans recognized that different cargoes might be more or less valuable, but they used tonnage sunk explicitly as a proxy. Dönitz wrote on April 15, 1942: "The enemy's shipping constitutes one single, great entity. It is therefore immaterial where a ship is sunk. Once it has been destroyed, it has to be replaced by a new ship; and that's that."[72] Hitler stated in April 1942 the "victory depends on destroying the greatest amount of Allied tonnage."[73] Dönitz argued that the only way to determine whether he and the organization had made good decisions was to observe their "measure of success."[74]

Given the dramatic drop in merchant ships sunk, and the Allies' increased ability to threaten U-boats (forcing them to spend more time on self-protection than hunting and destroying merchant ships), it is not surprising that the German naval assessment is the opposite of that of the British civilians and admirals. When the British admirals declared victory, Dönitz conceded defeat and altered German naval strategy, ordering that all U-boat activities be restricted to the Mediterranean Sea. The Mediterranean was less lethal to his U-boats because the Germans had better air cover there, and the Allies could not use their major surface ships for convoy escort. But the Mediterranean was also significantly less vital to the Allies' ability to conduct the war and to Great Britain's ability to survive.[75]

The rapid decrease in merchant ships sunk and increase in U-boats destroyed captures the factors influencing this change. Dönitz explicitly acknowledged the effect of these indicators. "Losses, even heavy losses, must be borne when they are accompanied by corresponding sinkings."[76] But without the corresponding sinkings of merchant ships, and in the face of rapid increases in U-boat losses, the situation was unacceptable.[77] Thus, in this situation, the dominant indicators not only represent the critical factors affecting German naval decision making but are themselves identified as being the crucial determinants of success and failure.

German decision makers not only relied on quantitative measures for assessment, they focused on the relative rate of change of their dominant indicator, the U-boat potential.[78] Furthermore, the Germans analyzed monthly indicator figures in terms of the recent previous months (instead of a seasonal comparison, or a moving average).[79]

The change in German naval strategy in May 1943—withdrawing from the Atlantic—occurred without a significant strategic change by the Allies. Successful Allied efforts, such as increasing the number of long-range patrols, continuing air patrols over the Bay of Biscay, and increasing the number of escort craft (in particular, escort carriers), altered the situation. Although none of these methods of antisubmarine warfare was new, the resources dedicated to them all increased incrementally, and their combined effect dramatically altered the submarine situation. The Germans were not reacting to a change in strategy by Britain and the United States but rather to a situation that rapidly deteriorated and convinced them that their current strategy was failing and they needed to adopt an alternative. This represents an example of strategic change occurring in response to altered environmental conditions rather than to specific adversarial strategic changes.

Finally, it is important to recognize that the German navy's employment of U-boats to sink Allied merchant shipping was also a strategic choice. By the German navy's measures, U-boats had been successful at commerce raiding in World War I. Thus, like the British admiralty, the Germans began World War II with the strategy that they used at the end of World War I. This did not have to be the case. The Japanese and the Americans (who initially refused to use convoys) began the war employing a different strategy from their ally's. The Japanese used their submarines exclusively as escorts for their naval ships and refused to convoy their own merchant shipping.[80] Unlike the Americans, however, the Japanese did not alter their strategy and adopt their ally's method of fighting. Instead, despite German pleas to the contrary, the Japanese used their submarines for fleet support during the entire war.

The lack of a major British antisubmarine strategy switch masks a changing and uncertain decision making environment for both civilian and naval leaders. Shipping losses were not monotonic as they had been in World War I, and the rapidly changing relation between U-boats, merchant shipping, and escorts resulted in frequent and sometimes radical alterations of assessment.

The dominant indicator approach effectively captures the four critical periods of British antisubmarine assessment. In 1940 both naval and civilian decision makers were concerned with the performance of the convoy strategy, and both organizations' dominant indicators suggested a rapidly deteriorating situation. In the summer of 1941 the admirals became increasingly concerned, while the civilians became increasingly pleased with the situation. During this time, the dominant indicators relied on by both organizations moved in divergent directions, capturing this split in assessments. In the winter of 1942 the civilians were concerned about the U.S. situation, and the admirals were generally conflicted. At this time, merchant shipping losses increased while for the only period of the war the admirals' two indicators of success—U-boats sunk and built—moved rapidly in different directions. Finally, in the spring of 1943 the British navy rapidly altered its assessment of convoy from extremely bad to extremely good.

The dominant indicator approach also helps us explain why the British admirals were so committed to a strategy of convoy at the start of the war. After World War I, the British navy determined that convoy, rather than sea patrol, was more effective at maximizing their key indicators of success. Thus, the admirals supported convoys because they increased the number of U-boats destroyed. Before World War II, the British navy's planning assumed that convoys would be used. In fact, the navy began to employ convoys before the war officially began. The admiralty demonstrated its commitment to convoys again, when it angered Admiral King with its adamant and persistent demands that the United States adopt the strategy. Thus, the admirals seem to be more committed to their assessment criteria (U-boats sunk) than to their earlier strategy (sea patrol). This case illustrates the importance of using a true comparative case study, as well as the usefulness of looking at decision making across time rather than at static, one-time snapshots.

Neither alternative approach effectively captures the environmental factors that influenced British decision making. As we have seen, decision makers reach positive and negative assessments in periods with both record and nonrecord absolute values of their indicators. Thus, the absolute-value model does not seem to provide a useful approach for explaining British assessments.

Unlike the World War I case, the action-reaction approach does not capture British or German decision making. The British changed assessments dramatically in times when the Germans made no strategic alterations. Similarly, following the German shift to Wolf Packs, the British did not fundamentally alter their assessment. Finally, during the spring of 1943, when the British admirals rapidly changed their assessments from intensely bad to good, they were not reacting to German changes.

Similarly, the Germans changed their naval strategy in the fall of 1940. This change was largely because of their acquisition of French Atlantic ports, an exogenous factor that none of the explanations examined here could have captured. And the British decision to start the war with a convoy strategy did not affect German decision making. Finally, the German decision to concede defeat in the Battle of the Atlantic did not follow from a British strategic change. Thus, the action-reaction explanation does not provide much empirical purchase in this case.

In World War II, British civilian and naval leaders dramatically altered their assessments of the effectiveness of convoy while continuously employing a convoy strategy. At the same time, German U-boat command, led by Dönitz, explicitly employed an assessment process based on a key, dominant indicator. On the basis of these indicators—and no other clearly observable phenomena—both Dönitz and the British declared the Allies victors in the Battle of the Atlantic. Ships would continue to be sunk, and sailors would continue to die, but after this time, neither British nor German leaders would question the effectiveness of Great Britain's convoy strategy, nor the eventual outcome of the naval battle.

At the climax of the Battle of the Atlantic, a variety of actors agreed about who was winning and losing. But sometimes organizational leaders from different countries—or even the same country—reach different conclusions about the performance of strategies. These differences can even extend into an organization itself, making the organization internally torn and gridlocked. This was the case for the Americans during the Vietnam War.

Chapter 5

U.S. Ground Strategy in the Vietnam War

Victory was a high body-count, defeat a low kill-ratio, war a matter of arithmetic.

—Philip Caputo, *A Rumor of War*

In spite of the vast amounts written on the Vietnam War, there are surprisingly few analyses that apply generalizable models to decision makers' strategic choices and assessments.[1] In particular, there are hardly any causal analyses of the strategic evaluations made by military and civilian decision makers during the U.S. ground war in South Vietnam. Without a general approach, it is difficult to determine which characteristics were unique to the Vietnam War and which were common to other wars. In addition, a causal analysis can help determine which of the many factors described by historians contributed most toward influencing U.S. behavior.

The Vietnam War is a particularly important case for the dominant indicator approach, because it is the best-known and most controversial example of actors deliberately using quantitative indicators to measure progress (although, as we have seen, British and German leaders also measured strategic success through quantitative indicators). Many have criticized the American leaders' reliance on quantitative data and, in particular, their employment of the number of enemy dead (the body count) to evaluate progress in the war. For example, Larry Cable claims that the "almost pornographic pandering to the American lust for numbers pretending to be facts assured that only the shortest of short-term criteria would be employed and that highly subjective data would be used to generate final numbers with the appearance of objectivity."[2] Alain Enthoven and K. Wayne Smith assert: "The highest officials in Washington and Saigon were blinded by the deluge of statistics showing only change and activity."[3] The criticism has been so intense that in 1995 former Secretary of Defense Robert McNamara defended the process of strategic assessment employed during the war. "Critics point to use of the body count as an example of my obsession with numbers. . . . But things you can count, you ought to count. Loss of life is one when you are fighting a war of attrition. *We tried to use body counts as a measurement to help us figure out what we should be doing in Vietnam to win the war* while putting our troops at least risk."[4] How do these concerns affect the applicability of the dominant indicator approach?

Arguments that America's reliance on such indicators as the body count led to bad Vietnam War decisions may be correct. The key for this study, however, is not whether the United States made the right decisions or chose the right indicator but whether the dominant indicator approach can help capture the environmental factors that influenced decision makers' strategic assessments.[5] If decision makers relied to an excessive degree on the information provided by their indicators, then an approach that tries to predict decision makers' strategic assessments by looking at the performance of these indicators should be appropriate. Thus, the Vietnam War is a critical case for the dominant indicator approach.

In this chapter, I analyze how the U.S. Army, Congress, and the Johnson Administration assessed the success of American ground strategy from 1966 to 1969. I have limited the scope of my analysis to ground warfare strategy from 1966 to 1969, with an emphasis on the Tet Offensive. During this time the three organizational actors that were potentially most critical to U.S. strategic decision making were the army (the U.S. Army in Vietnam and the Joint Chiefs of Staff), the Johnson Administration, and Congress (particularly the Senate). Although there were certainly other organizations involved in forming U.S. military policy in Vietnam, these three groups are seen by many analysts as the critical actors involved in formulating and assessing American ground warfare policy.[6] Limiting the time period facilitates analysis because the basic military and political goals did not change during these years. "When the Communist Tet Offensive came in early 1968, the formal objectives were still as set forth in NSAM [National Security Council Action Memo] 288 of March 1964."[7] Because the goals did not change but strategic assessments did, we can examine what environmental factors influenced these changes while controlling for other determinants.

THE SITUATION

By early 1964 a broad consensus formed among American policy makers that decisive U.S. action was necessary to prevent the South Vietnamese government from falling to the communists. The 16,000 American advisers in South Vietnam in 1964 were supposed to help build the Armed Forces of the Republic of Vietnam (ARVN) into a stable and effective fighting force. This was not working. American military and civilian leaders generally measured success in their advisory mission through indicators such as ARVN desertion rates, and Viet Cong (V.C.) initiated attacks. In early 1964, ARVN desertion rates began "spiraling," and there was a "dramatic increase in Viet-Cong initiated actions."[8] By most measures, the situation in South Vietnam, particularly after the anti-Diem coup of November 1963, was rapidly deteriorating. "Throughout 1964, the situation inside South Viet-Nam worsened considerably by every yardstick of insurgency measurement, from actual battle casualties to tonnage of rice not falling into Viet-Cong hands; from the size of enemy units to the desertion rate of the A.R.V.N. forces."[9] American decision makers from a variety of organizations recognized in 1964 that the ARVN and the government of South Vietnam were deteriorating at alarming rates and would not last without significant U.S. support.[10] The March 1964 National Security Council Action Memo and the August Gulf of Tonkin Resolution provided the United States with a legal mechanism to increase its involvement in the region.[11] But in order to minimize the political ramifications of American involvement, the Johnson Administration held off acting until after the November election. Developments in South Vietnam occurring in early 1965, however, made it clear that further delay would lead to a communist victory.

The V.C. destroyed two ARVN divisions in January 1965. In a January 27 memo from National Security Adviser McGeorge Bundy to President Lyndon Johnson, Bundy wrote that although there was some dissension in the administration on what the next step should be, there was complete agreement that "things are going very badly and that the situation is unraveling."[12] A February 10 official report noted that "continued and increasing Viet Cong success on the battlefield was demonstrated in report after report."[13] The rapid deterioration experienced in early 1965 led to the February initiation of the U.S. air war in Vietnam. On March 8, American combat units arrived in South Vietnam.

Later, American civilian and military decision makers would argue that U.S. bombing and troop deployments ended the ARVN's disintegration. President Johnson declared: "By the end of 1965 the worst crisis had ended; the downward slide had been stopped. Serious political and economic problems remained in the South, but on the military front things were looking up."[14] By almost all accounts, the United States stabilized the military situation in South Vietnam. Even though U.S. troop levels continued to increase, by most other measures the situation remained largely the same (many argued stalemated) until 1967.

During the advisory period, the U.S. mission to prevent the collapse of the ARVN fostered a common view of how to measure success. After the United States began to escalate its intervention this consensus ended. Once the ARVN was stabilized, there was less consensus on what American operational goals should be. Everyone agreed that the abstract goal was to preserve an independent South Vietnam, but as the Vietnam War expanded and organizations were given new, broad objectives, U.S. decision makers began to pursue a number of varied operational goals.

The United States essentially fought three connected, largely independent wars: a ground war, an air war, and a domestic war of pacification. Because different actors were involved in various aspects of each of these wars, they evaluated their performance through different measures of success. As Donald Mrozek notes, without an "agreed notion of what sort of war it was, it may have become inevitable for each party to reconceive the war in more limited terms—suited to the doctrinal familiarities of one's own subsection of the military, comfortable to one's own conditioned inclinations, and ultimately devoted to saving one's own institution from damage more than prosecuting the ill-defined and ambiguous larger war."[15] The complex and varied nature of the Vietnam War made it especially difficult to translate abstract, strategic goals into specific missions for individual organizations.

Even among the three major actors and within the narrow context of the ground war, the indicators and assessments of Congress, the army, and the Johnson Administration varied dramatically. Congress assessed success through minimizing U.S. casualties, the army evaluated performance through maximizing the number of enemy dead and enemy weapons captured, and the Johnson Administration based its assessments of U.S. effectiveness largely on U.S. and communist casualties. These measures, however, led to fundamentally different assessments of performance, particularly when the fighting dramatically increased during the Tet Offensive.

On January 31, 1968, during the Tet New Year cease-fire, the Viet Cong launched an enormous, widespread attack on U.S. and South Vietnamese forces throughout South Vietnam. Unlike previous V.C. attacks, which had taken place in rural areas and were uncoordinated, in the Tet Offensive the V.C. initiated coordinated, violent battles in dozens of cities throughout Vietnam. By almost all measures, the Tet Offensive represented a fundamental change in V.C. strategy and behavior.

The Tet Offensive, which lasted for more than a month, completely surprised the Americans.[16] This attack was more intense, more urban, and more coordinated than any up to this point of the war. During the battle the communists occupied the U.S. embassy grounds in Saigon for a short time, and the entire city of Hue for weeks. The toll in American lives was heavy. In the month of February, 2,124 Americans died, compared with 662 in February 1967. Yet the cost to the V.C. was more than thirty times greater; almost 70,000 V.C. were believed killed, compared with 7,300 a year earlier.

To the American public, the fighting seemed even more violent and deadly than these numbers suggest. Because it occurred in the cities, television and other media coverage was easier, and the coverage was broad and immediate. The attack seemed to nullify recent U.S. statements that the V.C. had been almost completely destroyed.[17] As a result, the Tet Offensive played a major role in shaping U.S. strategy in the remainder of the Vietnam War.

AMERICAN STRATEGIC ASSESSMENT

Debate still rages about the communists' motivation for launching the offensive. Captured communist documents reported that the attack had to be carried to the cities because "the cities are not only crucial places, but also places where the enemy has many weaknesses and where the U.S.-puppet rule is centered."[18] Traditional analysis has tended to see the Tet Offensive as an enormous victory for the communists, for it began the political process that led to U.S. withdrawal from Vietnam. Since the late 1980s, however, studies have suggested that the motivation for the offensive was more complex. These studies argue that the decision to launch the offensive was based not on the opportunity to exploit American public opinion but on a desperate effort by the North Vietnamese to halt a strategic situation that was rapidly becoming untenable. James Wirtz claims: "The desire to reverse a deteriorating military situation seems to have been the primary communist motivation behind the Tet offensive."[19] Michael Lanning and Don Cragg state that Tet was a "gamble aimed at reversing the losses."[20] In other words, the V.C. perceived that the situation was going badly and deteriorating at an increasing rate and therefore chose to implement an alternative strategy. If this is the case, then as Vietnamese archives become available, the type of approach employed here should be able to capture the factors that led communist leaders to decide that a new strategy was necessary. What is already clear, however, is that Tet represented a communist change in strategy that profoundly influenced the U.S. Congress's view of the war.

Congress

Members of Congress saw the war through the lens of domestic politics. They wanted to minimize the negative impact of the fighting on their constituency. As a result, Congress evaluated U.S. strategic performance in terms of the number of U.S. casualties and was particularly interested in minimizing the number of Americans killed in action in Vietnam.

Evidence for this concern is abundant. Between 1964 and 1968, Congress frequently questioned administration representatives, like Secretary of Defense McNamara and Secretary of State Dean Rusk, about the war, focusing on recent and potential future U.S. losses.[21] Specific examples of members of Congress expressing concern for U.S. casualties are also common. Stanley Karnow notes that "on a trip back from Asia to Washington in early 1966, I queried several members of Congress for their views on the war. Most of them seemed to be unsure; one of them expressed the prevailing sentiment when he confided to me that he would probably make up his mind *'when the casualties in my constituency become significant.'* "[22] Congressional concern about U.S. casualties also appears to make political sense *ex post.* John Mueller found that public attitudes toward the Korean and Vietnam wars changed as a function of U.S. losses.[23] Congressional interest in minimizing U.S. casualties appeared most clearly after Tet, but it was visible earlier. In fact, this concern, like much of the American political dynamics involved in the Vietnam War, represented a continuation of the politics previously practiced in Washington during the Korean War.[24]

Why did Tet so profoundly alter the congressional view of U.S. success in Vietnam? And why had Congress held such a benign view of Vietnam previously? Regarding the salience of Tet, analysts identify a number of characteristics of the attack, such as how the urban settings facilitated press coverage, the symbolic importance of the V.C. siege of the U.S. embassy in Saigon, and how the coordinated intensity of the attacks seemed to refute the assurances General William Westmoreland had given fewer than three months earlier in Washington. Although these factors and others probably did contribute to Congress's abrupt shift, they do not add up to an easily generalizable argument about what triggered the Congressional response. By analyzing the rate of change of Congress's dominant indicator set, we could have predicted its reaction.

Even though information on Vietnam was reported by the press on a daily basis, official Washington reports and assessments were largely based on monthly and quarterly figures.[25] Because U.S. decision makers attempted to minimize losses, a positive increase in the acceleration and change in acceleration of American losses would suggest that the situation was bad and getting increasingly worse.

In figure 5.1 we can see the number of Americans killed in action (KIA) per month and per quarter from January 1966 to the end of 1968.[26] The monthly figures suggest that U.S. losses increased, as did the rate of acceleration of losses in March and May 1967. In March 944 Americans were killed in action, compared with 662 the previous month and 507 in March 1966. This increase led to record increases in both acceleration and change in acceleration. In May 1,233 Americans were killed, again creating record, accelerating increases. In the winter quarter of 1967, 2,126 Americans were killed, a dramatic increase over the 1,247 killed the previous quarter or the 1,224 Americans killed in the winter of 1966. Not surprisingly, this rapid increase resulted in record positive acceleration and change in acceleration in the number of Americans killed in action.

In April 1967 Congress expressed serious concerns to President Johnson about the situation in Vietnam. In response, Johnson brought Westmoreland back to Washington to give "the first address to Congress by a battlefield commander during hostilities" on April 28.[27] Loss rates in March and May suggested that the situation was bad and becoming increasingly worse. The dramatic, accelerating increase in both months, as well as for the winter quarter of 1967, was sufficient to break Congress's previous silence on the war. Both June and August, however, showed dramatic, record-setting decreases in the rate at which Americans were killed in Vietnam. Not until the fall of 1967 did another month show positive acceleration and change in acceleration of U.S. killed in action. This helps explain why Congress, while clearly agitated about the situation in spring, returned to a position of support for the administration.

Previously, with the exception of a few senators who had been against the war from the beginning (such as Wayne Morse of Oregon, John Stennis, and William Fulbright), Congress as a body had essen-

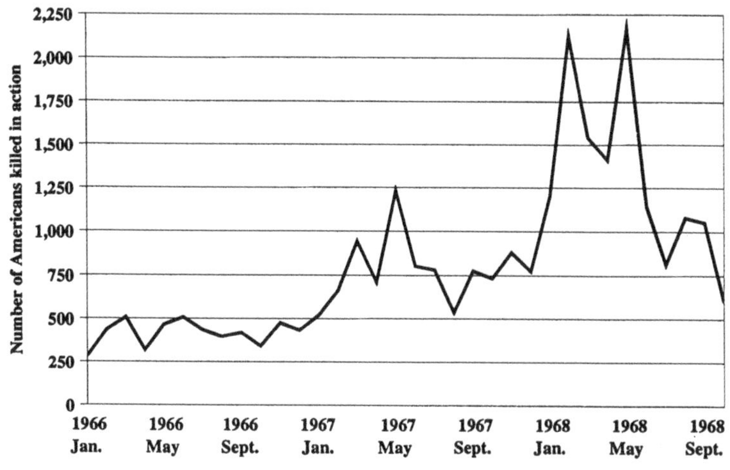

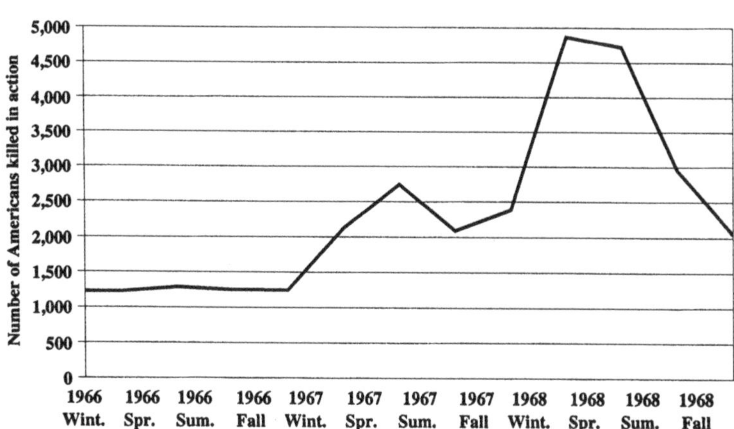

Figure 5.1 Americans Killed in Action During the Vietnam War, by Month and by Quarter

tially, if unenthusiastically, supported the war. "In any case the doves and hawks were both minorities. All in all, when the sound and the fury were penetrated it was actually clear that the dominant attitude in Congress was permissive and not all that different from the apprehensive but resigned persistence that characterized the President."[28] Congress expressed concerns about the fighting in the spring of 1967, but it still supported the administration's policies. Between 1965 and 1968 there were only three roll-call votes on the war in the Senate. All three were tied to appropriations bills and were designed to demonstrate congressional support for the war. Only two senators voted against any of them.[29] This acquiescence faded after the Tet Offensive.

The fighting of the Tet Offensive represented a dramatic and sudden increase in the deadliness of the Vietnam War. In February 1968 alone, 2,124 Americans died, almost twice as many as the worst previous month (May 1967) and more than a 220 percent increase from the February 1967 American KIA figure of 662. In January 1968, 1,202 Americans were killed—many of them on the last day of the month, the first day of the Tet Offensive. The impact of the battle can best be seen in the quarterly data. In the winter of 1968 there were 4,869 Americans KIA, 2,000 more than had been killed in any other quarter, and more than 2,500 more KIA than in the previous quarter. This resulted in record changes in both acceleration (2,481 KIA) and the change in acceleration (2,184 KIA). By the lens employed by Congress, the situation was going badly and deteriorating at an increasing, unprecedented rate.

The Tet Offensive triggered a tremendous amount of congressional criticism of the war and the beginning of an active search for alternative strategies. Liberal senators and representatives were calling for a fundamental reappraisal of U.S. strategy, and conservative senators who had favored the war (and even encouraged its escalation) were now calling for limiting, or even withdrawing, U.S. forces.[30] In March, "Senator Richard Russell, a close friend and mentor of Johnson's, one of the most powerful and conservative senators on Capital Hill, made a profound impression on [Secretary of Defense Clark] Clifford when he told him and General [Earle] Wheeler that he believed that the United States had made a serious mistake by involving itself in Vietnam in the first place. Clifford wondered, If Senator Russell and his fellow hawks did not support a troop increase, then who would?"[31] On March 11 and 12, Secretary of State Rusk testified for more than eleven hours before the Senate Foreign Relations Committee in the "most prolonged questioning of a Cabinet officer ever broadcast to the American people."[32] Unlike previous questionings, the attitude was harsh and skeptical, "the marathon hearing gave the public a unique insight into the mounting congressional misgivings toward the administration's Vietnam policies."[33] When President Johnson announced a change of strategy and peace talks in March, "most members of Congress welcomed the news."[34]

It is noteworthy that February 1968 was not the most lethal month of the war for Americans. In May 1968, 2,169 Americans were killed, which made May the record. This might appear confusing, because it is the Tet Offensive and the winter of 1968 that had the greatest influence on Congress.[35] But May does not represent a record-setting increase in acceleration; perhaps more important, the spring quarter, despite the 4,725 Americans killed in action, had a negative acceleration and change in acceleration in the rate of Americans killed. In other words, although almost as many Americans were killed in the spring of 1968 as in the winter, the winter quarter's sudden and dramatic increase had significantly more impact than the spring quarter, when the situation seemed to be improving. These assessments, however, differ markedly from those of the army.

The Army

Up to the early 1960s, U.S. Army planners focused on a conventional war scenario for fighting the USSR and developed the doctrine of "flexible response" in reaction to fears concerning U.S. nuclear doctrine, "massive retaliation." The political danger in South Vietnam, however, was fundamentally different from that posed to central Europe by Warsaw Pact forces. The Vietnam War was largely a civil war; the enemy was indigenous and attacked in small units on its own initiative: the enemy was simultaneously nowhere and everywhere. This was particularly true in the first years of American involvement (1965–1969). The

American strategic goal was not the destruction of an organized military machine armed with tanks, planes, helicopters, and war ships, for which the United States had prepared, but the preservation of a fragile regime from the lightly armed attacks of both its own people and the North Vietnamese. The U.S. Army had to apply and adapt its NATO-based strategies, equipment, training, and approach to a fundamentally different type of war, for which it was unprepared.

Not only was the foe the United States faced in Vietnam different, but the "multidirectional, nonlinear nature of military operations in Vietnam" did not lend itself to traditional military measurement of ground warfare.[36] In a more conventional war, armies organized themselves with fronts and rears to fight one another to acquire territory. Military actors frequently assess their performance by monitoring the geographical progress made by each side. This was the case in the ground war in World War II. Because each side attempts to control "real estate," the acquisition of geographical goals results in the destruction of enemy forces.[37] In a linear type of warfare, armies can set operational goals, like "be at that river by day *x*," and judge how successful their strategies are by how closely they meet their goals. For example, in World War II, "the invasion plan called for Allied forces to be on the line of the Seine River by 120 days after the Normandy landing."[38] In this type of situation, success and failure are easy to observe and measure.

In Vietnam, geographical measurements of strategic success did not apply; "looking at maps of the war in Vietnam never told anybody what was really happening until the very end."[39] This forced the military to come up with other measures of progress. "Some substitute had to be devised to measure progress in a guerrilla war."[40] In a remarkable consensus, primary and secondary accounts agree that the U.S. military measured performance by looking at the number of V.C. and North Vietnamese Army (NVA) troops killed—the body count—and the number of enemy weapons captured. George Herring notes: "In a war without front lines and territorial objectives, where 'attriting the enemy' was a major goal, the 'body count' became the index of progress."[41] Shelby Stanton asserted that on the basis of enemy casualties, officers, enlisted men, and units were "rewarded by promotions, medals, and time off from field duty. For example, General Westmoreland had issued a special commendation to the 11th Infantry Brigade based on its claim of 128 killed at My Lai."[42] Christian Appy writes that the "death tallies were constantly monitored and updated. In rear areas, command posts listed 'box scores' on large chalk boards. These scores were the number of people who had been killed on either side: the body count. Indeed, killing was the central focus of American policy, the heart of America's strategy of attrition."[43]

Reliance on body counts and enemy weapons captured was not new. Determination of a mission and the indicators of its success was one of the first acts undertaken by the U.S. military upon arriving in Vietnam.[44] Alain Enthoven (who headed McNamara's famed "whiz kids") notes, with Wayne Smith, that "from the beginning, the Vietnam conflict had been characterized as a 'war of attrition,' with heavy emphasis on enemy casualties, particularly the 'body count.'"[45] Furthermore, there is strong evidence that the army's employment of body counts in Vietnam represented the continuation of policies developed during the Korean War.[46]

In Korea, Commander-in-Chief Matthew Ridgway wrote to General James Van Fleet, who had recently replaced him as commander of the U.S. Eighth Army: "You will direct the efforts of your forces toward inflicting maximum personnel casualties and matériel losses on hostile forces in Korea, consistent with the maintenance intact of all your major units and the safety of your troops. . . . Acquisition of terrain itself is of little or no value."[47] The army's employment of body counts as a critical measure in the Korean and Vietnam wars derived from its pursuit of similar political objectives in the two. General Bruce Palmer wrote that in "both wars there was no territorial objective other than to defend the status quo ante; thus it was not possible to demonstrate or assess progress in terms of territory gained and held. Leaders quite naturally turned to other indicators of how the war was going, among them the number of enemy battle casualties."[48] This was especially true after April 1951, when General MacArthur was replaced by Ridgway, and the battle lines became increasingly static. The early employment of body counts as the army's primary means of assessment in Vietnam thus represents "a continuation of policies previously established during the Korean War."[49]

Despite its previous reliance, the army's employment of body counts as its critical means of assessment drew early and critical attention. As a result of prevailing skepticism, the army invested "considerable effort . . . to check the validity of the communist loss estimates."[50] Army decision makers concluded from these efforts that the body-count figures were accurate and represented their mission concerns. "The extreme emphasis on the body count as *the* measure of success led to various attempts to lend credence to the reported data. In one such attempt, General Westmoreland's intelligence chief reported in mid-1967 that his search of 70 captured enemy documents confirmed the 1966 body count to within 1.8 percent."[51]

Even after the war, army officers defended the logic of body counts as indicators of success. Westmoreland wrote that "statistics were, admittedly, an imperfect gauge of progress, yet in the absence of conventional frontlines, how else to measure it?"[52] After the war, one American general, Julian Ewell, even wrote a book whose major thesis was that body counts and weapons captured were the best indicators to use to evaluate strategic performance.[53]

Starting in 1965, with the arrival of significant U.S. ground forces, Westmoreland and the Joint Chiefs of Staff employed a strategy of search and destroy. With this strategy, U.S. forces conducted sweeps intended to find and fix enemy forces, allowing U.S. firepower and mobile forces to destroy them. These sweeps involved battalion-sized forces or larger. Search and destroy aimed to destroy the enemy, not control real estate. Hills and villages were frequently taken, abandoned, and retaken in order to kill enemy forces. The strategy of search and destroy emphasized locating the enemy. Upon arriving in Vietnam, General Westmoreland ordered General Stanley Larsen "to seek out the enemy and fight him wherever you can find him,"[54] and the army chief of staff sent General Harold Johnson off to Vietnam with the challenge, "Find the enemy!"[55] Once found, the strategy was to exploit U.S. superiority in firepower to destroy the enemy in numbers faster than they could be replaced. Avant notes: "The search-and-destroy missions which provided the basis for American military doctrine were an offensive attempt to bring as much firepower as possible to bear on the Communist forces."[56] The strategy was pithily described as "find the bastards and pile on."[57]

Throughout the war, the army's conviction that search and destroy represented the best strategy for its attrition mission did not change—despite substantial changes in the other actors' assessment of the war. Analyzing changes in the rates of enemy losses and enemy weapons lost provides a powerful yet parsimonious explanation for the consistency of U.S. military strategic evaluations.[58]

Between the introduction of troops in March 1965 and autumn 1967, the army concluded that it was doing well. These assessments were largely made through reliance on body counts and data about weapons captured.[59] In 1966 the army estimated that V.C.-NVA losses were 55,000 to 75,000, and in 1967 these losses were estimated to be between 100,000 and 140,000, from which the military concluded that "victory was just around the corner."[60] Cable captures the military's assessment of performance at this time, calling this period "Everything is Perfect and Getting Better."[61]

Although many scholars are highly critical of U.S. behavior, arguing that the military during this period established many of the fundamental and avoidable conditions that were to manifest themselves as problems in later years, virtually all analysts agree that without the U.S. presence South Vietnam would have fallen during the 1960s. U.S. intervention served to "stave off the total defeat of the Republic of Vietnam."[62] During this time, while the U.S. presence escalated, neither the United States, the V.C., nor the North Vietnamese made substantial shifts in their military strategy or goals.[63] This changed at the end of 1967.

In the fall of 1967 the NVA began to encircle a U.S. special forces outpost at Khe Sanh. Westmoreland reinforced the outpost with marines and dedicated a large percentage of U.S. artillery and B-52 raids to support the base. After January 31, 1968, the siege at Khe Sanh and the Tet Offensive ran concurrently. As the Khe Sanh siege and Tet continued, Westmoreland and Wheeler became increasingly satisfied with the military situation. Khe Sanh presented the U.S. military with the situation they had been trying to orchestrate: the presence of large numbers of NVA troops, fixed and targeted by the military's firepower. Westmoreland was "attempting to engage the enemy so that America's awesome firepower (everything from M-16 rifles to B-52 bombers) could be brought to bear. His objective was not to capture a hill or ridge line, but to destroy enemy soldiers and hostile units."[64]

Similar to antisubmarine warfare, the most difficult element of counterinsurgency is locating the enemy. The army was enormously effective at destroying NVA and V.C. forces once they were found and fixed. The siege of Khe Sanh, like the convoys, made it clear where the enemy was going to be. With the "searching" part over, the military could focus on "destroying" enemy forces.

In the winter of 1968, the U.S. Army counted 72,455 "enemy dead from hostile actions" (the body count). This was a tremendous increase from 21,872 the previous quarter or 22,756 in winter 1967. This increase resulted in record-setting, positive jumps in both acceleration (50,583 dead) and change in acceleration (48,798 dead). The number of enemy weapons captured took a similar dramatic increase during the Tet Offensive, increasing to 17,498 in the winter of 1968, up from 8,286 the previous quarter and 8,581 in winter 1967.

Most of these increases occurred in February 1968, the deadliest month of the war for communist soldiers. Army statistics counted 39,867 enemy dead, up from 15,217 in January and 7,341 in February 1967. This dramatic increase resulted in record acceleration and change in acceleration in the rate of communists killed in action. February resulted in more than 15,000 more communists killed in action than in any other month during the war (the next highest was May 1968). The number of enemy weapons captured in February, 8,677, was also the highest in the war, although it barely edged out May 1968, with 8,675 weapons captured (see figures 5.2 and 5.3).

The army declared Tet and Khe Sanh tremendous U.S. victories. The NVA took enormous losses at Khe Sanh, losing half of the troops with which it had begun the siege.[65] The U.S. military "estimated that the North Vietnamese lost 10,000 to 15,000 men in their vain attempt to restage Dien Bien Phu. The Americans lost 205."[66] Westmoreland wrote that Khe Sanh was "one of the most damaging, one-sided defeats among many that the North Vietnamese incurred" and added: "Khe Sanh will stand in history, I am convinced, as a classic example of how to defeat a numerically superior besieging force by coordinated application of firepower."[67]

Westmoreland and the army were also happy with the results of the Tet Offensive. He called Tet "a striking military defeat for the enemy on anybody's terms."[68] With regard to Tet, Wheeler could not understand "all the doom and gloom we see in the U.S. press."[69] Analyst Andrew Krepinevich wrote that "according to MACV's [Military Assistance Command, Vietnam] criterion, the Tet Offensive represented a disastrous failure for the Communists. The body count at the end of February was estimated at 37,000, with another 6,000 captured."[70] In figures 5.2 and 5.3 note the order of magnitude difference between KIA figures for Americans and communists. The data analysis confirms the message that jumps out from the graphs; at the end of 1967 and the beginning of 1968, the rate at which the U.S. Army killed communist soldiers and captured their weapons dramatically increased. By both measures, the situation was going extremely well for the army.

U.S. Army reactions to Tet and Khe Sanh reflect this positive assessment. After Tet and Khe Sanh, the military did not want to pursue an alternative strategy but rather to dedicate more resources to what they saw as the successful strategy in place. As Westmoreland put it: "A military commander must anticipate not only problems and likely moves by the enemy but also opportunities."[71] In May, Westmoreland presented Johnson with a request for 206,000 more troops so they could expand the war and pursue a failing enemy.[72] For political reasons, however, JCS chairman Earle Wheeler framed the request as a necessary way to avoid U.S. setbacks. This created the first split between Wheeler and Westmoreland.[73]

Westmoreland, Admiral Ulysses Grant Sharp, and other senior U.S. military decision makers argued that Khe Sanh and Tet were tremendous U.S. victories. How could their view be so diametrically opposed to that of Congress? If we analyze changes in the army's dominant indicator set we can see why the military was so optimistic. As

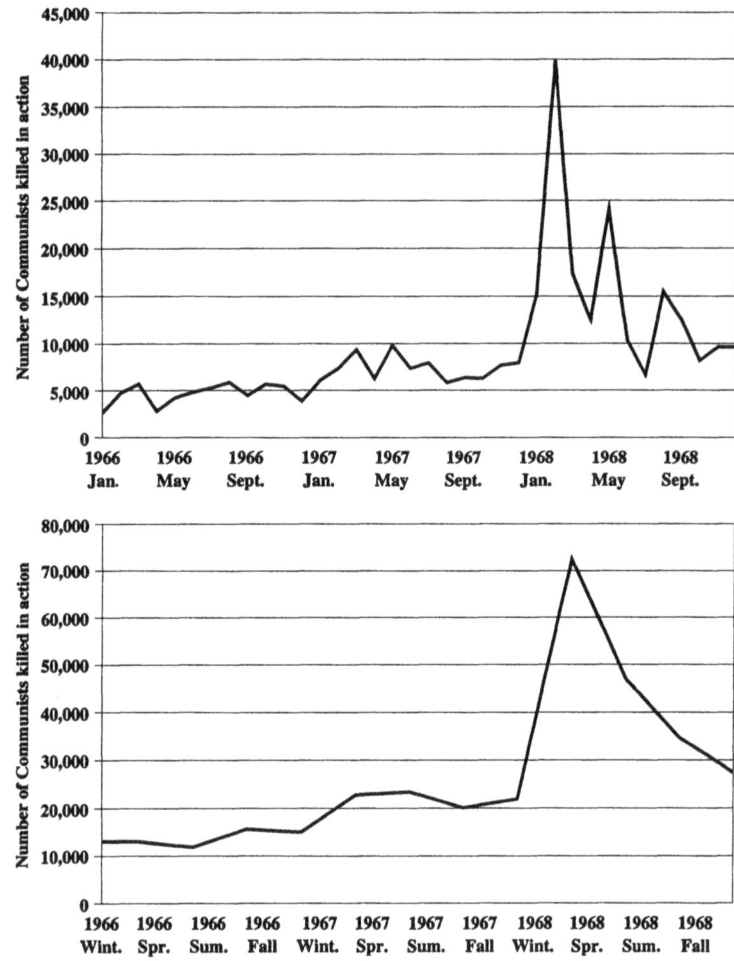

Figure 5.2 Communists Killed in Action During the Vietnam War, by Month and by Quarter

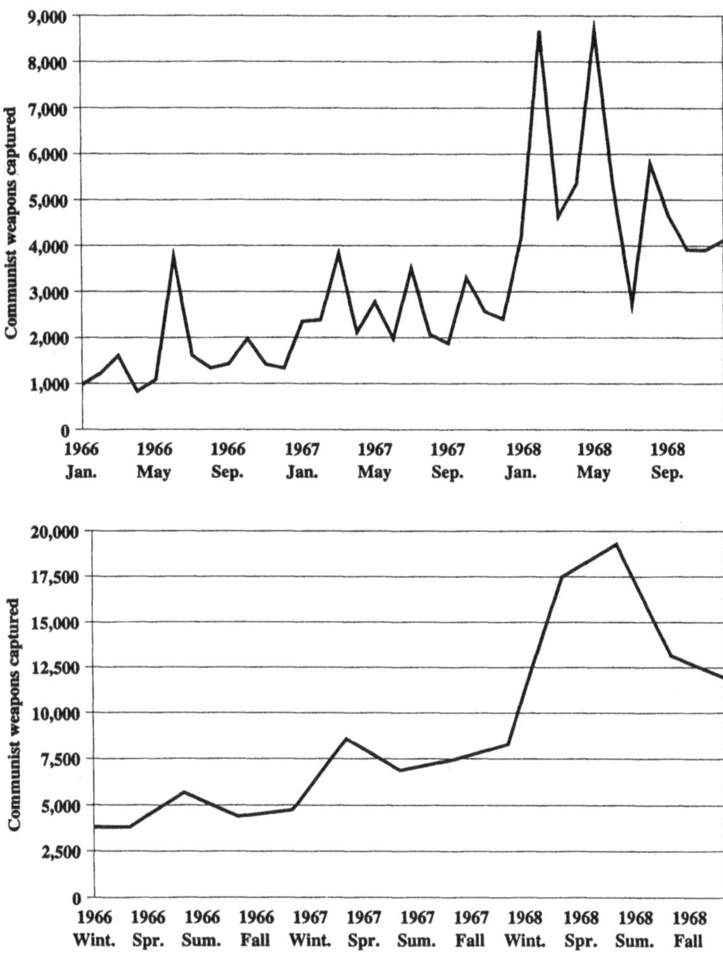

Figure 5.3 Communist Weapons Captured During the Vietnam War, by Month and by Quarter

figure 5.2 shows, enemy casualties dramatically increased at the end of 1967 and the beginning of 1968. The rate of enemy losses captures the military's assessment that the current situation was good and getting increasingly better. Army decision makers, monitoring this indicator to assess their strategy's progress, would see these signs as reason for optimism. Analysis of enemy weapons captured (see figure 5.3) adds additional support to this positive assessment. Through the lens of the military, the situation was excellent and getting better.

Analysis of the army's dominant indicators provides justification for the enthusiasm present in March and April 1968, as well as for the military's request for more troops (despite visible and growing public and congressional concerns). The army did not measure strategic success through U.S. casualties or American public opinion. In his summary report on Tet, General Wheeler stated that the military's post-Tet objectives were to destroy the NVA, restore security to the towns and countryside, and take the initiative against the enemy.[74] He never mentioned decreasing the rate of U.S. casualties. Douglas Kinnard, who served in the war and conducted the most extensive survey of Vietnam War generals, writes: "American public opinion simply was not considered by those who were actually planning how the war in the South was fought."[75]

The military was not indifferent to American casualties; it simply measured success through enemy dead and weapons captured. Westmoreland stated: "I had no illusions that Khe Sanh would be a brief fight lacking in American casualties, yet under the circumstances it was necessary to accept hardship and losses, as is so often the case in war."[76] Later in 1968, the army gave up the Khe Sanh outpost. Once again, army behavior was not motivated by concern about American casualties but by changes in enemy casualties, its dominant indicator set. Westmoreland wrote: "My successor, General Abrams, subsequently decided to evacuate Khe Sanh. The base no longer served to lure North Vietnamese soldiers to their deaths."[77] The military thus abandoned the base because it was not contributing to success as measured by their indicators, not because of the risk of loss of American lives. This would have been an ideal time for the military to score a propaganda success by arguing that it left Khe Sanh because it shared congressional and public concern for the Americans there. Instead, Westmoreland justified the decision in terms of the military's dominant indicators. This is a good example of how tightly organizations hold onto the lenses through which they assess policy and make decisions. But although both the army and the Congress reacted strongly and clearly to the Tet Offensive, the Johnson Administration's reaction was significantly more ambivalent.

The Johnson Administration

The Johnson Administration shared both Congress's political goals and the military's strategic objectives. The administration wanted to defeat communism in South Vietnam but was not willing to incur high human costs in doing so. Present throughout internal memos and memoirs of top Johnson administration civilians is the desire both to win the war and to minimize domestic political costs. Thus, the administration focused on indicators of military success and political concern, measuring success in the ground war in Vietnam through both enemy and American casualties.[78]

The administration was committed to evaluating progress in the war, with a particular reliance on quantitative data. Memos from Bundy, McNamara, and others to Johnson repeatedly framed success in terms of indicators. McNamara later wrote that "I insisted we try to measure progress. . . . It's not enough to conceive of an objective and a plan to carry it out; you must monitor the plan to determine whether you are achieving the objective. If you discover you are not, you either revise the plan or change the objective. I was convinced that, while we might not be able to track something as unambiguous as a front line, we could find variables that would indicate our success or failure. So we measured the targets destroyed in the North, the traffic down the Ho Chi Minh Trail, the number of captives, the weapons seized, the enemy body count, and so on."[79] As we shall see, Johnson himself frequently cited quantitative data when justifying the administration's position.

The Johnson Administration was interested in military success in Vietnam, but it did not micromanage the ground war as it did the air war, where Johnson was known to pick specific bombing targets. Thus, "senior decision makers of the Johnson Administration did not follow the course of ground combat in any except the most cursory manner, unless a particular engagement was unusually bloody or had captured a high degree of media attention."[80] The administration did, however, depend upon enemy dead to evaluate the military situation. Like the military, the civilians trusted the figures. Director of Central Intelligence Helms "provided the President with the . . . assurance that the U.S. strategy of attrition was working and that the reliance upon the body count of enemy dead was 'a useful indicator of the level of combat and a conservative, general estimate of the damage inflicted on the enemy.' Helms stated that he believed the enemy casualty counts to be reliable, conservative and verified."[81]

The administration was also concerned about U.S. losses. Johnson himself expressed this eloquently in the July 28, 1965, speech in which he announced the transfer of significant numbers of U.S. ground troops to Vietnam; "I do not find it easy to send the flower of our youth, our finest young men, into battle. I have spoken to you today of the divisions and the forces and battalions and the units, but I know them all, every one. I have seen them in a thousand streets, of a hundred towns, in every state in this Union—working and laughing and building, and filled with hope and life. I think I know too how their mothers weep and how their families sorrow. This is the most agonizing and most painful duty of your President."[82] Accounts by such scholars as Karnow, Larry Berman, and Doris Kearns frequently discuss the president's concern with U.S. casualties.[83] During Khe Sanh, Johnson was so concerned about the possibility of losing the besieged marines that he had a model of the post built in the White House situation room.[84] Throughout the siege, Dean Rusk said that every morning Johnson would "go down to the operations room and check on the casualties from Vietnam, each one of which took a little piece out of him."[85]

Like Congress, and unlike the military, the administration's decision makers were concerned about public opinion. Public opinion about Johnson and the war would affect both Johnson's likelihood of being reelected in 1968 and the administration's ability to sponsor and execute domestic policy, concerns not shared by the military.[86]

A number of key foreign policy appointees like Secretary of State Rusk and Secretary of Defense McNamara represented the administration's interests more intensely than they did their organizations' interests. The antipathy between McNamara and the military services is legendary. What is frequently forgotten, however, is the reason for McNamara's distrust. Even before U.S. combat troops were deployed to Vietnam, McNamara accused top admirals and generals of being insensitive to political concerns. Kinnard discusses McNamara's remarks to the Joint Chiefs of Staff, noting that the "ill-concealed contempt running thorough Secretary McNamara's remarks about the JCS suggested his views that the military services were insensitive to the political dimensions of war, but his view missed the fact that how one assessed a war's politics depended upon how one conceived of the war itself."[87] McNamara was clearly an active member in the administration's execution and evaluation of the war.

The administration relied on both military indicators, such as enemy body counts, and political indicators, such as U.S. casualties.[88] As we have seen, however, in 1968 these indicators suggested fundamentally different pictures of progress in the war. Since the administration's dominant indicator set included some indications that the situation was good and getting increasingly better and some indications that it was bad and getting increasingly worse, the dominant indicator theory predicts that the administration would become conflicted and unable to form a consensus around any single evaluation. This was exactly what occurred—gridlock: an outcome predicted by the dominant indicator approach but not by alternative explanations.

On the one hand, administration officials declared that Tet and Khe Sanh were American victories. Maxwell Taylor told a reporter in March: "I can't prove my case any more than the other side can be proved, but the indicators certainly are that the Tet offensive was not as destructive to the provinces as we feared at the outset; that the ARVN has not suffered the setback it looked as though it might have had and, indeed, we are resuming the offensive whereas the other side is avoiding combat."[89] President Johnson himself wrote that "in one month, the enemy sustained heavier losses than U.S. forces had suffered in nine years in Vietnam. Thousands more enemy soldiers were wounded or captured. The Tet offensive was, by any standard, a military defeat of massive proportions for the North Vietnamese and the Viet Cong."[90] And yet, the sharp increase in the rate of U.S. casualties caused by Khe Sanh and Tet greatly affected the civilian assessment of the war. Shortly after the siege of Khe Sanh began, Johnson wrote a memo saying that "we should review the conduct of military operations in South Vietnam with a view to reducing U.S. casualties, accelerating the turnover of responsibility to the GVN [government of South Vietnam] and working toward less destruction and fewer casualties in South Vietnam."[91] Perhaps the best expression of the belief that Khe Sanh and Tet were both successes and defeats for the U.S. was offered by Dean Rusk when he told the Senate Foreign Relations Committee on March 11 that "both sides suffered some severe setbacks in the course of the Tet offensive."[92]

The simultaneous assessments that things were going well and going badly profoundly affected the president and his administration. From the beginning of the siege of Khe Sanh to the end of the most intense fighting of Tet, the previously high level of consensus on Vietnam in the Johnson Administration dissolved and was replaced by division and discord.

At the end of October 1967, McNamara told Johnson that the current course of action was "dangerous, costly and unsatisfactory to our people."[93] On November 1 McNamara wrote a memo to Johnson entitled "Outlook if Present Course of Action Is Continued." In the memo he suggested that Johnson consider certain steps to reduce U.S. casualties, including changing the ground-war strategy so as to put more South Vietnamese and fewer U.S. servicemen in the field.[94] During the following months there were extensive debate and vacillation within the administration regarding the McNamara memo. The president fired McNamara as secretary of defense and replaced him with Clark Clifford, a well-known hawk.[95] Yet the new, hawkish secretary of defense soon agreed with McNamara's "dovish" position. Clifford states that by March he had concluded that "all we were going to do was waste our treasure and the lives of our men out there in the jungles."[96]

Accounts of what was going on at the White House emphasize the totally conflicted state of the administration. In Clifford's description: "The pressure grew so intense that at times I felt that the government might come apart at the seams. Leadership was fraying at its very center."[97] The administration seemed unable to determine whether the U.S. situation in Vietnam was good or bad. It was fundamentally torn in two.[98]

Not only did the administration no longer speak with one voice, but individuals within the administration held conflicting views. The president suffered from this cognitive dissonance. On the one hand, Johnson stated in March that "the curve was clearly upward."[99] On the other hand, unlike the military, Johnson was greatly disturbed by events in Vietnam, writing later that "my opinion had changed as a result of what I had heard from my advisers and what I saw happening on the ground in Vietnam." On March 12 he told a group of advisers that an evaluation of the effectiveness of U.S. strategy was in order. "I do think we should evaluate our strategy."[100]

During this period, a cloud of gloom and depression hung over the administration.[101] Under pressure from Congress and the public, the administration began to switch its position. Among the key leaders the consensus for the status quo rapidly turned to a consensus espousing change. In November, McNamara had been the only convert to George Ball's dovish position in the administration. But by the middle of March, only two key civilian advisers, Walt Rostow and Abe Fortas, remained fully in the hawk camp.[102] Secretary of State Rusk said on March 19 that "the element of hope has been taken away by TET. People don't think there is likely to be an end."[103] By March, Herring states that there was a consensus that "ground operations should be scaled down to reduce American casualties."[104] On March 23 President Johnson announced that Westmoreland had been removed as commander of U.S. forces in Vietnam and made army chief of staff, a move interpreted by some as a sign that "the strategy of search and destroy and a war of attrition had failed."[105]

On March 25 the so-called Wise Men, Johnson's collection of informal senior advisers, met and recommended that he fundamentally change U.S. policy in Vietnam. These were the same elder statesmen who only four and a half months earlier had strongly supported U.S. policy on the war. At this point, Johnson finally sided with the doves in his administration. He wrote that "if they had been so deeply influenced by the reports of the Tet offensive, what must the average citizen in the country be thinking?"[106] The shift of the Wise Men reflected the changing attitudes of the entire Johnson Administration. During the briefing and discussion with the Wise Men, Johnson's notes included the following: "Can no longer do the job we set out to do. . . . Adjust our course. . . . Move to disengage."[107] On March 31 Johnson announced that because of his concerns about "America's sons in the fields far away," he was withdrawing from the presidential campaign, and that he would fundamentally alter U.S. strategy in Vietnam.[108] These changes included all of McNamara's suggestions: a bombing halt, negotiations, and changes in force levels to reduce U.S. casualties. "Although the word *Vietnamization* was not coined until 1969, the planning had already started."[109]

After the sudden increase in U.S. casualties in May, Johnson appointed General Creighton Abrams commander in chief of U.S. forces in Vietnam. As Truman had done with Ridgway, Johnson provided his new field commander with a fresh objective. Johnson urged Abrams to "reduce United States combat losses and get the South Vietnamese Army back into the war's mainstream."[110] Abrams developed an alternative mission, the "one war" plan. For this mission the military developed new measures of performance. Although they still did not focus on U.S. casualties, "population security, not the body count, would be the criterion of success."[111]

Although much of the data collected and disseminated during the Vietnam War were either propaganda or simply inaccurate, the statistics played a significant role in forming decision makers' strategic evaluations. The accuracy of the figures employed is unimportant if they are the numbers that decision makers relied on; during the war, communists killed, weapons captured, and American dead were the critical indicators decision makers used to assess the situation. Vietnam analyst Thomas Thayer writes that "despite the problems the figures are useful and they must be addressed in any attempt to describe what happened in Vietnam."[112] And yet as late as 1991, Margaret Adams, electronic archivist at the National Archives, commented that few researches had ever used the quantitative evidence available from the Vietnam War.[113] National Archivist Donald Harrison notes that the Vietnam War "was the first war in military history to be run with the full-scale assistance of electronic data. . . . Collectively, this data provides evidence of what was available to decision makers. . . . However, one of the ironies of the historical analysis of the war in Vietnam has been an almost complete absence of computerized inquiry [using these data]."[114]

My analysis examines the data collected on U.S. and enemy killed in action, and enemy weapons captured, from 1966 through 1968. My approach accurately predicts that the military, focusing on such military indicators as enemy dead and enemy weapons captured, would see the significant increase in these indicators as a positive sign of U.S. strategic performance. The model also predicts that after Tet and Khe Sanh, Congress, reacting to the sudden increase in U.S. casualties, would shift from its passive stance to active opposition of U.S. policy in Vietnam.

Perhaps most important, the model predicts that the Johnson Administration, which was concerned with both military and political variables, would be unable to form a consensus on U.S. performance. This gridlock is fundamentally different from the lack of response that comes from apathy; instead, it accurately reflects the changing and divisive nature of the administration position. The model also picks up Johnson's concerns after the May increase in U.S. casualties.

The previous lack of significant increases in decision makers' dominant indicator sets helps to explain why none of the actors attempted to alter U.S. strategy before 1968. As discussed earlier, few approaches allow us to predict non-events. But sometimes these non-events, like congressional inaction before 1967, pose especially interesting historical questions. There were many months of record U.S. casualties in which Congress did not take action before March 1967. What made March and, later, February 1968 such critical months was not that they experienced record absolute values of U.S. losses but that these losses also represented a significant increase in the rate at which U.S. soldiers were being killed. With both positive acceleration and change in rate of acceleration, these periods conveyed to Congress the assessment that the situation was out of control and rapidly deteriorating. The standard approach, with its emphasis on record rates, is unable to capture that assessment.

The action-reaction approach also fails to explain the observed behavior. The North Vietnamese did not initiate a strategic change before spring 1967, when Congress became increasingly concerned with the situation. Furthermore, although Tet clearly does represent a strategic change on the part of the NVA, the action-reaction model is unable to explain why the army reached a strategic assessment diametrically opposite that of the Congress.

Finally, when comparing the three approaches, we see that only the dominant indicator approach allows us to predict that the Johnson Administration would become gridlocked, conflicted by internal dissension, and, unlike the other organizations, unable to reach a clear consensus during Tet. Neither the action-reaction nor the standard organization model has a mechanism for explaining this type of gridlocked behavior. Not only does the dominant indicator approach help to explain the Johnson Administration's period of organizational gridlock, but administration actors appear to have assessed the war, quite deliberately and self-consciously, in terms of rates of change of key indicators.

There is strong evidence that actors in the Vietnam War actually looked at changes in the rates of their key indicators to evaluate strategy. Recall Enthoven and Smith, that leaders "were blinded by the deluge of statistics showing only change and activity."[115] During the war, the Central Intelligence Agency developed and used advanced univariate, statistical modeling techniques. In a CIA report written for Rostow in 1967, analysts stated that the "Agency employed the technique of moving averages with several indicators to establish trends and turning points in the war between late 1963 and early 1967."[116] Even mathematically unsophisticated actors focused on changes in the trend of the figures they relied upon. Johnson claimed in March 1967 that "some South Vietnamese units were excellent, some were bad; but most were good—and getting better, which was the important thing."[117]

Both the administration's internal documentation and public appearances demonstrate a focus on changes in the rates of key quantitative indicators. In a November 17, 1967, news conference, Johnson argued that Americans "like that curve to rise like this (indicating a sharp rise) and they like the opposition to go down like this (indicating a sharply declining line)."[118] After the Tet Offensive, Rostow explained the situation to the president in a series of curves showing sharp drops versus incremental change.[119] Although I do not claim that the actors actually made calculations of derivatives, there is a large body of evidence that suggests that decision makers in both the military and the administration analyzed the war in terms of changes in the rates of key quantitative indicators. Thus the approach not only captures the primary factors structuring the actors' decisions, but it also reflects some of their behavior. Historical analysis of how decision makers used numbers has previously been restricted to the "order of battle" debate.

This analysis provides a different perspective to the order of battle controversy between the CIA and the army—among the longest-lasting debates of the war. The debate is over the communist order of battle, that is, the size of their forces. The CIA claimed during the war that the communist forces were much larger than the army believed. If the forces were larger, then the crossover point, where America was killing communists faster then the Vietnamese could replenish their forces, would have been considerably further in the future, or have required many more American forces. Thus, the communist order of battle was a critical quantitative assumption in projecting a time table for U.S. victory.

The debate over the enemy order of battle was first made public by Sam Adams in an article in *Harpers* magazine in May 1975.[120] The CBS news show "The Uncounted Enemy: A Vietnam Deception" (shown January 23, 1982) greatly inflamed interest in the controversy and resulted in a libel suit between Westmoreland and CBS. The suit was dropped by Westmoreland a week before the trial was scheduled to begin in February 1985.[121]

The controversy shows a critical element inherent in American decision making in the Vietnam War, one that is generally ignored by analysts. The debate about the size of the communist forces was not just important because one side was right and the other was wrong; the debate was also important because it shows that both military and civilian decision makers depended on the Vietnamese order of battle for evaluating the success of U.S. strategy. Although they disagreed on their assumption of how large the enemy was, both sides relied on changes in enemy dead to update their assessments of U.S. performance. The disagreement was over the size of the yardstick, not over what to measure.

The administration was committed to the goal of destroying the enemy through attrition and was aware that there was a debate among senior civilian and military analysts about how large the enemy order of battle was. However, this did not stop civilians from depending on these figures. In a memo to President Johnson dated January 20, 1967, Rostow wrote: "As you know, a debate continues on the absolute size of the enemy order of battle in Viet Nam. Whatever the size, you should know that official statistics now show for the first time a net decline in both VC main force and North Viet Nam army units for the fourth quarter of 1966. This is the first reversal of the upward trend since 1960."[122] Knowledge of the debate did not affect Rostow's and Johnson's use of changes in enemy dead, along with American casualties, as a critical measure of U.S. success. In 1968, when communist and U.S. dead *both* dramatically increased, the mixed signals sent by these two indicators catapulted the administration into a period of organizational gridlock.

The Vietnam War case demonstrated behavior parallel to that of World War I, where the military failed to see the situation as being as dire as many civilians did, as well as that of World War II, where divergent indicators facilitated organizational gridlock. Similar to the actors in these earlier cases, decision makers appear to have assessed performance deliberately through changes in the rates of key indicators.

Up to this point, I have examined actors from largely different organizations to discover how they assess strategic effectiveness in war. In the next chapter, I look at how similar types of organizations employing different dominant indicators reach contradictory assessments of performance, and how the dominant indicator approach applies to non-war decisions.

Chapter 6

Disagreement During the Vietnam War and the Hostage Rescue Attempt in Iran

The press will be looking at [the American hostage situation] in the context of the campaign. It'll be over in a few hours, but it could provide a nice contrast between Carter and our friend from Massachusetts in how to handle a crisis.

—Hamilton Jordan, November 4, 1979, *Crisis: The Last Year of the Carter Presidency*

Up to this point I have examined how the different lenses employed by different kinds of organizations can affect their evaluations of policy performance. Leaders do not have to come from different kinds of organizations, however, to employ separate lenses. Sometimes actors from similar kinds of organizations rely on different dominant indicators and reach fundamentally dissimilar evaluations of strategic performance. Two military organizations or two civilian organizations from the same country may make contradictory assessments based on common experiences.

In this chapter, I examine two cases. First, to illustrate how conflicts develop between similar types of organizations, I build on the analysis of the previous chapter to examine the different ways the U.S. Army and the Marine Corps measured success in the Vietnam War. Their employment of different indicators led to fundamentally different assessments of the Marine Corps's strategic success and fueled an intense bureaucratic conflict between the two organizations. Second, I examine the actions of a core White House political group that decisively influenced the decision to try to rescue the American hostages held in Iran, and I consider how their domestic politics lens helps explain the timing of the decision. This latter case shows that the dominant indicator approach can apply to non-war, civilian decision making situations and not just to wartime assessments.

MILITARY AGAINST MILITARY

Sometimes, similar military organizations in the same country, even given the same strategic objective, formulate different missions to achieve that objective and select different indicators to measure success. During the Vietnam War, the U.S. Army and the Marine Corps were both assigned the objective of maintaining a noncommunist South Vietnam. The two organizations, however, chose to translate this objective into different missions and measured success by different indicators.

Although it had fought in such global wars as World War I, World War II, and Korea, the Marine Corps had a traditional interest in fighting much smaller wars. Indeed, by 1940 the marines had developed a *Small War Manual.* The key theme of the manual was that in "small wars, the goal is to gain decisive results with the least application of force and the consequent minimum loss of life. The end aim is the social, economic, and political development of the people subsequent to the military defeat of the enemy insurgent."[1] During the 1950s, the Marine Corps became increasingly disenchanted with the army's strategies and tactics. The marines had historically seen their organizational essence as that of a small, mobile force that could react and adapt quickly. The Corps realized that the army design for a potential war between NATO and the Warsaw Pact in central Europe emphasized large units of heavy, armored forces, thus marginalizing the marines. Dissatisfied with this role in the army's scenario, the marines oriented their mission toward smaller conflicts in developing nations. As a result, during the late 1950s and early 1960s the Corps further developed its counterinsurgency strategy, training, and contingency planning. When marines arrived in Vietnam, the Corps had a well-articulated counterinsurgency strategy that emphasized local pacification.[2]

As we saw earlier, the army's attachment to the search-and-destroy strategy was intensified by its focus on preparing for a massive, modern military battle in central Europe. "The ground combat forces, in particular the Army, had developed a doctrine, a theory of victory, appropriate to combating the presumed major threat, a Warsaw Pact invasion of western Europe."[3] Thus, when the army arrived in Vietnam, it emphasized the physical destruction of the enemy and continued its Korean War policy of measuring success through enemy body counts.[4]

As stated in the 1940 *Small War Manual,* the Marine Corps was interested in social, political, and economic development. In Vietnam the Corps employed a strategy called "combined action platoons" (CAP) rather than the army's search-and-destroy policy. In the CAP strategy, the Corps dispersed small units of from ten to twelve marines to villages, where they would remain for long periods. In this, the marines were attempting to emulate some of the Viet Cong's strategies.[5] Their idea was to foster local stability. Marine Corps captain Jim Cooper summed up this strategy when he told a Vietnamese village that "henceforth the people would be protected from the VC, for he had come to stay."[6]

By using the CAP strategy, the marines attempted to convince Vietnamese peasants to stand up to V.C. threats. The peasants could challenge the V.C. because they would be confident that the U.S. military would have a continuous presence. Vietnamese hamlet leaders could ignore V.C. demands to provide soldiers, food, and supplies because the V.C. would be unable to terrorize the villagers. Previously, V.C. threats had been potent because the American presence was always temporary. Villagers knew that as soon as U.S. forces left, the V.C. would return and punish them for cooperating with the Americans or for not cooperating with the V.C. By maintaining a continual presence, the CAP strategy greatly increased the confidence of village leaders to stand up to the V.C.

Combined action platoons and search-and-destroy strategies could not be more different. The CAP strategy focuses on creating a permanent village presence, while the search-and-destroy strategy emphasizes movement: to find, fix, and destroy enemy forces. Not surprisingly, given these disparate objectives, the marines chose different indicators of performance from those employed by the army. The marines measured success by looking at indicators of village stability, like rice production.[7] If the villagers felt secure enough to buy rice seed, harvest it, and not turn it over to the V.C., then the Marine Corps interpreted this as a sign of success. Furthermore, as Marine Corps General Lewis Walt points out, "Each catty of rice . . . not going into Viet Cong bins meant that another catty had to be grown in North Vietnam and brought over the hundreds of miles of mountain trails by human bearers."[8] In addition, the Marine Corps's strategy resulted in an American casualty rate lower than that resulting from the army's search-and-destroy strategy. General Richard Clutterbuck wrote that while marine "casualties are high, they are only 50% of the casualties of the normal infantry or Marine battalions being flown around by helicopters on large scale operations."[9]

The object of the marines' strategy was for them to become a stable presence in the villages and thus deter communist attacks and village support of the V.C. The V.C. would thus either stay in the jungle (losing the support of the village) or be forced to fight the marines on prepared, defended terrain. Since the V.C. preferred ambush tactics and generally avoided attacking entrenched American positions, they would avoid protected villages. Thus, if the strategy was successful, the V.C. and marines were unlikely either to meet or to fight. Not surprisingly, a strategy that emphasized deterring V.C. attacks did not result in a high enemy body count. As a result, the army considered the CAP strategy a failure.

Army officers argued that the marine strategy was a failure and that the marines were afraid to fight. Army General Harry Kinnard stated that he was "absolutely disgusted" with the marines. He claimed they did not want to fight. "I did everything I could to drag them out . . . and get them to fight. . . . They just wouldn't play. They just *would not play.* They don't know how to fight on land, particularly against guerrillas."[10] Major General William Depuy noted that "the marines came in and just sat down and didn't do anything. They were involved in counterinsurgency of the deliberate, mild sort."[11] These officers' critical assessments were consistent with the army's official organizational evaluation of the marines' effectiveness. At the same time that the Marine Corps was deciding that their strategy was increasingly successful (rice production went up dramatically in CAP villages), the army was assessing it as a failure (Marine Corps body counts declined steeply).

In the fall of 1965, the army, which had command of the theater, forced the marines to alter their strategy and operate its way, practicing search-and-destroy missions. The declining body count and army indifference to such economic and political measures as rice production were the critical factors in this decision. As Deborah Avant writes, the marines' program was canceled "because of its *low* success rate—it did not kill enough Communists."[12] Douglas Kinnard notes: "Certain members of the MACV staff, though not objecting to pacification activities, felt nevertheless that Marines should give greater attention to search-and-destroy operations. Westmoreland was persuaded in November, 1965 to send the commander of the Marine Amphibious Force a letter which in effect requested that he conduct offensive operations of the search-and-destroy type with greater frequency."[13] The marines had failed to demonstrate success through the army's dominant indicators. This provides a demonstration of the power of those indicators in determining how organizations measure success. The marines' "efforts were not recognized as successful by the army. The army's dominance of the planning and implementation was also dominance over expertise, especially *measures of success*."[14]

Although it would be impossible to prove that the employment of the marines' approach by the army would have changed the outcome of the war, it is clear that the two strategies and means of assessment dramatically influenced how the war was fought. The marines' pacification mission emphasized political, social, and economic development, while the army's attrition mission emphasized killing as many of the enemy as possible. Because the V.C. was a political group—and virtually impossible to separate from the population at large—the strategy of search and destroy frequently facilitated indiscriminate killing of Vietnamese civilians. "When asked if the bombing did not sometimes kill civilians, an American sergeant responded with a laugh: 'What does it matter? They're all Vietnamese.'"[15] This is not to say that all army soldiers were capricious killers or that marines were sensitive social workers. It does suggest, however, that both the callous accidental killing of civilians in battle and the significantly rarer, deliberate massacre of civilians—such as occurred at My Lai—had roots in the incentive structure created by the army's mission of attrition. On the one hand, it seems unlikely that either the wanton destruction of civilians or the callous attitude toward Vietnamese deaths would have developed had most military units employed the CAP strategy and adopted marine dominant indicators. On the other hand, had the marine strategy dominated U.S. military action, the V.C. might have altered their strategy in a way that would have made CAP less effective.

Even within the same country, then, similar types of organizations (here, military) given identical strategic goals (stop a communist takeover of South Vietnam) can develop different operational missions. Furthermore, the development of different missions can lead these organizations to rely on different indicators to evaluate success. Reliance on different indicators could lead two or more military organizations to the same types of disagreements that can occur between military and civilian organizations.

Like civilian leaders, military leaders intervene when they think that a subordinate's strategy is not working. The army believed that the Marine Corps's strategy was failing because it did not result in large body counts. Thus the army, which had strategic command over the ground war in Vietnam, chose to intervene and force the marines to change their strategy in much the same way that Lloyd George had imposed convoys on the British admiralty in 1917.

If Cult of the Offensive arguments are correct, and military groups have fixed preferences in strategies, then bureaucratic conflicts between organizations should not develop. The army should either approve or disapprove of the marines' strategy from the beginning. After the marines changed their strategy and increased their body counts, the army was largely pleased with the Corps's performance. Thus, the results of strategy implementation clearly influenced the army's assessment of marine performance. Although the distinction between offensive and defensive is frequently difficult to make, I do not think one could argue that CAP was an offensive strategy. Thus, this case is inconsistent with the military behavior suggested by the Cult of the Offensive.

This case also appears inconsistent with the action-reaction model. The army assessed the marines' strategy as unsuccessful without there being a noticeable change in communist strategy. It was on the basis of its own dominant indicators that the army judged the marines as failing to implement an effective strategy.

Organizations not only use indicators to assess strategic performance in wartime, they also rely on indicators when evaluating the success of policies in peacetime. One such assessment came during the American hostage crisis in Iran.

CIVILIAN AGAINST CIVILIAN

The line between peacetime and wartime decision making is frequently difficult to draw. This distinction becomes particularly difficult to make when civilian leaders contemplate the use of force. When do decision makers become dissatisfied with diplomatic and other nonmilitary efforts to solve an international problem and determine that they must use force and risk lives? President Jimmy Carter faced this decision after the U.S. embassy in Iran was seized in November 1979. Although military leaders played a role in creating various options, the decision to launch a hostage rescue attempt was largely political. By identifying the pivotal organizational actors and their dominant indicators, we can explain the timing of the U.S. switch from diplomacy to force.[16]

On November 4, 1979, Iranian students overran the U.S. embassy and took sixty-six State Department personnel hostage.[17] Six months later, the United States attempted a rescue mission that failed to free the hostages and led to the deaths of eight Americans in the desert of Iran. Scholars and participants have conducted a number of postmortems on the rescue effort, but few have examined what triggered President Carter's decision to employ military force.

The U.S. civilian organizations that are critical in the assessment and implementation of foreign policy include the State Department, the Department of Defense, the National Security Council, and White House political advisers. Analyst Steve Smith groups advisers to President Carter who were central to foreign policy issues into three groups: "hawks," "doves," and "presidential supporters."[18]

The hawks included the National Security Council (NSC, led by National Security Adviser Zbigniew Brzezinski), the Department of Defense (DOD, directed by Secretary of Defense Harold Brown), and the Joint Chiefs of Staff (chaired by General David Jones). These leaders proposed from the onset of the embassy takeover that the president take decisive, military action. The advisers were generally concerned that lack of U.S. action would convey to the world that the United States was weak. In many ways, their concerns mirrored those of President Johnson during the Vietnam War. The hawks believed that the hostage crisis was linked to other issues and that a lack of decisive action would show a lack of U.S. resolve to pursue its foreign policy interests. This belief intensified after the Soviet invasion of Afghanistan on December 27. The hawks thus supported military options from the beginning and became increasingly strong advocates of military force as the crisis continued.[19] At the March 22, 1980, NSC meeting where the rescue was first presented in what would be its final form, Brzezinski argued that "there were only three choices: negotiating ad infinitum, bombing (perhaps the worst solution of all), and the rescue, a more surgical solution."[20]

The central dove organization was the State Department (directed by Secretary of State Cyrus Vance and also represented by Deputy Secretary of State Warren Christopher). Vance and Christopher were primarily concerned with protecting the lives of their State Department colleagues who were held captive.[21] The fact that their organization's people were being held gave them a different mission from that of the other organizations: for the State Department, the protection of its people was paramount. From the beginning, Vance and Christopher consistently opposed military action because they believed that it would unnecessarily endanger the hostages' lives. Five days after the hostages were taken, Vance argued: "We're dealing with a volatile, chaotic situation in Iran, and negotiation is the only way to free them. The President and this nation will ultimately be judged by our restraint in the face of provocation, and on the safe return of our hostages. . . . We have to keep looking for ways to reach [Ayatollah] Khomeini and peacefully resolve this."[22]

Such advisers as Brzezinski and Vance saw the result of inactivity in fundamentally different ways. In his advice to the president, Vance "harked back to the *Pueblo* incident, which had plagued the Johnson Administration but which had been resolved honorably and without loss of life." Brzezinski, appalled, blurted out, "But that went on for over a year!"[23] A year of inactivity did not bother the doves; the key was to get the hostages out alive.

Smith calls the third group the presidential supporters. It included people in top White House positions like Hamilton Jordan, Walter Mondale, Robert Strauss, and Jody Powell, who were primarily interested in how events in Iran would influence President Carter's reelection prospects. These advisers lacked specific foreign policy agendas. Instead, their main interest was presidential politics and winning in 1980. "Mondale, Powell and Jordan seem to have been neither 'hawks' nor 'doves' in their views of the Iranian action; rather, their policy proposals show that their concern was first and foremost with the effect of the crisis on the Carter presidency."[24]

The presidential supporters evaluated the hostage crisis in terms of their mission of reelecting the president. Even on the day the Iranians took the embassy, Jordan and Powell were discussing the event in the context of the election: "Jody's hard-nosed judgment rang true. What was all this going to do to the President's image and his prospects for reelection?"[25]

The key indicator that the presidential supporters focused on was the president's national popularity.[26] Politicians and pollsters usually measure presidential popularity by examining responses to the question "Do you approve or disapprove of the way that [the president] is handling his job as President?"[27] The Gallup organization regularly conducts these surveys: presidential popularity figures are available on a monthly basis for the months between October 1979 and May 1980. These figures include the percentage of respondents that approve, disapprove, or have no opinion about how the president handles his job. The presidential supporters tracked these figures carefully. By analyzing this polling data, we can capture the key systematic elements that determined the supporters' position.

Foreign policy played a major role in respondents' attitudes toward

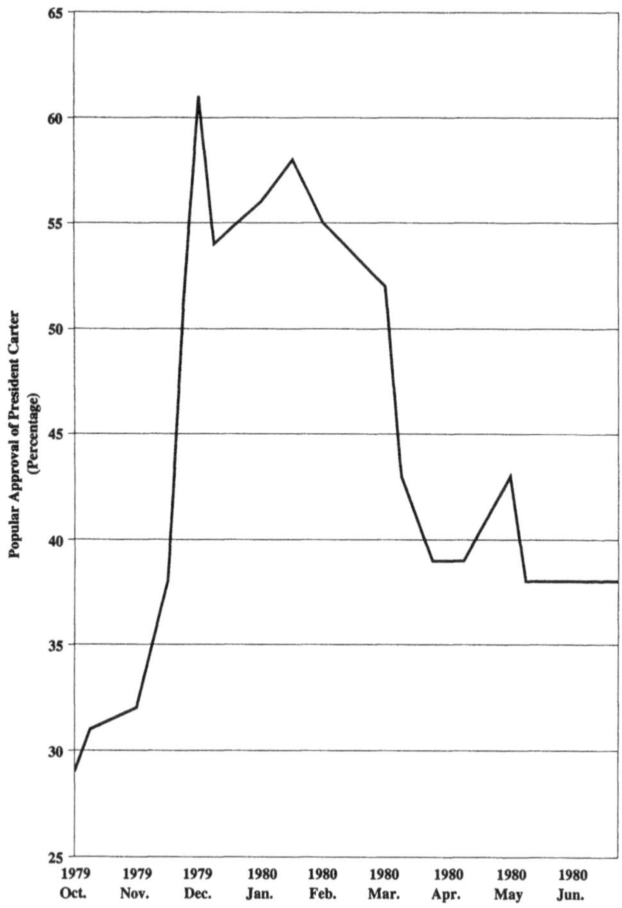

Figure 6.1 Hostage Rescue: President Carter's Popularity

the president in late 1979 and early 1980. Figure 6.1 shows that President Carter's popularity shot up in November and December, dropped in January, and remained constant until March, when it plummeted. In November and December, the public rallied around the president. Presidential supporters saw this as evidence that the firm but diplomatic approach was working. Robert Strauss said in November: "The American people like the way Carter's handled this hostage thing so far." He continued: "He's been decisive and firm. But it won't last. At some point their patience will run out."[28] With the president's popularity shooting up from 29 percent at the beginning of October to 61 percent at the beginning of December, the presidential supporters could only be pleased with how Carter was handling the hostage situation.[29]

Carter's popularity fell precipitously in the first week of January, following the Soviet invasion of Afghanistan. The American public and Jimmy Carter were shocked by the invasion. Carter compared it to the hostage crisis, remarking to his chief of staff that the invasion was "more serious, Hamilton. Capturing those Americans was an inhumane act committed by a bunch of radicals and condoned by a crazy old man. But this is deliberate aggression that calls into question detente and the way we have been doing business with the Soviets for the past decade."[30] The Soviet invasion acted as an exogenous shock, dissipating the effect that the sudden dip in popularity might have had on the presidential supporters' view of diplomatic solutions to the hostage crisis. Polls show that public approval of Carter's handling of the Iranian situation remained at 61 percent.[31] Thus, the presidential supporters could control for the effect of both the Iranian and Afghanistan crises on the president's approval rating.

By mid-January, the president's popularity stabilized, hovering in the high-50-percent range. Carter decisively won most of the primaries and caucuses but lost two of the important ones, New York and Connecticut. During this time, the presidential supporters seemed to hold moderate views in favor of the status quo.

Smith argues that in April the presidential supporters quickly changed their view to one of support for the use of military force. Furthermore, their position switch was critical in the decision to go forward with the rescue. "The change came about because the 'presidential supporters' and President Carter himself felt that the situation had altered significantly."[32] Critical to my argument is the fact that the presidential supporters changed their position because of their concerns about the domestic political situation rather than international politics. Smith writes that because of the "domestic criticism of Carter's inaction . . . the presidential supporters felt it was time to act."[33]

Although Smith well documents the presidential supporters' switch, he provides no evidence for exactly what triggered the timing of their decision—that is, why in April? The president's ratings had been falling since February. What occurred at this time to change the political supporters' and the president's assessment of the efficacy of diplomatic policy and the need for military force?

As we have seen, by the end of March, the president's popularity had plummeted, with dramatic increases in acceleration and the rate of acceleration.[34] The president's popularity, which had peaked at 61 percent in December 1979, had slowly descended to 52 percent by the first week of March. Between the first and last week of March, however, Carter's popularity dropped to 39 percent, a sudden and dramatic dive. Both the acceleration (−13 percent) and the change in the rate of acceleration (−10 percent) suggested that the situation was bad and getting increasingly worse. Since the presidential supporters focused on how the president was perceived by the public, this sudden drop would be cause for extreme alarm. Indeed it was; by all accounts, the presidential supporters rapidly and decisively changed their view to support for military action. Note, however, that as poor a rating as 39 percent was, it was ten points higher than his previous October approval rating of 29 percent. Thus, it was not the absolute value of the approval rating that so worried the presidential supporters but the rate at which it was falling.

Statements by presidential supporters confirm Smith's contention that their perceptions of the president's political standing radically changed between March 22 and April 11 and that this made them alter their policy assessments. Before the March 22 meeting, there was still a consensus in support of the status quo. Powell wrote of the March 22 meeting that although the rescue option looked "impressive . . . no one seemed to feel that this was the correct choice at the time."[35] Yet after essentially the same briefing on April 11, Powell wrote that he "sensed that the men around the table, including the president, were leaning strongly toward ordering the plan to be implemented. The comments that followed confirmed my hunch. I added my endorsement. . . . The only partial demurral came from Deputy Secretary of State Warren Christopher."[36] In a chapter entitled "From Bad to Awful," Powell later summed up this change in conditions, by noting that "if the attitude of the press toward Jimmy Carter was bad during the first half of the 1980 primary campaign, it turned terrible during the first week in April."[37] Jordan wrote that by April, action had become necessary, both in order to release the hostages and to help the president's approval rating.[38]

Hawk organizations like the DOD and NSC favored military options from the start. By April 1980 the White House had changed its position; it now also supported a military option. But unlike these organizations, the State Department never favored implementation of a military option. Although many saw the conditions in April as forecasting the end to diplomacy and the implementation of military force, Vance did not think that the conditions warranted changing the status quo. Recognizing that the situation had existed for six months, he nonetheless believed that diplomatic effort should be continued. He advised President Carter that "we have all been repeatedly disappointed, as we seemed to be on the verge of a breakthrough only to see it all fall apart. This is a particularly difficult time, but my strong feeling is that we should not be discouraged; we must continue to look for ways to negotiate. I am strongly opposed to a rescue mission."[39] From November 4 through April 24, when the rescue attempt was implemented, Vance opposed the use of military force. He was so adamant about his position that he resigned immediately after the decision to try a rescue was made—*before* the rescue failed.[40]

All accounts suggest that, with the exception of the State Department's Christopher and Vance, a consensus had formed supporting military action by April 11. After conferring with Jordan, Mondale, and Powell,[41] President Carter determined that "we could no longer afford to depend on diplomacy. I decided to act."[42] On that same day, Carter ordered that the military go ahead with the ill-fated rescue attempt. Given that the hawks were consistently in favor of the military option and the doves consistently against, the presidential supporters, who changed their position, "likely played the critical role in determining the outcome."[43] Examining the president's deteriorating popularity provides an explanation of what triggered the change.

President Carter depended heavily on his three groups of advisers in dealing with the Iranian hostage situation. From the beginning, the hawks and the doves fundamentally disagreed on the utility of military force. By reacting to the sudden drop in the polls and actively turning against the diplomatic approach, the third group, the presidential supporters, seemed to have decisively tipped the balance in favor of military force. By looking at the dominant indicator set of the key swing group, we can explain the timing of this domestic politics decision. Ironically, Secretary of State Vance early on feared exactly this development. Jordan wrote of a November 9 meeting between Jordan, Powell, and Vance that Vance was "worried that Jody and I are so preoccupied with Carter's re-election that we might encourage him to do something foolish because of political pressures. I assured him that I agreed with the present strategy and the ultimate objective of returning the hostages, but we also had to think about the posture of both the president and the nation."[44] If scholars like Smith are correct that the presidential supporters' switch tipped the decision in favor of the rescue attempt, then this model helps to capture the shift in the structural forces that triggered the switch.

Scholars have offered two explanations for the timing of the decision. The first is that Carter employed the military option as soon as it was available.[45] But the empirical record does not support this in terms of either the rescue or alternative military options. Two days after the hostages had been taken, President Carter discussed possible military actions with his military advisers.[46] The administration developed military options that included air strikes, harbor mining, and rescue attempts. The Joint Chiefs of Staff considered a number of military options, including the rescue effort, as feasible before April 24. Before April 15 the military had already put the Delta hostage rescue team on alert seven times.[47] Furthermore, the mission described at the March 22 briefing, where no action was taken, was virtually identical to the mission presented at the April 11 briefing—after which the president decided to launch the operation.[48]

Little was gained from this twenty-day delay. The plan was never fully tested; there was no full-scale run-through involving what we now know to be the critical area—the operations at Desert One. Plans called for U.S. Delta commandos to conduct a complicated transfer from transport planes to helicopters and to refuel the helicopters at a point called Desert One, hundreds of miles inside Iranian territory.[49] The commandos had never practiced this complex, joint operation, which involved navy, marine, air force, and army personnel and equipment, because they were afraid that a rehearsal would endanger the operation's secrecy. The Desert One operation failed: eight U.S. servicemen were killed, and the United States was forced to abort the mission. Therefore, arguments that the military option needed organization time do not convincingly explain the timing of Carter's decision to use force.

A second argument, frequently made by Carter Administration participants, suggests that by April the president had "had enough."[50] A number of participants in the decision—Jordan, Powell, and Colonel Charlie Beckwith, field commander of the rescue operation—have argued that the rescue decision was not triggered by any specific policy failure. Instead they say that by April, President Carter had become generally dissatisfied with the situation. "President Carter understood where we were coming from. He'd been driven to the end of his patience. Now it was time to act."[51] The record, however, does not support this argument.

U.S. officials had tried a long sequence of nonmilitary actions, which all failed. "So it had gone, for six months, as America tried diplomacy, approached Iranian moderates, imposed various economic sanctions, appealed for help from allies, turned to the Red Cross, requested United Nations assistance, and finally cut diplomatic relations."[52] Between November and April, the Carter Administration attempted numerous diplomatic initiatives to free the hostages, involving several negotiation partners, a multitude of sanctions, and various attempts to encourage allies to assist U.S. efforts to apply pressure to Iran. They all failed. It is difficult to see why the cumulative effect of failures was sufficient only at this point to trigger action.

An additional problem with this explanation is that although it might be true, it is unfalsifiable and begs the question. Neither the availability of alternative options nor the failure of diplomatic efforts was unique in April. Why did the president not use military force in the six months before April 24, and why did he choose to use force then? Put differently, statements that the president had "had enough" and had "lost his patience" are measures of our *dependent* variable—strategic assessment. They are not measures of the *independent* variable. Thus, it is impossible for this type of argument to explain why the assessment changed. Instead, the dominant indicator approach provides a more convincing explanation for the decision.

Analysis of the Carter decision to launch a rescue effort demonstrates that the model can be applied to non-war, civilian decision making situations as well as military scenarios. By looking at the critical indicators relied on by the group most interested in Carter's reelection, I can show how a sharp drop in the public opinion polls triggered this group of advisers to switch positions and advocate action. Analysis of record values or other traditional criteria are unable to explain why the political faction lost patience with the situation at the end of March—and not during the previous six months of dropping polls, lost primaries, *Nightline* (originally called *Day [. . .] : America Held Hostage*), and the hostage crisis. This case shows that the dominant indicator approach can advance our knowledge of domestic political policy assessment.

Chapter 7

Decision Making in War

War is the greatest test of a bureaucratic organization.

—James Q. Wilson, *Bureaucracy: What Government Agencies Do and Why They Do It*

The battlefield provides leaders with information that helps them assess their strategies. We can think of strategy as a policy implemented by organizations to pursue desired goals. Leaders view the world through their organizations' lenses and thus can reach conflicting policy assessments from common experiences. A critical element in an organization's lens is the set of quantitative indicators on which it relies—its dominant indicators. By looking at sudden and dramatic changes in an organization's dominant indicators, we can capture the influence of environmental changes on decision makers' policy assessments, a critical factor in policy change. The model combines rational choice techniques with traditional organizational methods and can be applied to a variety of decision making situations.

The substantive question that motivates this study is: How can we represent the battlefield factors that influence decision makers' strategic assessments in war? Strategic assessment represents a crucial element in a state's ability to adapt strategy to the changing wartime situation, which in turn plays a critical role in determining the outcome and costs of wars. In the empirical chapters of this book, I focused on critical strategic aspects of World War I, World War II, and the Vietnam War to see how different organizations from Great Britain, the United States, and Germany assessed strategy. What have we learned?

GENERAL EMPIRICAL CONCLUSIONS

In this study, I come to four general conclusions:

- Organizations use indicators.
- Organizations periodically update their beliefs about a strategy's performance.
- Decision makers react to dramatic changes in their indicators.
- Militaries act more rationally than supporters of the Cult of the Offensive would predict.

Organizations employ indicators to assess policy performance. In World War I, the British civilians and German navy relied on the tonnage of British and Allied merchant shipping lost, while the British navy saw success through the number of German U-boats sunk. In World War II, British civilians assessed success through the destruction and construction of Allied merchant shipping. The British admirals evaluated strategy through the destruction and construction of German U-boats; while the German navy measured success through the "U-boat potential"—the number of merchant ships sunk per ship at sea. In the Vietnam War, the U.S. Army measured success through the number of communists killed and communist weapons captured; the U.S. Congress measured success through the number of Americans killed in action; and the Johnson Administration relied on both U.S. and communist killed-in-action figures. The U.S. Marine Corps initially evaluated performance through measures of South Vietnamese social stability, like success of rice harvests, a method that put the Corps at odds with the army and eventually led to a bureaucratic battle that the Corps lost. Finally, we saw that President Carter's supporters saw success through the lens of public approval of the president. Indicators thus played a key role in the assessment process of actors from a variety of organizations, countries, types of war, and political situations (both war and non-war), as well as across a sixty-six-year time span (1914–1980).

Strategic assessments change: organizations update their beliefs about the efficiency and likelihood of success of their strategies, both during and after conflicts. In particular, this book shows that contrary to the arguments made by scholars supporting the Cult of the Offensive, the information generated by war influences the preferences in strategy of military organizations. Instead of having fixed preferences, the military and civilian groups in this study appear to have had fixed criteria, including their dominant indicators, upon which they assessed strategies. The British admiralty became strong supporters of convoy in both world wars after it discovered that convoy performed better than sea patrol in the sinking of U-boats. Similarly, the presidential supporters in the Carter Administration did not have a preference for the type of policy employed to deal with foreign policy crises like the U.S. hostage situation. Instead, when success—as measured by their dominant indicator, presidential approval—began to change rapidly, they evaluated the diplomatic approach as a failure and opted for an alternative approach.

Both civilian and military organizations react to sudden and dramatic changes in dominant indicators. Their reactions are both self-conscious and deliberate, with decision makers frequently invoking the accelerating rates of their indicators as cause for dissatisfaction or satisfaction. Lloyd George was concerned that the "alarming rate at which our ships were being sunk was rapidly increasing," while Churchill wrote in a letter to Roosevelt that "were this diminution [of merchant ships] to continue at this rate, it would be fatal."[1] President Johnson stated that "some South Vietnamese units were excellent, some were bad; but most were good—and getting better, which was the important thing."[2] Leaders base their concern or satisfaction on the accelerating change in the indicators they are using to monitor performance.

Decision makers frequently depict the variation of their indicators explicitly through graphs and curves, and employ language that focuses on rates of growth and acceleration. The German navy assessed its performance by looking at graphs of the U-boat potential over time, which provided "an accurate picture of the relative rise or fall of the potential."[3] Churchill wrote about his fear manifested in the "charts, curves and statistics," while Johnson assessed the situation by saying that "the curve was clearly upward" and stated in a press conference that Americans liked the "curve to rise like this (indicating a sharp rise) and they like the opposition to go down like this (indicating a sharply declining line)."[4] In all these cases, decision makers described both extremely good and extremely poor assessments in terms of curvilinear changes in key indicators.

Finally, I conclude that military organizations act more rationally than Cult of the Offensive arguments would suggest. Military organizations' strategic assessments largely varied along with their indicators. The indicators may not appear to us *ex post* as the most appropriate measures, but military organizations appear to use the information generated from the battlefield to act purposefully and rationally (in a procedural sense, at least) to maximize their interests. When a military organization's indicators suggested that its strategy was performing well, the organization embraced the policy (as did the U.S. Army after Tet), and when they suggested that a strategy was performing poorly, the organization searched for alternatives (as did the British navy in early 1943). Although military organizations clearly used indicators as propaganda, I found *no* instances where organizations formed policy assessments that obviously contradicted the evaluation one could predict from their policy assessment process. That is, no organization stated that the situation was going extremely well when one of their indicators suggested that it was going poorly and deteriorating at record rates. Given that in all cases, at least some of the evidence for an organization's selection of indicators was *ex ante,* my finding suggests that military organizations act more rationally than could be expected from Cult of the Offensive arguments.

In addition, I have generally found that civilian and military actors differed widely at the time on what constituted "offensive" and what "defensive" tactics. Specifically, each wartime case produced behavior that does not correspond with the Cult of the Offensive claims. In World War I tremendous pressure on the British navy to become increasingly "offensive" and "adventurous" came from civilians. In World War II the British navy began the war employing a strategy of convoy and strenuously urging the Americans to do the same. A convoy strategy would probably be coded a "defensive" strategy by Cult of the Offensive supporters. And in the Vietnam War, the marines supported a strategy of combined action platoons that would also probably be seen as defensive by Cult of the Offensive supporters. Furthermore, in at least three cases, allied militaries (the British and American navies and the German and Japanese navies in World War II, and the U.S. Marine Corps and Army in Vietnam) held extremely divergent views on what strategy to employ and how to measure success, suggesting that approaches that assume a monolithic military miss critical political issues.

The empirical analysis consists of four main cases, incorporating a total of eleven central actors and 178 observations (64 for World War I; 69 for World War II; 36 for Vietnam; and 9 for the hostage rescue attempt). With this limited number of observations, actors, and cases, it would be inappropriate to judge the lack of support for the Cult of the Offensive approach as conclusive. At the same time, my analysis spans a variety of organizations and wars, and includes more observations than most of the Cult of the Offensive studies. It thus reveals serious empirical and theoretical flaws in the Cult of the Offensive argument. But how does my method compare with the alternative models? An analysis of strategic assessments allows us to evaluate the effectiveness of the dominant indicator, the action-reaction, and the standard organization models.

THE MODELS' EXPLANATORY POWERS

In my model, I have incorporated elements central to each of the three alternative models. The standard organization model contributed the notion that organizational lenses provide a critical perspective on what decision makers perceive. Like that in the action-reaction model, my analysis paid special attention to situations where states' strategies changed and to how this influenced strategic assessments. In all the cases, decision makers' assessments were analyzed in terms of the movement of their dominant indicators. Each of the models has comparative advantages and disadvantages.[5] Analysis of each shows both their strengths and weaknesses in explaining the specific cases and suggests that the dominant indicator approach provides a superior method for explaining strategic assessment.

The Action-Reaction Model

The action-reaction model resembles arguments made by Robert Jervis and Kimberly Zisk and assumes that decision makers react to strategic changes made by their adversaries.[6] It is a highly parsimonious approach that explains some of the observed strategic behavior evident in our cases. In World War I, Germany changed its submarine strategy three times (implementing and retracting unrestricted submarine warfare in 1915, and reimplementing it in 1917). Each change resulted in a change in civilian assessment. The approach, however, does not explain why the British civilians and admirals saw convoy as an immediate success, why the admirals failed to react to the German actions, or why the Germans failed to react to the British strategic change.

In World War II, the action-reaction model does not help explain a critical lack of reaction by the British and an important change in strategic assessment by the Germans. First, the British did not react to the Germans' implementation of Wolf Packs by changing their naval strategy. And second, in what is arguably the most important naval strategic assessment of the war, Admiral Dönitz's evaluation that the U-boat campaign had been lost in spring 1943 was due only to incremental changes in escort convoys and air patrol and not to a dramatic change in strategy by the Allied forces. The World War II case highlights two problems with the action-reaction approach. First, as occurred in the spring of 1943, assessments on both sides (in this case, the German and British) can alter rapidly and radically as a result of their strategic interaction but not as a product of policy change (such as the implementation of unrestricted submarine warfare). Second, and more important, how did the British know that the Germans had switched to a Wolf Pack strategy in the summer of 1940? The Germans did not announce their new strategy; instead, the British could only observe the *effects* of the change. In order to capture how organizations react to unobservable strategic change, we need to examine how they assess performance. In other words, the action-reaction approach assumes that a state will always know that its adversary has changed strategies. This is not always the case. Some strategic changes manifest themselves only through their influence on an organization's measures of performance—

a process captured by the dominant indicator approach or something like it. The action-reaction approach had equally mixed success in predicting results in the American cases.

During the Vietnam War, both Congress and the Johnson Administration reacted strongly to the Tet Offensive. But the action-reaction approach does not help explain congressional concern in spring of 1967, why the communist forces launched the Tet Offensive in the winter of 1968, why the U.S. Army saw Tet as a victory, or how the organizational gridlock occurred in the Johnson Administration.

Finally, in the hostage rescue case, no specific action spurred the presidential supporters to change their endorsement of a diplomatic to support of a military approach. They did not react to a specific Iranian change but rather to a deteriorating political situation.

Together, these cases suggest mixed results for the action-reaction approach. Distinct, visible strategic changes influenced decision makers' assessments. However, organizations, both civilian and military, sometimes altered their assessments without there having been a change in their adversary's strategy, something that the action-reaction model does not predict. Furthermore, when the approach accurately predicts a strategic change, it cannot explain which organizations will react or whether an organization will become gridlocked. These restrictions are a trade-off for the model's simplicity; this parsimonious approach does specify conditions sufficient for a change in assessment.

The Standard Organization Approach

The standard organization approach, which I also call the absolute-value model, applies the type of organization model proposed by Herbert Simon, Richard Cyert, James March, and Anthony Downs to an indicator approach.[7] This parsimonious approach states that organizations will be satisfied with their policy when their indicators set records in the desired direction and dissatisfied when their indicators set records in the undesired direction. This approach captures many of the manifestations of strategic assessment, such as British civilian discontent in World War I before April 1917, congressional concern following the Tet Offensive, and U.S. Army satisfaction resulting from Tet. This approach was much less effective, however, at capturing British military organizations' assessments in the two world wars and the Carter Administration's policy assessments.

The approach has two problems. First, it forecasts many extreme assessments that we do not observe. This is particularly true of negative assessments from indicators that decision makers wish to minimize or positive assessments from indicators that decision makers wish to maximize. In World War I there were twelve record values of British and Allied shipping sunk before April 1917. Although it is likely that British civilians were unhappy with the situation during all the months before the implementation of convoy, the standard approach does not provide a mechanism for separating out the general levels of unhappiness from the extreme discontent that resulted in costly political actions. In other words, the absolute-value model predicts that civilians would be dissatisficed twelve times, when in fact there were only four months when extreme civilian dissatisfaction was visible: civilian concerns voiced in the summer of 1915, the fall of the Asquith government in 1916, and Lloyd George's actions in February and April 1917. In the other eight months civilians did not act in a way that would suggest extreme displeasure with the antisubmarine situation. The approach thus captures the four visible assessments, but it also predicts eight other extreme assessments at times when nothing unusual was observed. This is a common problem with the standard organization approach. While it is generally quite effective at capturing observed change, it also makes a large number of false predictions.

At the same time, the standard organization approach can make too few predictions. In the hostage rescue case, before the rescue decision, the president's approval rating had never reached its October 1979 low. Thus the approach would not predict that the presidential supporters would be dissatisfied with the diplomatic approach. This type of situation is especially likely in war, where a country's mobilization and experience at warfare tend to lead to an increase in destructiveness.

If a war becomes increasingly violent after its initial battles (because actors mobilize greater resources or learn how to destroy each other more effectively), then the smallest values for most of the indicators occur in the first few observation periods. When this is the case, the standard organization model will not work effectively. Although this empirical condition is not a rule, it was the case in the data analyzed in this study and affected the absolute-value model's ability to predict decision makers' strategic assessments. Returning to the World War I case, we saw that both civilian and military decision makers were extremely satisfied with convoys. For the admirals, convoy led to record values of U-boats sunk; therefore, the standard model works. But for the civilians, no month after April 1917 shows fewer than 118,000 tons of shipping lost, almost six times higher than the lowest month on record, November 1914, in which just 19,413 tons were sunk. This is not a surprising condition. As wars are fought, militaries get better at inflicting damage on one another. It is extremely unusual to replicate at a later stage the low levels of damage experienced early in the war. But the standard model would predict that the civilians would have been dissatisfied with the situation and pushed for strategic change every month after November 1914! Thus, not only does the standard model fail to signify that the civilians were extremely pleased by the performance of convoy, it is highly unlikely that conditions could exist where the model would signify satisfaction after showing record levels of dissatisfaction.

When these two situations are analyzed together, one sees that the standard organization model is asymmetrically biased. If the organization is trying to minimize the indicator, it will overpredict states of dissatisfaction and underpredict states of satisfaction. If the organization is trying to maximize the indicator, the standard organization model will do the opposite; it overpredicts states of satisfaction and underpredicts dissatisfaction. Thus, this approach is likely to make too many predictions of either satisfaction or dissatisfaction and too few of the other. A superior approach would treat increases and decreases in dominant indicators more symmetrically.

A second problem with the absolute-value model is that it treats all record values uniformly, regardless of the marginal change in value of the indicator that created it. The Tet Offensive, for example, was not just a record value in all the actors' dominant indicators; it represented a tremendous increase in the rate at which these indicators moved. And, as we saw in both the empirical analyses and earlier in this chapter, decision makers recognize changes in the rate at which their indicators change and point to rapid increases or decreases in their indicators when supporting their positions. By looking at whether something is a record value, the absolute-value approach fails to include information on the rate of indicator variation, as the dominant indicator model does. As we have seen, these rates represent a critical factor in some decision makers' calculus. Conversely, we have also seen that decision makers are frequently insensitive to small changes, even if those changes produce records.

Finally, the absolute-value model does not work well with proportional indicators. If an organization from a country that was overrun by an adversary measured success through the percentage of country reclaimed from the aggressor (this is an indicator that the Kuwaiti Army might have used in 1991), then a record value would never be set, for it would have to exceed 100 percent. This problem, however, did not appear in the cases examined.

Unlike the action-reaction model, which does not include indicators, both the dominant indicator model and the absolute-value model share a basic indicator approach. The key difference between them is the evaluation of what type of record indicator value was necessary for decision makers to assess a situation as succeeding or failing. Although the standard organization model can capture some of the observed data, an approach that is both more symmetrical in respect to increases and decreases and that incorporates the size of the change that creates a record value would be more effective. The dominant indicator approach provides just this type of model.

The Dominant Indicator Model

The dominant indicator model argues that decision makers react to sudden and dramatic changes in their environment and that these changes are represented by record increases in the acceleration and change in acceleration of their dominant indicators, rather than by record absolute values. In the cases studied, this model predicted many of the observed strategic assessments; in addition, it predicted few unobserved changes in assessments. The success of the model can be seen by analyzing how well it did in explaining strategic assessments in each case.

The dominant indicator model effectively captures the periods of civilian dissatisfaction with the strategy of sea patrol—the summer of 1915, the fall of 1916, and the winter of 1917—as well as the civilian satisfaction with convoy after its introduction. In particular, the model helps to explain why Lloyd George put pressure on the British admirals in February and April 1917 but not in March. The model also helps us understand why before April 1917 the admirals failed to see the situation as being as dire as the civilians thought but joined them in applauding the performance of convoys afterward.

Overall, the dominant indicator model outperforms the other two models in explaining British antisubmarine assessments in World War II. As we saw earlier, the action-reaction model offers no help in the World War II case, and the absolute-value model does not work well in assessing the rapidly changing Battle of the Atlantic. The dominant indicator model was particularly helpful in understanding the rapid alterations in strategic assessment by the British navy in the winter and spring of 1943. No other model can explain why the admirals first became despondent and considered abandoning the convoy strategy, and then, soon after, celebrated their victory over the German U-boats. The model also captures most of the conditions that influenced civilian decision making.

In the Vietnam War, the dominant indicator model accurately predicted that Congress would react negatively to the events of the spring of 1967 and would see the Tet Offensive as creating an unsatisfactory situation. Similarly, the model also captures the army's positive assessments before and during Tet. Finally, the model accurately predicted that the Tet Offensive would push the Johnson Administration into a condition of organizational gridlock. The action-reaction model cannot predict gridlock, and the standard organization model would predict that the Johnson Administration was gridlocked during virtually the entire Vietnam conflict. Only the dominant indicator model correctly captures the conditions that led to this unique condition.

Finally, in the Iranian hostage rescue decision, a situation quite different from the wartime cases, the dominant indicator model captured the rapid drop in approval rating that triggered the presidential supporters to action.

In each of these cases, the dominant indicator model captured most of the extreme assessments of organizational satisfaction or dissatisfaction. At the same time, the dominant indicator model made fewer errant predictions (forecasting behavior that was not observed) than the standard organization model. Also, unlike the standard organization approach, the model applied symmetrically to both gains and losses. And by relying on the rate of change of indicators, the model indicated the same type of environmental changes that decision makers themselves, both at the time and later, pointed to when supporting their strategic assessments.

In addition to the empirical advantages, the dominant indicator approach contains a number of theoretical strengths. First, it combines both rational choice and bounded rationality approaches to decision making, creating a model that I consider complementary to both. As well, this approach combines historical, case study, and quantitative empirical methods.

Another strength of this approach is that it examines the conditions under which actors change their preferences about policies, rather than whether those policies were the best way to achieve the actors' desired outcome. That is, the approach relies on *ex ante* information to determine actors' assessments of policies and not *ex post* analysis to determine the appropriateness and accuracy of actors' policy choices. This facilitates analysis of non-events, in which an organization wishes to alter a policy but is overruled by some other organization.

This analysis introduces a number of concepts, such as dissatisfaction and noise, that can be transported to other studies. Instead of simply examining the conditions under which decision makers are satisficed, as do most organization approaches, I introduce the notion of being dissatisficed. When a decision maker is dissatisficed, he or she is extremely dissatisfied and would like to change policies. In my analysis, dissatisfaction occurs when a policy is "going poorly and getting increasingly worse," and the decision maker believes that the policy is performing at the worst level possible.

As well, I show that we could use the time period inherent in indicators to represent decision makers' expectations of the noise present in their data. Because of the tremendous pressure on them, particularly in war, to evaluate strategies as quickly as possible, decision makers choose the shortest possible time frame for their indicators. The longer an indicator's time period, the more data decision makers need before they can make useful evaluations of their policies. An approach that predicts decision makers' policy assessments complements particularly well approaches that predict policy outcomes.

Finally, when examining historical data, it is sometimes difficult to determine which indicators decision makers used, because most of the sources available after an event are influenced by knowledge of the outcome of that event. Similarly, an analysis requires the actual data used by the decision maker, not the "corrected" data. (Frequently, historical data have been "corrected," which makes it difficult to determine what figures decision makers actually employed.) This is a general problem for historical analysis, but it facilitates *ex ante* prediction of future events.

The dominant indicator approach requires that we determine, *ex ante,* decision makers' indicators. Given these indicators, we can predict how decision makers will react to environmental changes. It thus follows the form of procedural rationality arguments.[8] But as in all such analyses, there is a danger that history might contaminate the available data. Specifically, both the indicators employed by organizations and the values of these indicators might be "revised" or "corrected" through the historical process. Analysts employing the dominant indicator approach (or any procedural rationality approach) therefore need to be careful when using historical data. The analysis of current decision making provides a historically unbiased context for predicting policy assessment. The dominant indicator approach might thus be best applied to current policy evaluations rather than to the analysis of past decision making—certainly an unusual situation for decision analysis.

Although this book has focused on military strategy, the dominant indicator approach can also apply to nonconflict policy evaluations. In particular, the dominant indicator approach can help us better understand the conditions under which different civilian organizations reach conflicting assessments of their domestic policies. Decision makers in the United States, for example, have been grappling with the problem of evaluating how effective the government has been in its "war on drugs."[9] The agencies involved agree that the overall strategic goal is to decrease drug use in America, but various agencies, with dissimilar missions, measure effectiveness in fundamentally different ways. Government law-enforcement agencies, whose mission is largely one of interdiction, tend to focus on supply measurements. The most important measures used by organizations like the Drug Enforcement Administration, the Federal Bureau of Investigation, and state and local enforcement agencies are arrests and "drugs on the table"—the amount and value of the drugs confiscated, usually measured in kilograms and street-value prices (these drugs are frequently laid out on a table for reporters and officials to see). Thus, law-enforcement organizations believe that their policies are successful when the quantity and value of the drugs they confiscate increases.

Health organizations, such as the Centers for Disease Control or city-based health-education programs, emphasize the effects drugs have on people. They frequently look at demand-based indicators, like the number of drug-overdose cases, injuries reported by hospitals, or child drug use. Thus, if the number of drug overdoses reported decreases, these organizations see it as a sign of success.

Because they focus on different indicators of performance, these organizations frequently reach fundamentally different assessments about the government's drug efforts. These differences were particularly strong during the Reagan Administration. Enforcement agencies like the FBI reallocated resources that had previously been dedicated to counterespionage and other Cold War activities to the drug-interdiction effort. This resulted in an increase in arrests and amount of confiscated drugs. At the same time, the Reagan Administration cut back on drug rehabilitation and education programs just as crack cocaine use was increasing dramatically in the inner cities. This resulted in a large increase in the number of drug-related injuries and deaths. Thus, by the late 1980s, the two key groups involved in the drug war had reached fundamentally different evaluations about the effectiveness of the Reagan Administration's policies for combating drugs.

I began this study by stating that the battlefield informs decision makers' strategic assessments. But we have seen that the battlefield can also confuse decision makers. Rather than resulting from pathological or malignant forces, this confusion may derive from organizations doing their jobs as best they know how under difficult and uncertain conditions. When actors choose different lenses through which to evaluate their policies, they can share a common wartime experience, yet reach contradictory assessments.

Rather than being solved, this problem will become exacerbated by technology. On the information battlefield of the future, wartime leaders will know more, faster, than ever before. But like those who have already fought, those whose battles are yet to come will still have to decide which information to rely on and which to discard. As the availability of information grows, so do the chances that actors will see the world through different lenses. Thus, the study of how nations fight wars will increasingly become the study of how nations use information in war.

Appendix A: World War I Data

A.1 Number of U-boats Lost, by Month

		U-boats	Acceleration	Change in Acceleration
1914	Aug.	2	—	—
	Sept.	0	−2	—
	Oct.	0	0	2
	Nov.	1	1	1
	Dec.	2	1	0
1915	Jan.	3	1	0
	Feb.	0	−3	−4
	Mar.	3	3	6
	Apr.	1	−2	−5
	May	1	0	2
	Jun.	3	2	2
	July	3	0	−2
	Aug.	3	0	0
	Sept.	2	−1	−1
	Oct.	1	−1	0
	Nov.	2	1	2
	Dec.	0	−2	−3
1916	Jan.	0	0	2
	Feb.	0	0	0
	Mar.	2	2	2
	Apr.	3	1	−1
	May	4	1	0

A.1 Continued

		U-boats	Acceleration	Change in Acceleration
	Jun.	0	−4	−5
	July	3	3	7
	Aug.	2	−1	−4
	Sept.	1	−1	0
	Oct.	0	−1	0
	Nov.	5	5	6
	Dec.	3	−2	−7
1917	Jan.	2	−1	1
	Feb.	5	3	4
	Mar.	4	−1	−4
	Apr.	1	−3	−2
	May	7	6	9
	Jun.	2	−5	−11
	July	9	7	12
	Aug.	5	−4	−11
	Sept.	11	6	10
	Oct.	5	−6	−12
	Nov.	8	3	9
	Dec.	8	0	−3
1918	Jan.	10	−6	2
	Feb.	2	−8	−10
	Mar.	7	5	13
	Apr.	6	−1	−6
	May	16	10	11
	Jun.	3	−13	−23
	July	6	3	16
	Aug.	7	1	−2
	Sept.	9	2	1
	Oct.	19	10	8

A.2 Gross Tons of Allied Shipping Lost, by Month

		Shipping	Acceleration	Change in Acceleration
1914	Aug.	62,767	–	–
	Sept.	98,378	35,611	–
	Oct.	87,917	−10,461	−46,072
	Nov.	19,413	−68,504	−58,043
	Dec.	44,197	24,784	93,288
1915	Jan.	47,981	3,784	−21,000
	Feb.	59,921	11,940	8,156
	Mar.	80,775	20,854	8,914
	Apr.	55,725	−25,050	−45,904
	May	120,058	64,333	89,383
	Jun.	131,428	11,370	−52,963
	July	109,640	−21,788	−33,158
	Aug.	185,866	76,226	98,014
	Sept.	151,884	−33,982	−110,208
	Oct.	88,534	−63,350	−29,368
	Nov.	153,043	64,509	127,859
	Dec.	123,141	−29,902	−94,411
1916	Jan.	81,259	−41,882	−11,980
	Feb.	117,547	36,288	78,170
	Mar.	167,097	49,550	13,262
	Apr.	191,667	24,570	−24,980
	May	129,175	−62,492	−87,062
	Jun.	108,855	−20,320	42,172
	July	118,215	9,360	29,680
	Aug.	162,744	44,529	35,169
	Sept.	230,460	67,716	23,187
	Oct.	353,660	123,200	55,484
	Nov.	311,508	−42,152	−165,352
	Dec.	355,139	43,631	85,783
1917	Jan.	368,521	13,382	−30,249
	Feb.	540,006	171,485	158,103
	Mar.	593,841	53,835	−117,650

A.2 Continued

		Shipping	Acceleration	Change in Acceleration
	Apr.	881,027	287,186	233,351
	May	596,629	−284,398	−571,584
	Jun.	687,507	90,878	375,276
	July	557,988	−129,519	−220,397
	Aug.	511,730	−46,258	83,261
	Sept.	351,748	−159,982	−113,724
	Oct.	458,558	106,810	266,792
	Nov.	289,212	−169,346	−276,156
	Dec.	399,111	109,899	279,245
1918	Jan.	306,658	−92,453	−202,352
	Feb.	318,957	12,299	104,752
	Mar.	342,597	23,640	11,341
	Apr.	278,719	−63,878	−87,518
	May	295,520	16,801	80,679
	Jun.	255,587	−39,933	−56,734
	July	260,967	5,380	45,313
	Aug.	283,815	22,848	17,468
	Sept.	187,881	−95,934	−118,782
	Oct.	118,559	−69,322	26,612

Appendix B: World War II Data

B.1 U-boats Lost

			By Month			By Quarter		
			Losses	Accel-eration	Change in Accel-eration	Losses	Accel-eration	Change in Accel-eration
		Sept.	2	—	—			
	Fall	Oct.	5	3	—	7	—	—
		Nov.	1	−4	−7			
		Dec.	1	0	4			
1940	Wint.	Jan.	2	1	1	9	2	—
		Feb.	4	2	1			
		Mar.	3	−1	−3			
	Spr.	Apr.	5	2	3	6	−3	−5
		May	1	−4	−6			
		Jun.	0	−1	3			
	Sum.	July	2	2	3	5	−1	2
		Aug.	3	1	−1			
		Sept.	0	−3	−4			
	Fall	Oct.	1	1	4	3	−2	−1
		Nov.	2	1	0			
		Dec.	0	−2	−3			
1941	Wint.	Jan.	0	0	2	5	2	4
		Feb.	0	0	0			

B.1 Continued

			By Month			By Quarter		
			Losses	Accel-eration	Change in Accel-eration	Losses	Accel-eration	Change in Accel-eration
		Mar.	5	5	5			
	Spr.	Apr.	2	−3	−8	7	2	0
		May	1	−1	2			
		Jun.	4	3	4			
	Sum.	July	1	−3	−6	6	−1	−3
		Aug.	3	2	5			
		Sept.	2	−1	−3			
	Fall	Oct.	2	0	1	17	11	12
		Nov.	5	3	3			
		Dec.	10	5	2			
1942	Wint.	Jan.	3	−7	−12	11	−6	−17
		Feb.	2	−1	6			
		Mar.	6	4	5			
	Spr.	Apr.	3	−3	−7	10	−1	5
		May	4	1	4			
		Jun.	3	−1	−2			
	Sum.	July	11	8	9	31	21	22
		Aug.	10	−1	−9			
		Sept.	10	0	1			
	Fall	Oct.	16	6	6	34	3	−18
		Nov.	13	−3	−9			
		Dec.	5	−8	−5			
1943	Wint.	Jan.	6	1	9	40	6	3
		Feb.	19	13	12			
		Mar.	15	−4	−17			
	Spr.	Apr.	15	0	4	73	33	27
		May	41	26	26			
		Jun.	17	−24	−50			

B.1 Continued

			By Month			By Quarter		
			Losses	Acceleration	Change in Acceleration	Losses	Acceleration	Change in Acceleration
	Sum.	July	37	20	44	71	−2	−35
		Aug.	25	−12	−32			
		Sept.	9	−16	−4			
	Fall	Oct.	26	17	33	53	−18	−16
		Nov.	19	−7	−24			
		Dec.	8	−11	−4			
1944	Wint.	Jan.	15	7	18	60	7	25
		Feb.	20	5	−2			
		Mar.	25	5	0			
	Spr.	Apr.	21	−4	−9	68	8	1
		May	22	1	5			
		Jun.	25	3	2			
	Sum.	July	23	−2	−5	80	12	4
		Aug.	36	13	15			
		Sept.	21	−15	−28			
	Fall	Oct.	13	−8	7	34	−46	−58
		Nov.	7	−6	2			
		Dec.	14	7	13			
1945	Wint.	Jan.	14	0	−7	68	34	80
		Feb.	22	8	8			
		Mar.	32	10	2			
	Spr.	Apr.	55	23	13			
		May	28	−27	−50			

B.2 U-boats Built

		New U-boats	Acceleration	Change in Acceleration
1940	Wint.	7	—	—
	Spr.	4	−3	—
	Sum.	9	5	8
	Fall	15	6	1
1941	Wint.	22	7	1
	Spr.	30	8	1
	Sum.	47	17	9
	Fall	53	6	−11
1942	Wint.	69	16	10
	Spr.	49	−20	−36
	Sum.	59	10	30
	Fall	61	2	−8
1943	Wint.	69	8	6
	Spr.	69	0	−8
	Sum.	71	2	2
	Fall	61	−10	−12
1944	Wint.	78	17	27
	Spr.	62	−16	−33
	Sum.	53	−9	7
	Fall	49	−4	5
1945	Wint.	65	16	20

B.3 Allied Shipping Lost, by Month

			Global	Pacific Losses	Allied Losses	Acceleration	Change in Acceleration
		Sept.	194,845	0	194,845	—	—
	Fall	Oct.	196,355	0	196,355	1,510	—
		Nov.	174,269	0	174,269	−22,086	−23,596
		Dec.	189,768	0	189,768	15,499	37,585
1940	Wint.	Jan.	214,506	0	214,506	24,738	9,239
		Feb.	226,920	0	226,920	12,414	−12,324
		Mar.	107,009	0	107,009	−119,911	−132,325
	Spr.	Apr.	158,218	0	158,218	51,209	171,120
		May	288,461	0	288,461	130,243	79,034
		Jun.	585,496	19,196	566,300	277,839	166,792
	Sum.	July	386,913	0	386,913	−179,387	−495,618
		Aug.	397,229	12,180	385,049	−1,864	208,899
		Sept.	448,621	0	448,621	63,572	41,076
	Fall	Oct.	442,985	7,203	435,782	−12,839	−57,028
		Nov.	385,715	33,996	351,719	−84,063	−51,634
		Dec.	349,568	26,956	322,612	−29,107	21,123
1941	Wint.	Jan.	320,240	0	320,240	−2,372	6,819
		Feb.	403,393	0	403,393	83,153	112,481
		Mar.	529,706	287	529,419	126,026	43,160
	Spr.	Apr.	687,901	0	687,901	158,482	31,882
		May	511,042	0	511,042	−176,859	−335,054
		Jun.	432,025	0	432,025	−79,017	97,842
	Sum.	July	120,975	0	120,975	−311,050	−232,033
		Aug.	130,699	21,378	109,321	−11,654	320,774
		Sept.	285,942	4,793	281,149	171,828	145,519
	Fall	Oct.	218,289	0	218,289	−62,860	−222,896
		Nov.	104,640	0	104,640	−113,649	−45,996
		Dec.	583,706	431,673	152,033	47,393	592,715
1942	Wint.	Jan.	419,907	71,054	348,853	196,820	−127,652
		Feb.	679,632	181,247	498,385	149,532	423,524
		Mar.	834,164	183,773	650,391	152,006	−105,193

B.3 Continued

			Global	Pacific Losses	Allied Losses	Acceleration	Change in Acceleration
	Spr.	Apr.	674,457	13,913	660,544	10,153	−314,239
		May	705,050	16,959	688,091	27,547	190,300
		Jun.	834,196	31,416	802,780	114,689	98,553
	Sum.	July	618,113	31,722	586,391	−216,389	−345,229
		Aug.	661,133	1,553	659,580	73,189	259,103
		Sept.	567,327	3,188	564,139	−95,441	−136,826
	Fall	Oct.	637,833	13,691	624,142	60,003	164,312
		Nov.	807,754	0	807,754	183,612	99,415
		Dec.	348,902	0	348,902	−458,852	−628,773
1943	Wint.	Jan.	261,359	9,227	252,132	−96,770	−566,609
		Feb.	403,062	19,351	383,711	131,579	229,246
		Mar.	693,389	6,161	687,228	303,517	148,624
	Spr.	Apr.	344,680	35,168	309,512	−377,716	−639,036
		May	299,428	33,472	265,956	−43,556	303,457
		Jun.	123,825	1,248	122,577	−143,379	−130,351
	Sum.	July	365,398	0	365,398	242,821	417,176
		Aug.	119,801	4,476	115,325	−250,073	−487,170
		Sept.	156,419	9,977	146,442	31,117	282,215
	Fall	Oct.	139,861	7,176	132,685	−13,757	−53,176
		Nov.	144,391	6,711	137,680	4,995	21,088
		Dec.	168,524	0	168,524	30,844	19,603
1944	Wint.	Jan.	130,635	0	130,635	−37,889	−62,022
		Feb.	116,855	0	116,855	−13,780	24,109
		Mar.	157,960	0	157,960	41,105	54,885
	Spr.	Apr.	82,372	0	82,372	−75,588	−116,693
		May	27,297	0	27,297	−55,075	20,513
		Jun.	104,084	0	104,084	76,787	131,862
	Sum.	July	78,756	0	78,756	−25,328	−102,115
		Aug.	118,304	0	118,304	39,548	64,876
		Sept.	44,805	0	44,805	−73,499	−113,047
	Fall	Oct.	11,668	7,176	4,492	−40,313	40,362

B.3 Continued

			Global	Pacific Losses	Allied Losses	Acceleration	Change in Acceleration
		Nov.	37,980	7,247	30,733	26,241	59,449
		Dec.	134,913	43,100	91,813	61,080	70,621
1945	Wint.	Jan.	82,897	7,176	75,721	−16,092	−148,949
		Feb.	95,316	0	95,316	19,595	64,435
		Mar.	111,204	0	111,204	15,888	3,469
	Spr.	Apr.	104,512	22,822	81,690	−29,514	−22,580
		May	17,198	7,176	10,022	−71,668	−80,622

B.4 Allied Shipping Lost, By Quarter

		Shipping Lost	Acceleration	Change in Acceleration
	Fall	560,392	—	—
1940	Wint.	548,435	−11,957	—
	Spr.	1,012,979	464,544	476,501
	Sum.	1,220,583	207,604	−256,940
	Fall	1,110,113	−110,470	−318,074
1941	Wint.	1,253,052	142,939	253,409
	Spr.	1,630,968	377,916	234,977
	Sum.	511,445	−1,119,523	−1,497,439
	Fall	474,962	−36,483	1,083,040
1942	Wint.	1,497,629	1,022,667	1,059,150
	Spr.	2,151,415	653,786	−368,881
	Sum.	1,810,110	−341,305	−995,091
	Fall	1,780,798	−29,312	311,993
1943	Wint.	1,323,071	−457,727	−428,415
	Spr.	698,045	−625,026	−167,299
	Sum.	627,165	−70,880	554,146
	Fall	438,889	−188,276	−117,396
1944	Wint.	405,450	−33,439	154,837
	Spr.	213,753	−191,697	−158,258
	Sum.	241,865	28,112	219,809
	Fall	127,038	−114,827	−142,939

Appendix C: Vietnam War Data

C.1 U.S. Killed in Action, by Month

		U.S. Killed in Action	Acceleration	Change in Acceleration
1966	Jan.	282	—	—
	Feb.	435	153	—
	Mar.	507	72	−81
	Apr.	316	−191	−263
	May	464	148	339
	Jun.	507	43	−105
	July	435	−72	−115
	Aug.	396	−39	33
	Sept.	419	23	62
	Oct.	340	−79	−102
	Nov.	475	135	214
	Dec.	432	−43	−178
1967	Jan.	520	88	131
	Feb.	662	142	54
	Mar.	944	282	140
	Apr.	710	−234	−516
	May	1,233	523	757
	Jun.	803	−430	−953
	July	781	−22	408
	Aug.	535	−246	−224
	Sept.	775	240	486
	Oct.	733	−42	−282

C.1 Continued

		U.S. Killed in Action	Acceleration	Change in Acceleration
	Nov.	881	148	190
	Dec.	774	−107	−255
1968	Jan.	1,202	428	535
	Feb.	2,124	922	494
	Mar.	1,543	−581	−1,503
	Apr.	1,410	−133	448
	May	2,169	759	892
	Jun.	1,146	−1,023	−1,782
	July	813	−333	690
	Aug.	1,080	267	600
	Sept.	1,053	−27	−294
	Oct.	600	−453	−426
	Nov.	703	103	556
	Dec.	749	46	−57

C.2 U.S. Killed in Action, by Quarter

		Killed in Action	Acceleration	Change in Acceleration
1966	Wint.	1,224	—	—
	Spr.	1,287	63	—
	Sum.	1,250	−37	−100
	Fall	1,247	−3	34
1967	Wint.	2,126	879	882
	Spr.	2,746	620	−259
	Sum.	2,091	−655	−1,275
	Fall	2,388	297	952
1968	Wint.	4,869	2,481	2,184
	Spr.	4,725	−144	−2,625
	Sum.	2,946	−1,779	−1,635
	Fall	2,052	−894	885

C.3 Enemy Body Count, by Month

		Body Count	Acceleration	Change in Acceleration
1966	Jan.	2,648	—	—
	Feb.	4,727	2,079	—
	Mar.	5,685	958	−1,121
	Apr.	2,818	−2,867	−3,825
	May	4,239	1,421	4,288
	Jun.	4,815	576	−845
	July	5,297	482	−94
	Aug.	5,860	563	81
	Sept.	4,459	−1,401	−1,964
	Oct.	5,665	1,206	2,607
	Nov.	5,447	−218	−1,424
	Dec.	3,864	−1,583	−1,365
1967	Jan.	6,064	2,200	3,783
	Feb.	7,341	1,277	−923
	Mar.	9,351	2,010	733
	Apr.	6,227	−3,124	−5,134
	May	9,808	3,581	6,705
	Jun.	7,354	−2,454	−6,035
	July	7,923	569	3,023
	Aug.	5,810	−2,113	−2,682
	Sept.	6,354	544	2,657
	Oct.	6,272	−82	−626
	Nov.	7,662	1,390	1,472
	Dec.	7,938	276	−1,114
1968	Jan.	15,217	7,279	7,003
	Feb.	39,867	24,650	17,371
	Mar.	17,371	−22,496	−47,146
	Apr.	12,515	−4,856	17,640
	May	24,086	11,571	16,427
	Jun.	10,319	−13,767	−25,338
	July	6,653	−3,666	10,101
	Aug.	15,478	8,825	12,491

C.3 Continued

	Body Count	Acceleration	Change in Acceleration
Sept.	12,543	−2,935	−11,760
Oct.	8,168	−4,375	−1,440
Nov.	9,632	1,464	5,839
Dec.	9,600	−32	−1,496

C.4 Enemy Body Count, by Quarter

		Body Count	Acceleration	Change in Acceleration
1966	Wint.	13,060	—	—
	Spr.	11,872	−1,188	—
	Sum.	15,616	3,744	4,932
	Fall	14,976	−640	−4,384
1967	Wint.	22,756	7,780	8,420
	Spr.	23,389	633	−7,147
	Sum.	20,087	−3,302	−3,935
	Fall	21,872	1,785	5,087
1968	Wint.	72,455	50,583	48,798
	Spr.	46,920	−25,535	−76,118
	Sum.	34,674	−12,246	13,289
	Fall	27,400	−7,274	4,972

C.5 Enemy Weapons Captured

			By Month	By Quarter	Acceleration	Change in Acceleration
1966	Wint.	Jan.	979			
		Feb.	1,219			
	Spr.	Mar.	1,607	3,805	—	—
		Apr.	829			
		May	1,087			
	Sum.	Jun.	3,761	5,677	1,872	—
		July	1,614			
		Aug.	1,342			
	Fall	Sept.	1,430	4,386	−1,291	−3,163
		Oct.	1,977			
		Nov.	1,423			
1967	Wint.	Dec.	1,338	4,738	352	1,643
		Jan.	2,360			
		Feb.	2,395			
	Spr.	Mar.	3,826	8,581	3,843	3,491
		Apr.	2,118			
		May	2,781			
	Sum.	Jun.	1,979	6,878	−1,703	−5,546
		July	3,508			
		Aug.	2,068			
	Fall	Sept.	1,877	7,453	575	2,278
		Oct.	3,303			
		Nov.	2,579			
1968	Wint.	Dec.	2,404	8,286	833	258
		Jan.	4,187			
		Feb.	8,677			
	Spr.	Mar.	4,634	17,498	9,212	8,379
		Apr.	5,351			
		May	8,675			
	Sum.	Jun.	5,259	19,285	1,787	−7,425
		July	2,730			
		Aug.	5,787			
	Fall	Sept.	4,643	13,160	−6,125	−7,912

Appendix D: President Carter's Approval Rating

D.1 President Carter's Approval Rating

		Overall Approval Rating			Approval of Handling of Iran	
		Approval	Acceleration	Change in Acceleration	Approval	Disapproval
1979	Oct.	29	—	—	—	—
	Nov.	32	3	—	—	—
	Dec.	61	29	26	—	—
1980	Jan.	56	−5	−34	61	30
	Feb.	55	−1	4	—	—
	Mar., Week 1	52	−3	−2	—	—
	Mar., Week 4	39	−13	−10	40	50
	Apr.	—	—	—	46	42
	May, Week 1	43	4	17	—	—
	May, Week 4	38	−5	−9	—	—

NOTES

CHAPTER 1: STRATEGY AND ORGANIZATION

1. Paul Kennedy, "Britain in the First World War," in Allan Millet and Murray Williamson (eds.), *Military Effectiveness* (Boston: Allen and Unwin, 1988), 53.
2. Geoffrey Perret, *There's a War to Be Won: The United States Army in World War II* (New York: Ballantine, 1991), 156, fn.
3. Gregg Herken, *Counsels of War* (New York: Knopf, 1985); Fred Kaplan, *The Wizards of Armageddon* (New York: Simon and Schuster, 1983).
4. Randolph M. Siverson and Harvey Starr, *The Diffusion of War: A Study of Opportunity and Willingness* (Ann Arbor: University of Michigan Press, 1991), 3.
5. For a discussion of this debate, see Stephen Peter Rosen, *Winning the Next War: Innovation and the Modern Military* (Ithaca: Cornell University Press, 1991); Kimberly Martin Zisk, *Engaging the Enemy: Organization Theory and Soviet Military Innovation, 1955–1991* (Princeton: Princeton University Press, 1993); and Deborah D. Avant, *Political Institutions and Military Change: Lessons from Peripheral Wars* (Ithaca: Cornell University Press, 1994).
6. Herbert Simon, *Administrative Behavior* (New York: Free Press, 1976); Richard Cyert and James March, *A Behavioral Theory of the Firm* (Englewood Cliffs, N.J.: Prentice-Hall, 1963); James March and Herbert Simon (with Harold Guetzkow), *Organizations* (New York: John Wiley and Sons, 1958); Anthony Downs, *Inside Bureaucracy* (Boston: Little, Brown, 1967).
7. Randall L. Calvert, "The Rational Choice Theory of Social Institutions: Cooperation, Coordination, and Communication," in Jeffrey S. Banks and Eric A. Hanushek (eds.), *Modern Political Economy: Old Topics, New Directions* (Cambridge: Cambridge University Press, 1995), 225.
8. Eric Rasmusen, *Games and Information: An Introduction to Game Theory* (Cambridge, Mass.: Basil Blackwell, 1990), 21.

9. For an analysis of the effects of information and expectations on war outcomes, see Scott S. Gartner and Randolph M. Siverson, "War Expansion and War Outcome," *Journal of Conflict Resolution* Vol. 40, No. 1 (March 1996).
10. Robert Axelrod, *The Evolution of Cooperation* (New York: Basic, 1984).
11. Richard Betts, "Analysis, War and Decision: Why Intelligence Failures Are Inevitable," *World Politics* Vol. 31, No. 1 (October 1978), 64.
12. Zisk, 3–4.
13. Betts, "Analysis, War and Decision," 68
14. Rosen, 22.
15. Fahd, quoted in H. Norman Schwarzkopf and Peter Petre, *It Doesn't Take a Hero* (New York: Bantam, 1992), 306.
16. Donna J. Nincic and Miroslav Nincic, "Commitment to Military Intervention: The Democratic Government as Economic Investor," *Journal of Peace Research* Vol. 32, No. 4 (November 1995), 413.
17. Colin L. Powell and Joseph E. Persico, *My American Journey* (New York: Ballantine, 1995), 380.
18. Aaron Friedberg, *The Weary Titan* (Princeton: Princeton University Press, 1988), 288.
19. Carl von Clausewitz, *On War* (New York: Penguin, 1985), 162.
20. Fred Charles Ikle, *Every War Must End* (New York: Columbia University Press, 1971), 35.
21. Bernard Brodie, *War and Politics* (New York: Macmillan, 1973), 452.
22. Richard Overy, *Why the Allies Won* (London: Jonathan Cape, 1995), 320.
23. Clausewitz, 163.
24. Thomas C. Thayer, *War Without Fronts: The American Experience in Vietnam* (Boulder, Colo.: Westview Press, 1985), 3.
25. Simon, *Administrative Behavior,* 51.
26. Richard Neustadt and Harvey Fineberg, *The Epidemic That Never Was: Policy-Making and the Swine Flu Affair* (New York: Vintage, 1983).
27. Stuart Hill, *Democratic Values and Technological Choices* (Stanford: Stanford University Press, 1992), 3–4. Italics in original.
28. John Keegan, *The Second World War* (New York: Viking, 1989), 91.
29. Göring, quoted in Williamson Murray, *Luftwaffe* (Baltimore: Nautical and Aviation Publishing, 1985), 47.
30. Murray, 53.
31. Keegan, *The Second World War,* 96.

32. Gerhard L. Weinberg, *A World at Arms: A Global History of World War II* (Cambridge: Cambridge University Press, 1994), 149.
33. Murray, 54.
34. Murray, 59.
35. The following discussion is taken from Scott Sigmund Gartner and Marissa Edson Myers, "Body Counts and 'Success' in the Vietnam and Korean Wars," *Journal of Interdisciplinary History* Vol. 25, No. 3 (Winter 1995), 377–395.
36. Gartner and Myers, 382.
37. David Halberstam, *The Fifties* (New York, Villard, 1993), 83.
38. Russell Weigley, *The History of the United States Army* (Bloomington: University of Indiana Press, 1984), 521–522.
39. George Donelson Moss, *Vietnam: An American Ordeal* (Englewood Cliffs, N.J.: Prentice-Hall, 1990), 395.
40. General Bruce Palmer, Jr., *The 15-Year War: America's Military Role in Vietnam* (Lexington: University of Kentucky Press, 1984).
41. Robert A. Pape, Jr., "Coercive Air Power in the Vietnam War," *International Security* Vol. 15, No. 2 (Fall 1990), 144.
42. Pape, 131.
43. Pape, 146.
44. Baron de Jomini, *The Art of War,* translated by G. H. Mendell and W. P. Craighill (Westport, Conn.: Greenwood Press, 1971), 59 and 62.
45. Clausewitz, 173. Italics removed.
46. Brodie, 452.
47. Harry G. Summers, *On Strategy: A Critical Analysis of the Vietnam War* (New York: Dell, 1982), 25.
48. Barry R. Posen, *The Sources of Military Doctrine: France, Britain, and Germany Between the World Wars* (Ithaca: Cornell University Press, 1984), 13. Italics in the original. Jack Snyder, *The Ideology of the Offensive: Military Decision Making and the Disasters of 1914* (Ithaca: Cornell University Press, 1984); Stephen Van Evera, "The Causes of War" (Ph.D. diss., University of California, Berkeley, 1984).
49. Allan C. Stam III, *Win, Lose, or Draw* (Ann Arbor: University of Michigan Press, 1996); Posen, *The Sources of Military Doctrine.*
50. Moss (1990); Phillip B. Davidson, *Vietnam at War: The History, 1946-1975* (New York: Oxford University Press, 1988).

51. Elizabeth Kier, "Culture and Military Doctrine: France Between the Wars," *International Security* Vol. 19, No. 4 (Spring 1995), 65–93; Posen (1984); Snyder (1984); Van Evera (1984).
52. William P. Mako, *U.S. Ground Forces and the Defense of Central Europe* (Washington, D.C.: Brookings Institution Press, 1983).
53. Richard Betts, *Soldiers, Statesmen and Cold War Crises* (Cambridge: Harvard University Press, 1977), 12.
54. Hans J. Morgenthau, *Politics Among Nations* (New York: Knopf, 1954), 112; Maarten Ultee, *Adapting to Conditions* (Tuscaloosa: University of Alabama Press, 1986), 11.
55. General D. K. Palit, *Return to Sinai: The Arab-Israeli War, 1973* (Salisbury: Compton, 1974), 118–119; Rod Paschall, *The Defeat of Imperial Germany: 1917–1918* (Chapel Hill: Algonquin, 1989), 128–162.
56. Posen, 16. Italics in original.
57. D. Scott Bennett and Allan C. Stam III, "The Duration of Interstate Wars, 1916–1985," *American Political Science Review* Vol. 90, No. 2 (June 1996), 239–257; T. N. Dupuy, *Numbers, Predictions, and War: The Use of History to Evaluate and Predict the Outcome of Armed Conflict* (Fairfax, Va.: Hero, 1985).
58. Stam, *Win, Lose, or Draw*, 52.
59. John Mearsheimer, *Conventional Deterrence* (Ithaca: Cornell University Press, 1983).
60. William Manchester, *Goodbye Darkness* (New York: Laurel, 1979), 358.
61. Mearsheimer, 27.
62. Betts, *Soldiers, Statesmen and Cold War Crises*, 12.
63. Posen (1984); Snyder, *The Ideology of the Offensive*, and "Civil Military Relations and the Cult of the Offensive," *International Security* Vol. 9, No. 1 (Summer 1984), reprinted in Steven Miller (ed.), *Military Strategy and the Origins of the First World War* (Princeton: Princeton University Press, 1985); Van Evera, *The Causes of War*, and "The Cult of The Offensive and the Origins of the First World War," *International Security* Vol. 9, No. 1 (Summer 1984), reprinted in Miller, *Military Strategy*.
64. Jack S. Levy, "The Causes of War: A Review of Theories and Evidence," in Philip E. Tetlock, Jo L. Husbands, Robert Jervis, Paul C. Stern, and Charles Tilly (eds.), *Behavior, Society, and Nuclear War*, Vol. 1 (New York: Oxford University Press, 1989), 276.
65. Posen, 50.

66. Stephen Van Evera, "Why States Believe Foolish Ideas: Non-Self-Evaluation by Government and Society," paper presented at the annual meeting of the American Political Science Association, Washington, D.C., September 1988, pp. 3–4.
67. As I shall discuss in Chapter 2, I believe that organizations do use propaganda but that the use of propaganda does not preclude policy assessment.
68. Scott Sagan, "The Perils of Proliferation," *International Security* Vol. 18, No. 4 (Spring 1994), 104.
69. Examples include: Deborah D. Avant, "The Institutional Sources of Military Doctrine: Hegemons in Peripheral Wars," *International Studies Quarterly* Vol. 37, No. 4 (December 1993), 409–430; Dani Reiter, "Learning, Realism, and Alliances: The Weight of the Shadow of the Past," *World Politics* Vol. 46, No. 4 (July 1994); and Scott Sagan, *The Limits of Safety* (Princeton: Princeton University Press, 1993).
70. Rosen, 3.
71. Robert Jervis, "The Drunkard's Search," in Shanto Iyengar and William McGuire (eds.), *Explorations in Political Psychology* (Durham, N.C.: Duke University Press, 1993); Arthur L. Stinchcombe, *Information and Organizations* (Berkeley: University of California Press, 1990).
72. Gartner and Myers (1995).
73. Zisk, 6.
74. Barry Weingast and Mark Moran, "Bureaucratic Discretion or Congressional Control: Regulatory Policymaking by the Federal Trade Commission," *Journal of Political Economy* Vol. 91 (1983). Cited in Terry M. Moe, "Political Institutions: The Neglected Side of the Story," *Journal of Law, Economics and Organization* Vol. 6 (1990), 225.
75. Glenn Hastedt, "Organizational Foundations of Intelligence Failure," in Alfred Mauer, Marlon Tunstall, and James Keagle (eds.), *Intelligence Policy and Practice* (Boulder, Colo.: Westview Press, 1985), 153.
76. Overy, 1.

CHAPTER 2: THE DOMINANT INDICATOR APPROACH

1. Posen (1984); Snyder (1984); Van Evera (1984).
2. William H. Riker, "Political Science and Rational Choice," in James Alt and Kenneth Shepsle (eds.), *Perspectives on Positive Political Economy* (Cambridge: Cambridge University Press, 1990).

3. Simon (1976); Cyert and March (1963); March and Simon (1958); Downs (1967).
4. Jonathan Bendor, "A Model of Muddling Through," *American Political Science Review* Vol. 89, No. 4 (December 1995), 820.
5. Bruce Bueno de Mesquita, *The War Trap* (New Haven: Yale University Press, 1981), 17.
6. David Stockman, *Triumph of Politics* (New York: Harper and Row, 1986), 296–298.
7. Posen (1984); Snyder (1984); Van Evera (1984); Simon (1976); Cyert and March (1963); March and Simon (1958); Downs (1967).
8. Morton Halperin, *Bureaucratic Politics and Foreign Policy* (Washington, D.C.: Brookings Institution Press, 1974), 28.
9. Simon, *Administrative Behavior,* 112.
10. For a discussion of the theoretical importance of specifying this type of trade-off, see the analysis of the trade-offs countries make between autonomy and security in James Morrow, "Alliances and Asymmetry: An Alternative to the Capability Aggregation Model of Alliances," *American Journal of Political Science* Vol. 35, No. 4 (November, 1991), 904.
11. Michael Specter, "City Dwellers Want U.S. Park Funds to Go East," *New York Times* (July 27, 1992), A:1.
12. Linda Greenhouse, "Pennsylvania Recalls the Century of Steam," *New York Times* (November 19, 1995), XX:8
13. Michael de Courcy Hinds, "As 'Steamtown' Grows, So Does Parks Debate," *New York Times* (November 23, 1991), A:1.
14. Ridenour, quoted in Hinds, A:8. Congress won, and Steamtown opened on July 1, 1995.
15. For an example of the U.S. military turning down funds for similar reasons, see Robert Pear, "Disputed Military Aircraft Crashes; 7 Aboard Lost," *New York Times* (July 21, 1992), A:1.
16. Eric Schmitt, *New York Times* (May 24, 1995), C:18.
17. For a discussion of how changes in the objectives imposed on an organization lead to changes in its missions, see Gartner and Myers (1995).
18. Zisk, 13.
19. Simon, *Administrative Behavior,* xxxiv.
20. Lunney, quoted in Charles Murray and Catherine Bly Cox, *Apollo: The Race*

to the Moon (New York: Touchstone, 1989), 262. Parenthetical remarks removed.

21. Allen Millet, Williamson Murray, and Kenneth Watman, "The Effectiveness of Military Organizations," in Allan Millet and Williamson Murray (eds.), *Military Effectiveness.* Volume 1: *The First World War* (Boston: Allen and Unwin, 1988), 3.
22. Keegan, *The Second World War,* 171.
23. Downs, 50; Cyert and March, 32.
24. Graham Allison, *Essence of Decision: Explaining the Cuban Missile Crisis* (Boston: Little, Brown, 1971), 67.
25. James March and Johan Olsen, "Garbage Can Models of Decision Making in Organizations," in James March and Roger Weissinger-Baylon (eds.), *Ambiguity and Command: Organizational Perspectives on Military Decision Making* (Marshfield, Mass.: Pitman, 1986), 16. For a more recent, critical examination of rational choice approaches, see Donald P. Green and Ian Shapiro, *Pathologies of Rational Choice Theory: A Critique of Applications in Political Science* (New Haven: Yale University Press, 1994). For a critique of Green and Shapiro, see Barry O'Neill, "Weak Models, Nil Hypotheses, and Decorative Statistics," *Journal of Conflict Resolution* Vol. 39, No. 4 (December 1995), 731–748.
26. Terry M. Moe, "Politics and the Theory of Organization," *Journal of Law, Economics and Organization,* Vol. 7 (1991), 110.
27. Herbert Simon, *The Sciences of the Artificial* (Cambridge: MIT Press, 1981), 138.
28. Robert Axelrod, *Framework for a General Theory of Cognition and Choice* (Berkeley: Institute of International Studies, No. 18, 1972), 43.
29. Cyert and March, 80.
30. Simon, *Administrative Behavior,* xxx.
31. James G. March, "Bounded Rationality, Ambiguity, and the Engineering of Choice," *Bell Journal of Economics* Vol. 9, No. 2 (Autumn 1978).
32. Axelrod, 43.
33. Downs, 171–172.
34. March and Simon, 183.
35. For a more extensive treatment of this point, see Scott Sigmund Gartner, "Predicting the Timing of Carter's Decision to Initiate a Hostage Res-

cue Attempt: Modeling a Dynamic Information Environment," *International Interactions* Vol. 18, No. 14 (1993).

36. John Harsanyi, "Games with Incomplete Information Played by 'Bayesian' Players, I: The Basic Model," *Management Science* Vol. 14, No. 3 (November 1967), 159–82; John Harsanyi, "Games with Randomly Distributed Payoffs: A New Rationale for Mixed Strategy Equilibrium Points," *International Journal of Game Theory* Vol. 2, No. 1 (1973), 1–23; Reinhard Selten, "The Chain-Store Paradox," *Theory and Decision* Vol. 9, No. 2 (April 1978), 127–159.
37. Rasmusen, *Games and Information: An Introduction to Game Theory* (Cambridge, Mass.: Basil Blackwell, 1990), 22. Italics removed.
38. Rasmusen, 53. Italics removed.
39. James D. Morrow, *Game Theory for Political Scientists* (Princeton: Princeton University Press, 1994), 161.
40. Edi Karni, *Decision Making Under Uncertainty* (Cambridge: Harvard University Press, 1985), 12.
41. Robert Komer, "What 'Decade of Neglect'?" *International Security* Vol. 79 (Fall 1985).
42. Ken Binmore, *Essays on the Foundations of Game Theory* (Cambridge, Mass: Basil Blackwell, 1990), 156.
43. David M. Kreps, *Game Theory and Economic Modeling* (Oxford: Clarendon Press, 1990); Binmore (1990).
44. Binmore, 21 and 154.
45. Riker (1990); Robert Jackman, "Rationality and Political Participation," *American Journal of Political Science* Vol. 37, No. 1 (February 1993), 282.
46. Riker, 174.
47. Riker, 172.
48. Jackman, 282.
49. Terry M. Moe, "Politics and the Theory of Organization," 110.
50. Riker (1990).
51. Van Evera (1984); Posen (1984); Aaron Wildavsky, "The Self-Evaluating Organization," *Public Administration Review* Vol. 32 (September–October 1972), 509.
52. Van Evera, "Causes of War," 8.
53. Zisk, 15.
54. Friedberg, 285.
55. George Akerlof, "The Economics of Caste and of the Rat Race and Other

Woeful Tales," *Quarterly Journal of Economics* Vol. 90, No. 4 (November 1976), 599. Italics in the original.

56. Jervis (1993).
57. Rosen, 146.
58. James L. Stokesbury, *A Short History of World War I* (New York: William Morrow, 1981), 203.
59. Lawrence Freedman, *The Evolution of Nuclear Strategy* (New York: St. Martin's, 1983), 246.
60. Friedberg, 284. Italics added.
61. Rosen, 34.
62. Randall Calvert, "The Value of Biased Information: A Rational Choice Model of Political Advice," *Journal of Politics* Vol. 47 (1985), 552.
63. Calvert (1985).
64. Brodie, 439.
65. Downs, 50.
66. Downs, 167.
67. Friedberg, 283; Jervis, "The Drunkard's Search," 340.
68. March and Olsen, 17.
69. Michael Handel, "Strategic Surprise: The Politics of Intelligence and the Management of Uncertainty," in Alfred Mauer, Marlon Tunstall, and James Keagle (eds.), *Intelligence Policy and Practice* (Boulder, Colo.: Westview Press, 1985), 245.
70. Stinchcombe, 10.
71. Posen, 234.
72. March, quoted in Zisk, 16.
73. James Schampel, "Change in Material Capabilities and the Onset of War: A Dyadic Approach," *International Studies Quarterly* Vol. 37, No. 4 (December 1993), 397. Italics in the original.
74. Cabeza, quoted in Nathaniel C. Nash, "As World Crowds In, an Island Shields Its Culture," *New York Times* (February 6, 1993), A:2.
75. Donald A. Schon, *Beyond the Stable State* (New York: Norton, 1971).
76. Charles Doran and Wes Parsons, "War and the Cycle of Relative Power," *American Political Science Review* Vol. 74 (1980); A. F. K. Organski and Jacek Kugler, *The War Ledger* (Chicago: University of Chicago Press, 1980); Schampel (1993).
77. March and Simon, 121.

78. Cyert and March, 167.
79. Jervis, "The Drunkard's Search," 340.
80. For example, during the Gulf War, the U.S. military in Saudi Arabia created an index to measure the air war's effects on enemy capabilities. See Schwarzkopf and Petre (1992).
81. A fourth model, which examines the acceleration of indicator movement (as opposed to the acceleration and the change in acceleration) can be found in Scott Sigmund Gartner, "Strategic Assessment in War: A Bounded Rationality Model of How Organizations Evaluate Policy Effectiveness" (Ph.D. diss., University of Michigan, 1992).
82. Zisk (1993); Robert Jervis, *Perception and Misperception in International Politics* (Princeton: Princeton University Press, 1976).
83. Bruce Bueno de Mesquita, David Newman, and Alvin Rabushka, *Forecasting Political Events: The Future of Hong Kong* (New Haven: Yale University Press, 1985).
84. I discuss this more extensively in Chapter 7.
85. Charles Lindblom and David Braybrooke, *A Strategy of Decision* (London: Free Press, 1963), 83.
86. Schampel (1993); Gartner (1993). See also Doran and Parsons (1980).
87. One could also subtract the value at time_{t+1} from the value at time_t. Because I am interested in creating *ex ante* expectations, I used time_t and time_{t-1}: decision makers at time_t do not know what the value of the indicator will be at time_{t+1}.

CHAPTER 3: BRITISH ANTISUBMARINE DECISION MAKING IN WORLD WAR I

1. A third strategy, discussed at the end of this chapter, was to attack German U-boat bases.
2. Kennedy, 44.
3. David Lloyd George, *War Memoirs of David Lloyd George: 1916–1917* (Boston: Little, Brown, 1934), 81.
4. B. H. Liddell Hart, *The War in Outline* (New York: Random House, 1936), 61.
5. Dan Van der Vat, *The Atlantic Campaign: World War II's Great Struggle at Sea* (New York: Harper and Row, 1988), 18.
6. Bryan Ranft, "The Royal Navy and the War at Sea," in John Turner (ed.), *Britain and the First World War* (London: Unwin Hyman, 1988), 64.

7. Corbett, quoted in Richard Hough, *The Great War at Sea* (Oxford: Oxford University Press, 1989), 62.
8. Stokesbury, 87; Van der Vat, 40.
9. Hart, *The War in Outline,* 180.
10. All data for this chapter come from John Terraine, *The U-Boat Wars: 1916–1945* (New York: Henry Holt, 1989). Where possible, these figures were checked against numbers discussed by Admiral John Jellicoe and Prime Minister Lloyd George. All calculations were performed by the author. The data can be found in Appendix A, unless noted otherwise. "World shipping losses" include the countries of Great Britain, its allies, and the neutrals.
11. John Rushworth Jellicoe, *The Crisis of the Naval War* (London: Cassell, 1920), 223.
12. V. E. Tarrant, *The U-Boat Offensive 1914–1945* (London: Arms and Armour Press, 1989), 18.
13. Arthur Marder, *From the Dreadnought to Scapa Flow,* Vol. 4 (London: Oxford University Press, 1969), 160.
14. Van der Vat, 29.
15. A. J. P. Taylor, *The First World War* (New York: Perigree Books, 1963), 180.
16. Taylor, 181. Italics added.
17. David Lloyd George, *War Memoirs of David Lloyd George: 1917* (Boston: Little, Brown, 1934), 455.
18. Marder, 63.
19. Lloyd George, *War Memoirs: 1916-1917,* 77. Another factor was American naval construction, which, although not a manipulatable policy for the British, did help address their shipping concern.
20. Marder, 109. Italics added.
21. Van der Vat (1988).
22. Francis A. March, *History of the World War* (Philadelphia: United Publishers of the United States and Canada, 1919), 732.
23. Marder, 156–157.
24. Van der Vat, 32
25. Van der Vat, 23.
26. David Lloyd George, *War Memoirs of David Lloyd George: 1915–1916* (Boston: Little, Brown, 1937), 125.

27. *The Times History of the War,* Vol. 14 (London: Times, 1918), 148; Van der Vat, 30.
28. Van der Vat, 30.
29. Lloyd George, quoted in *Times History of the War,* 148.
30. Lloyd George, quoted in *Times History of the War,* 149.
31. Lloyd George, *War Memoirs: 1916–1917,* 96.
32. Lloyd George, *War Memoirs: 1916–1917,* 96. Italics added.
33. *Times History of the War,* 149. The *Times* presentation makes it unclear if this is a quote or a paraphrase.
34. Lloyd George, *War Memoirs: 1916–1917,* 85.
35. Lloyd George, *War Memoirs: 1916–1917,* 81.
36. Lloyd George, *War Memoirs: 1916–1917,* 90.
37. Beatty and his staff (the "serving officers"), who had no specific organizational responsibility in U-boats or merchant shipping, frequently disagreed with the admirals. Lloyd George gained a great deal of information about the viability of convoy by discussing it with the serving officers.
38. Jellicoe, *Crisis of the Naval War,* 169.
39. John Rushworth Jellicoe, *The Submarine Peril: The Admiralty Policy in 1917* (London: Cassell, 1934), 35.
40. The total number of U-boats involved in World War I was, and continues to be, hotly debated (Jellicoe, *The Submarine Peril,* 184; Jellicoe, *Crisis of the Naval War,* 37; Van der Vat, 41).
41. Beesly and Marder, quoted in Terraine, 87.
42. Another possible figure, the number of U-boats at sea, was not used by the British. "Nobody noticed that the number of ships lost related directly to the number of submarines at sea" (Van der Vat, 40).
43. Jellicoe, *The Crisis of the Naval War,* 33.
44. Jellicoe, *The Submarine Peril,* 184.
45. Admiralty memo, quoted in Jellicoe, *The Crisis of the Naval War,* 52–53.
46. Van der Vat, 33.
47. Lloyd George, *War Memoirs: 1916–1917,* 133, 131–132.
48. C. R. M. F. Cruttwell, *A History of the Great War* (Oxford: Clarendon Press, 1961), 387.
49. Marder, 106.
50. Jellicoe, *The Submarine Peril,* 45.

51. John Keegan, *The Price of Admiralty: The Evolution of Naval Warfare* (New York: Viking, 1989), 219.
52. Holger Herwig, "The Dynamics of Necessity: German Military Policy During the First World War," in Allan Millet and Williamson Murray (eds.), *Military Effectiveness*, Vol. 1: *The First World War* (Boston: Allen and Unwin, 1988), 104.
53. Jellicoe, *The Submarine Peril*, 14.
54. Jellicoe, *The Crisis of the Naval War*, 179.
55. Terraine, 33.
56. Doveton Sturdee, "A Few Remarks on the Main Naval Strategy of the War," November 1916 appendix to chapter 3 of Jellicoe's *The Submarine Peril*, 25.
57. Marder, 110.
58. Lloyd George, *War Memoirs: 1916-1917*, 116–117.
59. Lloyd George, *War Memoirs: 1916-1917*, 117.
60. Marder, 167.
61. Marder, 168–169.

CHAPTER 4: BRITISH ANTISUBMARINE DECISION MAKING IN WORLD WAR II

1. The British navy dedicated a large percentage of its resources, in particular destroyers, to defend against a possible German invasion of Great Britain. This diversion helped the U-boats achieve a high average number of kills per boat. Peter Flemming, *Operation Sea Lion* (New York: Simon and Schuster, 1957), 160.
2. Van der Vat, 339.
3. Keegan, *The Second World War*, 123.
4. Winston Churchill, *The Grand Alliance* (Boston: Houghton Mifflin, 1950), 123.
5. Winston Churchill, *Their Finest Hour* (Boston: Houghton Mifflin, 1949), 598.
6. S. W. Roskill, *The War at Sea: 1939-1945*, Vol. 3, Part 2: *The Offensive* (London: HMSO, 1961), 305.
7. S. W. Roskill, *The War at Sea: 1939-1945*, Vol. 2: *The Period of Balance* (London: HMSO, 1956), 355.
8. John D. Hayes, "Developments in Naval Warfare," in Vincent Esposito (ed.), *A Concise History of World War II* (New York: Praeger, 1964), 322.
9. Terraine, 243.
10. Terraine, 244.

11. Van der Vat, 81.
12. S. W. Roskill, *The War at Sea: 1939-1945,* Vol. 1: *The Defensive* (London: HMSO, 1954), 92.
13. Charles Sternhell and Alan Thorndike, *Antisubmarine Warfare in World War II: Report No. 51 of the Operations Evaluation Group* (Washington: Office of the Chief of Naval Operations, Operations Evaluation Group, United States Navy, 1946, declassified), 5.
14. Roskill, Vol. 1, 91–92; Terraine, 286.
15. Keegan, *The Price of Admiralty,* 219.
16. Jellicoe, *The Crisis of the Naval War,* 51.
17. Sternhell and Thorndike, 18.
18. Cohen and Gooch, 63.
19. Roskill, Vol. 2, 97.
20. Oliver Warner, *The British Navy: A Concise History* (London: Thames and Hudson, 1975), 147; Van der Vat, 81.
21. Roskill, Vol. 1, 481.
22. Quoted in Roskill, Vol. 2, 98.
23. Rosen, 37.
24. Churchill, *Their Finest Hour,* 563.
25. Where possible, data were taken from Roskill's official histories. Supplementary sources include Terraine (1989) and Churchill's *Second World War.* The data are listed in Appendix B. World Shipping refers to U.N. and neutral forces.
26. Karl Dönitz, *Ten Years and Twenty Days* (London: Weidenfeld and Nicolson, 1959) 104.
27. Churchill, *Their Finest Hour,* 398.
28. Churchill, *Their Finest Hour,* 398.
29. Churchill, *Their Finest Hour,* 402.
30. Van der Vat, 141.
31. Van der Vat, 141.
32. Vincent Esposito (ed.), *A Concise History of World War II* (New York: Praeger, 1964), 70.
33. Churchill, *Their Finest Hour,* 398, 403, 404.
34. Chamberlain, quoted in Winston S. Churchill, *The Gathering Storm* (Boston: Houghton Mifflin, 1948), 658.

35. Keegan, *The Second World War,* 77; Weinberg, 118.
36. Keegan, *The Second World War,* 107.
37. Roskill, Vol. 1, 467.
38. Churchill, *Their Finest Hour,* 599.
39. Roskill, Vol. 1, 467.
40. B. H. Liddell Hart, *History of the Second World War* (New York: Capricorn, 1972), 387.
41. Roskill, Vol. 1, 134.
42. Van der Vat, 232.
43. Terraine, 578.
44. Terraine, 579.
45. Quoted in Terraine, 253.
46. There are insufficient data to derive meaningful figures on the rate of change of quarterly U-boat construction until the last quarter of 1940. Roskill, Vol. 1, 614.
47. Churchill, *Their Finest Hour,* 401.
48. Arthur Hezlet, *The Submarine and Sea Power* (New York: Stein and Day, 1967), 171; Terraine, 308–309.
49. Van der Vat, 272.
50. Roskill, Vol. 1, 467.
51. Weinberg (1994) argues that this change was due to German setbacks on the Eastern front, resulting in a greater demand for tank production and diversion of scarce steel resources.
52. Terraine, 428.
53. Van der Vat, 275.
54. Liddell Hart, *History of The Second World War,* 370; Van der Vat, 339; Hezlet, 183; Roskill, Vol. 2, 368. An exception is John Keegan, who believes that the crux occurred in the summer of 1942 (Keegan, *The Second World War,* 113).
55. Van der Vat, 322.
56. Hezlet, 182.
57. Roskill, Vol. 2, 367.
58. Roskill, Vol. 2, 368.
59. Van der Vat, 337.
60. May 24, 1943, diary entry, Dönitz, 341.
61. For example, see Van der Vat, 270, 339.

62. Keith R. Tidman, *The Operations Evaluation Group: A Story of Naval Operations Analysis* (Annapolis: Naval Institute Press, 1984), 80; S. W. Roskill, *The War at Sea: 1939-1945*, Vol. 3, Part 1: *The Offensive* (London: HMSO, 1960), 15.
63. Hezlet, 183.
64. Tidman, 80.
65. Gunther Hessler, *U-Boat War in the Atlantic: 1939-1945* (London: Crown, 1989), 10.
66. Dönitz, 196.
67. Dönitz, 150–151.
68. Edward P. Von der Porten, *The German Navy in World War II* (New York: Crowell, 1969), 188; Hayes, 321; Hezlet, 182–183.
69. This was sometimes called the "U-boat potential."
70. Dönitz, 102. Note that by specifying days, the Germans expected less noise than the British admirals did in their use of months and quarters.
71. Dönitz, 130.
72. Dönitz, 228.
73. Overy, 45.
74. Dönitz, 102.
75. Van der Vat, 337.
76. Dönitz, 263.
77. Roskill, Vol. 3, Part 1, p. 15.
78. Dönitz, 129.
79. Dönitz, 130.
80. Weinberg, 383–384.

CHAPTER 5: U.S. GROUND STRATEGY IN THE VIETNAM WAR

1. Exceptions to this include John Mueller, "Trends in Popular Support for the Wars in Korea and Vietnam," *American Political Science Review* Vol. 65 (June 1971), and Avant (1994).
2. Larry Cable, *Unholy Grail: The U.S. and the Wars in Vietnam, 1965–68* (London: Routledge, 1991), 201.
3. Alain C. Enthoven and K. Wayne Smith, *How Much Is Enough? Shaping the Defense Program, 1961–1969* (New York: Harper and Row, 1971), 307.
4. Robert S. McNamara (with Brian Van De Mark), *In Retrospect: The Tragedy and Lessons of Vietnam* (New York: Random House, 1995), 238. Italics added.

5. For an analysis of the relation between indicators and strategy, see Stam (1996).
6. Avant (1993); Andrew Krepinevich, *The Army and Vietnam* (Baltimore: Johns Hopkins University Press, 1986). The Marine Corps had a short-lived independence from army command in Vietnam that I discuss in the next chapter.
7. Douglas Kinnard, *The War Managers* (Wayne, N.J.: Avery, 1985), 23.
8. George Herring, *America's Longest War: The United States and Vietnam, 1950–1975* (New York: Knopf, 1979), 117–118; Cable, 80.
9. Bernard B. Fall, "Viet-Nam—The Agonizing Reappraisal," in Bernard B. Fall and Marcus G. Raskin (eds.), *The Vietnam Reader* (New York: Random House, 1965), 335.
10. Shelby Stanton, *The Rise and Fall of an American Army* (New York: Dell, 1985), 7.
11. This NSAM was sent from McGeorge Bundy, national security adviser, to Dean Rusk and other administration foreign policy decision makers. It established the goals and mechanisms of the multi-agency U.S. intervention in South Vietnam. The memo can be found in Jeffrey T. Richelson, *Presidential Directives on National Security from Truman to Clinton* (Alexandria, Va.: Chadwyck-Healey, 1994).
12. McNamara, 166.
13. Cable, 91.
14. Lyndon Baines Johnson, *The Vantage Point: Perspectives on the Presidency, 1963–1969* (New York: Holt, Rinehart, and Winston, 1971), 232.
15. Donald J. Mrozek, *Air Power and the Ground War in Vietnam: Ideas and Actions* (Maxwell Air Force Base, Ala.: Air University Press, 1988), 171.
16. For a discussion of how the United States was surprised, see James J. Wirtz, *The Tet Offensive: Intelligence Failure in War* (Ithaca: Cornell University Press, 1991).
17. For a highly critical view of how this belief was formed, see Peter Braestrup, *Big Story: How the American Press and Television Reported and Interpreted the Crisis of Tet 1968 in Vietnam and Washington* (New Haven: Yale University Press, 1977).
18. Patrick J. McGarvey (ed.), *Visions of Victory: Selected Communist Military Writings, 1964–1968* (Stanford: Hoover Institution on War, Revolution, and Peace, 1969), 54.

19. Wirtz, 270.
20. Michael Lee Lanning and Dan Cragg, *Inside the VC and the NVA: The Real Story of North Vietnam's Armed Forces* (New York: Ballantine, 1992), 231.
21. Stanley Karnow, *Vietnam: A History* (New York: Penguin, 1991), 343, 357.
22. Karnow, 498. Italics added.
23. Mueller, 366.
24. Gartner and Myers (1995).
25. For example, see William Westmoreland and Ulysses S. Grant Sharp, *Report on the War in Vietnam: As of June 30, 1968,* 120.
26. Original data are from Ralph Littauer and Norman Uphoff (eds.), *The Air War in Indochina* (Boston: Beacon Press, 1972) and Thomas C. Thayer, *A Systems Analysis View of the Vietnam War: 1965–1972,* Vols. 1–8 (Washington D.C.: Department of Defense, declassified May 9, 1977). All calculations were performed by the author. The data can be found in Appendix C.
27. William C. Westmoreland, *A Soldier Reports* (Garden City, N.Y.: Doubleday, 1976), 277.
28. Leslie Gelb with Richard Betts, *The Irony of Vietnam: The System Worked* (Washington, D.C.: Brookings Institution Press, 1979), 159.
29. Doris Kearns, *Lyndon Johnson and the American Dream* (New York: Signet, 1976), 341–342.
30. Karnow, 570.
31. Moss, 262.
32. Johnson, 403.
33. Karnow, 572.
34. Gelb and Betts, 219.
35. For example, see Congressman Ronald Dellums's statements during the testimony of Sam Adams before the Select Committee on Intelligence, U.S. House of Representatives, Ninety-fourth Congress, September 18, 1975, 695.
36. Stanton, 76.
37. Cable, 173.
38. Kinnard, 69.
39. Thayer, *War Without Fronts,* 4.
40. Kinnard, 69.
41. Herring, 153–154.
42. Stanton, 259.

43. Appy, 144.
44. Cable, 173.
45. Enthoven and Smith, 295.
46. For an extensive analysis of the use of body counts in the Korean War, see Gartner and Myers (1995).
47. Matthew Ridgway, *The Korean War* (Garden City, N.Y.: Doubleday, 1967), 167.
48. Palmer, 164.
49. Gartner and Myers, 381.
50. Thayer, *War Without Fronts,* 102.
51. Enthoven and Smith, 295–296. Italics in original. These authors' Pentagon-based civilian unit, Systems Analysis, concluded that the "body count was overstated by at least 30 percent" (296).
52. Westmoreland, 332.
53. Julian Ewell and Ira Hunt, *Sharpening the Combat Edge: The Use of Analysis to Reinforce Military Judgment* (Washington, D.C.: Department of the Army, 1974).
54. Kinnard, 23.
55. Joseph McChristian, *The Role of Military Intelligence: 1965-1967* (Washington, D.C.: Department of the Army, 1974), 3.
56. Avant, "The Institutional Sources of Military Doctrine," 419–420.
57. Lance Corporal Roger Reynolds, quoted in Thayer, *War Without Fronts,* 89.
58. The other key military statistic, the infiltration rate, measured the success of the air war against North Vietnam, rather than the ground war in the south. The number of infiltrators did, however, affect the crossover point: the point at which the United States was killing communists faster than the Vietnamese could replace them.
59. Cable, 179.
60. Enthoven and Smith, 297.
61. Cable, 39.
62. Stanton, 7.
63. Herring, 206.
64. Mrozek, 79–81.
65. John Schlight, *The War in South Vietnam: The Years of the Offensive, 1965-1968* (Washington, D.C.: Office of Air Force History, U.S. Air Force, 1988), 285.
66. Westmoreland, 422.

67. Westmoreland, 408.
68. Westmoreland, 404.
69. Johnson, 417.
70. Krepinevich, 239.
71. Westmoreland, 428.
72. Karnow, 564–565; Johnson, 405. Expanding the war meant that Westmoreland and Wheeler wanted to increase the number of U.S. search-and-destroy operations (they had been consistently calling for expanding the geographic limits put on the ground war by Johnson).
73. Westmoreland, 433–434.
74. Wheeler's 1968 report to President Johnson after Tet, in Neil Sheehan et al., *The Pentagon Papers: New York Times Edition* (New York: Bantam, 1971), 620.
75. Kinnard, 161.
76. Westmoreland, 412.
77. Westmoreland, 423.
78. The administration also had to deal with such foreign policy events as North Korea's January 23, 1968, seizure of the *Pueblo.*
79. McNamara, 237–238.
80. Cable, 187.
81. Cable, 181.
82. Johnson, 153.
83. Karnow (1991); Kearns (1976); Larry Berman, *Lyndon Johnson's War* (New York: Norton, 1989).
84. Karnow, 529.
85. Berman, 142.
86. Kinnard, 162.
87. Kinnard, 62.
88. Berman, 149–151.
89. Taylor, quoted in Gelb and Betts, 318.
90. Johnson, 383.
91. Johnson, 601.
92. Rusk, quoted in Gelb and Betts, 318.
93. McNamara, quoted in Johnson, 372.
94. Other suggestions included a bombing halt and negotiations. Johnson, 372, 601.
95. Actually, he was never asked to resign. Johnson announced that McNamara

had become head of the World Bank. McNamara learned of his move from the press.

96. Clifford, quoted in Karnow, 568.
97. Clifford, quoted in Karnow, 560.
98. Berman, 190.
99. Johnson, 397.
100. Johnson, 406.
101. Berman, 149.
102. Berman, 185.
103. Rusk, quoted in Berman, 189.
104. Herring, 206.
105. Berman, 191.
106. Johnson, 418.
107. Berman, 199.
108. Johnson, 435.
109. Stanton, 205. Italics in original.
110. Stanton, 205.
111. Krepinevich, 253.
112. Thayer, *War Without Fronts,* 30.
113. Margaret O'Neill Adams, "Electronic Records: Vietnam Records and the National Archives," *Prologue* Vol. 23, No. 1 (Spring 1991), 78.
114. Donald Fisher Harrison, quoted in M. Adams, 76.
115. Enthoven and Smith, 307.
116. Cable, 179.
117. Johnson, 261.
118. Berman, 115.
119. Berman, 149–151.
120. Sam Adams, *War of Numbers: An Intelligence Memoir* (South Royalton, Vt.: Steerforth Press, 1994).
121. Adams, *War of Numbers,* xxx.
122. Walt Rostow to President Johnson, White House Memorandum, 1/20/67, University of California, Davis, Archive 6-2-37.

CHAPTER 6: VIETNAM AND THE HOSTAGE RESCUE ATTEMPT

1. Krepinevich, 172.
2. Cable, 200.

3. Cable, 238.
4. Gartner and Myers (1995).
5. Morris Janowitz, *The Professional Soldier* (New York: Free Press, 1971), xlv.
6. Krepinevich, 173.
7. Wirtz, 43.
8. Walt, quoted in Krepinevich, 174.
9. Krepinevich, 174.
10. Harry Kinnard, quoted in Krepinevich, 175. Italics in original.
11. Depuy, quoted in Krepinevich, 175.
12. Avant, "The Institutional Sources of Military Doctrine," 420. Italics in original.
13. Douglas Kinnard, 61.
14. Avant, "The Institutional Sources of Military Doctrine," 420. Italics in original.
15. Herring, 163.
16. An expanded version of this analysis appeared in Gartner (1993).
17. On November 19 and 20, the Iranians released thirteen black and female hostages (Joseph Nathan Kane, *Facts About the Presidents* [New York: H. W. Wilson, 1981], 301).
18. Steve Smith, "Policy Preferences and Bureaucratic Position: The Case of the American Hostage Rescue Mission," in David C. Kozak and James M. Keagle (eds.), *Bureaucratic Politics and National Security* (Boulder, Colo.: Lynne Rienner, 1988), 138.
19. Paul B. Ryan, *The Iranian Rescue Mission: Why It Failed* (Annapolis, Md.: Naval Institute Press, 1985).
20. Daniel P. Bolger, *Americans at War: 1975–1986, An Era of Violent Peace* (Novato, Calif.: Presidio, 1988), 138.
21. Cyrus Vance, *Hard Choices: Critical Years in America's Foreign Policy* (New York: Simon and Schuster, 1983); Warren Christopher, "Introduction," in Paul H. Kreisberg (ed.), *American Hostages in Iran: The Conduct of a Crisis* (New Haven: Yale University Press, 1985).
22. Cyrus Vance, quoted in Jordan, 45.
23. Jordan, 45. After Brzezinski's comment, Jordan (incorrectly) adds: "And Johnson wasn't in the middle of a re-election campaign."
24. Smith, 132.
25. Jordan, 36.

26. They also considered polls and results from the race between Carter and his Democratic rival, Edward Kennedy. Between November and April, however, the Gallup organization conducted only two polls that asked respondents to rate both candidates, so they are not applicable to the analysis of rates of change. The primaries and caucuses, however, did provide important information. The first was in January 1980 in Iowa.
27. George Gallup, *The Gallup Poll: Public Opinion 1980* (Wilmington, Del.: Scholarly Resources, 1981), 3.
28. Strauss, quoted in Jordan, 60.
29. All figures and graphs are from Gallup (1981). All calculations are my own.
30. Carter, quoted in Jordan, 99.
31. Gartner, "Predicting the Timing of Carter's Decision," 376.
32. Smith, 138.
33. Smith, 138.
34. This poll, conducted on the last two days of March, is as close as the Gallup organization comes to the first week of April.
35. Jody Powell, *The Other Side of the Story* (New York: William Morrow, 1984), 225.
36. Powell, 227.
37. Powell, 209.
38. Jordan, 288–289.
39. Jordan, 252.
40. Gartner, "Predicting the Timing of Carter's Decision," 373.
41. Zbigniew Brzezinski, *Power and Principle: Memoirs of the National Security Adviser, 1977-1981* (New York: Farrar, Straus, and Giroux, 1985), 493.
42. Jimmy Carter, *Keeping Faith: Memoirs of a President* (New York: Bantam, 1982), 506.
43. Gartner, "Predicting the Timing of Carter's Decision," 377.
44. Jordan, 53. Italics removed.
45. Bolger (1988).
46. Carter diary entry, November 6, 1979, in Carter, 458.
47. Charlie A. Beckwith and Donald Knox, *Delta Force* (New York: Harcourt, Brace, Jovanovich, 1983), 252.
48. Powell, 227.
49. Bolger, 149.
50. Jordan, 250. Italics removed.

51. Beckwith and Knox, 258.
52. Bolger, 103.

CHAPTER 7: DECISION MAKING IN WAR

1. Lloyd George, *Memoirs: 1915–1916,* 380; Churchill, *Their Finest Hour,* 561.
2. Johnson, 261.
3. Dönitz, 129.
4. Churchill, quoted in Keegan, *The Price of Admiralty,* 226; Johnson, 397; Berman, 115.
5. As I stated in Chapter 2, because it predicted no military change in assessments and did not specify how to account for civilian evaluations, I did not identify the Cult of the Offensive approach as an alternative model.
6. Jervis (1976); Zisk (1993).
7. Simon (1957); March and Simon (1958); Cyert and March (1963); Downs (1967).
8. Riker (1990).
9. Information in this section was drawn from my experiences in the Federal Bureau of Investigation, the National Institute of Justice (where I was a Social Science Program Specialist for the Drugs, Alcohol, and Crime division), and the Georgia Bureau of Investigation (where I was a member of the Governor's Task Force on Drug Interdiction).

Bibliography

Adams, Margaret O'Neill. 1991. "Electronic Records: Vietnam Records and the National Archives." *Prologue* 23:76–84.

Adams, Sam. 1975. "Testimony Before the Select Committee on Intelligence." *Proceedings of the U.S. House of Representatives,* Ninety-fourth Congress, September 18.

———. 1994. *War of Numbers: An Intelligence Memoir.* South Royalton, Vt.: Steerforth Press.

Akerlof, George. 1976. "The Economics of Caste and of the Rat Race and Other Woeful Tales." *Quarterly Journal of Economics* 90:599–617.

Allison, Graham. 1971. *Essence of Decision: Explaining the Cuban Missile Crisis.* Boston: Little, Brown.

Appy, Christian G. 1993. *Working-Class War: American Combat Soldiers and Vietnam.* Chapel Hill: University of North Carolina Press.

Avant, Deborah D. 1993. "The Institutional Sources of Military Doctrine: Hegemons in Peripheral Wars." *International Studies Quarterly* 37:409–430.

———. 1994. *Political Institutions and Military Change: Lessons From Peripheral Wars.* Ithaca: Cornell University Press.

Axelrod, Robert. 1972. *Framework for a General Theory of Cognition and Choice.* Berkeley, Calif.: Institute of International Studies.

———. 1984. *The Evolution of Cooperation.* New York: Basic Books.

Beckwith, Charlie A., and Donald Knox. 1983. *Delta Force.* New York: Harcourt, Brace, Jovanovich.

Bendor, Jonathan. 1995. "A Model of Muddling Through." *American Political Science Review* 89:819–840.

Bennett, D. Scott, and Allan C. Stam III. 1996. "The Duration of Interstate Wars, 1916–1985." *American Political Science Review* 90:239–257.

Berman, Larry. 1989. *Lyndon Johnson's War.* New York: W. W. Norton.

Betts, Richard. 1977. *Soldiers, Statesmen, and Cold War Crises.* Cambridge: Harvard University Press.

———. 1978. "Analysis, War and Decision: Why Intelligence Failures Are Inevitable." *World Politics* 30:61–89.

Binmore, Ken. 1990. *Essays on the Foundations of Game Theory.* Cambridge, Mass.: Basil Blackwell.

Bolger, Daniel P. 1988. *Americans at War, 1975–1986: An Era of Violent Peace.* Novato, Calif.: Presidio.

Braestrup, Peter. 1977. *Big Story: How the American Press and Television Reported and Interpreted the Crisis of Tet 1968 in Vietnam and Washington.* New Haven: Yale University Press.

Brodie, Bernard. 1973. *War and Politics.* New York: Macmillan.

Brzezinski, Zbigniew. 1985. *Power and Principle: Memoirs of the National Security Adviser, 1977–1981.* New York: Farrar, Straus, and Giroux.

Bueno de Mesquita, Bruce. 1981. *The War Trap.* New Haven: Yale University Press.

———. 1992. "The Game of Conflict Interactions: A Research Program." In *Theoretical Research Programs: Studies in the Growth of Theories of Group Process,* ed. Joseph Berger and Morris Zelditch. Stanford: Stanford University Press.

Bueno de Mesquita, Bruce, David Newman, and Alvin Rabushka. 1985. *Forecasting Political Events: The Future of Hong Kong.* New Haven: Yale University Press.

Cable, Larry. 1991. *Unholy Grail: The U.S. and the Wars in Vietnam, 1965–68.* London: Routledge.

Calvert, Randall L. 1985. "The Value of Biased Information: A Rational Choice Model of Political Advice." *Journal of Politics* 47:531–555.

———. 1995. "The Rational Choice Theory of Social Institutions: Cooperation, Coordination, and Communication." In *Modern Political Economy: Old Topics, New Directions,* ed. Jeffrey S. Banks and Eric A. Hanushek. Cambridge: Cambridge University Press.

Carter, Jimmy. 1982. *Keeping Faith: Memoirs of a President.* New York: Bantam Books.

Christopher, Warren. 1985. "Introduction." In *American Hostages in Iran: The Conduct of a Crisis,* ed. Paul H. Kreisberg. New Haven: Yale University Press.

Churchill, Winston S. 1948. *The Second World War: The Gathering Storm.* Boston: Houghton Mifflin.

———. 1949. *The Second World War: Their Finest Hour.* Boston: Houghton Mifflin.

———. 1950. *The Second World War: The Grand Alliance.* Boston: Houghton Mifflin.

Clausewitz, Carl von. 1985. *On War.* New York: Penguin.

Cohen, Eliot A., and John Gooch. 1990. *Military Misfortunes: The Anatomy of Failure in War.* New York: Free Press.

Cruttwell, C. R. M. F. 1961. *A History of the Great War.* Oxford: Clarendon Press.

Cyert, Richard, and James March. 1963. *Behavioral Theory of the Firm.* Englewood Cliffs, N.J.: Prentice Hall.

Davidson, Phillip B. 1988. *Vietnam at War: The History, 1946–1975.* New York: Oxford University Press.

Dönitz, Karl. 1959. *Memoirs: Ten Years and Twenty Days.* London: Weidenfeld and Nicolson.

Doran, Charles, and Wes Parsons. 1980. "War and the Cycle of Relative Power." *American Political Science Review* 74:947–965.

Downs, Anthony. 1967. *Inside Bureaucracy.* Boston: Little, Brown.

Enthoven, Alain C., and K. Wayne Smith. 1971. *How Much Is Enough? Shaping the Defense Program, 1961–1969.* New York: Harper and Row.

Esposito, Vincent, ed. 1964. *Concise History of World War I.* New York: Praeger.

Ewell, Julian, and Ira Hunt. 1974. *Sharpening the Combat Edge: The Use of Analysis to Reinforce Military Judgment.* Washington, D.C.: Department of the Army.

Fall, Bernard. 1965. "Viet-Nam—The Agonizing Reappraisal." In *The Vietnam Reader,* ed. Bernard B. Fall and Marcus G. Raskin. New York: Random House.

Flemming, Peter. 1957. *Operation Sea Lion.* New York: Simon and Schuster.

Freedman, Lawrence. 1983. *The Evolution of Nuclear Strategy.* New York: St. Martin's.

Friedberg, Aaron. 1988. *The Weary Titan.* Princeton: Princeton University Press.

Gallup, George. 1981. *The Gallup Poll: Public Opinion 1980.* Wilmington, Del.: Scholarly Resources.

Gartner, Scott Sigmund. 1992. "Strategic Assessment in War: A Bounded Rationality Model of How Organizations Evaluate Policy Effectiveness." Ph.D. Diss. University of Michigan.

———. 1993. "Predicting the Timing of Carter's Decision to Initiate a Hostage

Rescue Attempt: Modeling a Dynamic Information Environment." *International Interactions* 18:365–386.

Gartner, Scott Sigmund, and Marissa Edson Myers. 1995. "The Myth of Uniqueness: An Analysis of the United States Army's Reliance on Body Counts in the Vietnam and Korean Wars." *Journal of Interdisciplinary History* 25:377–395.

Gartner, Scott Sigmund, and Randolph M. Siverson. 1996. "War Expansion and War Outcome." *Journal of Conflict Resolution* 40:4–15.

Gelb, Leslie, with Richard Betts. 1979. *The Irony of Vietnam: The System Worked.* Washington, D.C.: Brookings Institution Press.

Green, Donald P., and Ian Shapiro. 1994. *Pathologies of Rational Choice Theory: A Critique of Applications in Political Science.* New Haven: Yale University Press.

Greenhouse, Linda. 1995. "Pennsylvania Recalls the Century of Steam." *New York Times,* November 19, XX:8.

Halberstam, David. 1993. *The Fifties.* New York: Villard.

Halperin, Morton. 1974. *Bureaucratic Politics and Foreign Policy.* Washington, D.C.: Brookings Institution Press.

Handel, Michael. 1985. "Strategic Surprise: The Politics of Intelligence and the Management of Uncertainty." In *Intelligence Policy and Process,* ed. Alfred Maurer, Marlon Tunstall, and James Keagle. Boulder, Colo.: Westview Press.

Harsanyi, John. 1967. "Games with Incomplete Information Played by 'Bayesian' Players, I: The Basic Model." *Management Science* 14:159–182.

———. 1973. "Games with Randomly Distributed Payoffs: A New Rationale for Mixed Strategy Equilibrium Points." *International Journal of Game Theory* 2:1–23.

Hastedt, Glenn. 1985. "Organizational Foundations of Intelligence Failures." In *Intelligence Policy and Practice,* ed. Alfred Maurer, Marlon Tunstall, and James Keagle. Boulder, Colo.: Westview Press.

Hayes, John D. 1964. "Developments in Naval Warfare." In *A Concise History of World War II,* ed. Vincent Esposito. New York: Praeger.

Herken, Gregg. 1985. *Counsels of War.* New York: Knopf.

Herring, George. 1979. *America's Longest War: The United States and Vietnam, 1950–1975.* New York: Knopf.

Herwig, Holger. 1988. "The Dynamics of Necessity: German Military Policy During the First World War." In *Military Effectiveness,* volume 1: *The First*

World War, ed. Allan Millet and Williamson Murray. Boston: Allen and Unwin.

Hessler, Gunther. 1989. *U-Boat War in the Atlantic: 1939–1945*. London: Crown.

Hezlet, Arthur. 1967. *The Submarine and Sea Power*. New York: Stein and Day.

Hill, Stuart. 1992. *Democratic Values and Technological Choices*. Stanford: Stanford University Press.

Hinds, Michael de Courcy. 1991. "As 'Steamtown' Grows, So Does Parks Debate." *New York Times*, November 23, A:1.

Hough, Richard. 1989. *The Great War at Sea*. Oxford: Oxford University Press.

Hughes, Wayne P., Jr. 1986. "Garbage Cans at Sea." In *Ambiguity and Command: Organizational Perspectives on Military Decision Making*, ed. James March and Roger Weissinger-Baylon. Marshfield, Mass.: Pitman.

Ikle, Fred Charles. 1971. *Every War Must End*. New York: Columbia University Press.

Jackman, Robert. 1993. "Rationality and Political Participation." *American Journal of Political Science* 37:279–290.

Janowitz, Morris. 1971. *The Professional Soldier*. New York: Free Press.

Jellicoe, John Rushworth. 1920. *The Crisis of the Naval War*. London: Cassell.

———. 1934. *The Submarine Peril: The Admiralty Policy in 1917*. London: Cassell.

Jervis, Robert. 1976. *Perception and Misperception in International Politics*. Princeton: Princeton University Press.

———. 1993. "The Drunkard's Search." In *Explorations in Political Psychology*, ed. Shanto Iyengar and William McGuire. Durham, N.C.: Duke University Press.

Johnson, Lyndon Baines. 1971. *The Vantage Point: Perspectives on the Presidency, 1963–1969*. New York: Holt, Rinehart, and Winston.

Jomini, Baron de. 1971. *The Art of War*, trans. G. H. Mendell and W. P. Craighill. Westport, Conn.: Greenwood Press.

Jordan, Hamilton. 1982. *Crisis: The Last Year of the Carter Presidency*. New York: Putnam.

Kane, Joseph Nathan. 1981. *Facts About the Presidents*. New York: H. W. Wilson.

Kaplan, Fred. 1983. *The Wizards of Armageddon*. New York: Simon and Schuster.

Karni, Edi. 1985. *Decision Making Under Uncertainty*. Cambridge: Harvard University Press.

Karnow, Stanley. 1991. *Vietnam: A History*. New York: Penguin.

Kearns, Doris. 1976. *Lyndon Johnson and the American Dream*. New York: Signet.

Keegan, John. 1989. *The Price of Admiralty: The Evolution of Naval Warfare.* New York: Viking.

———. 1989. *The Second World War.* New York: Viking.

Kennedy, Paul. 1988. "Britain in the First World War." In *Military Effectiveness,* volume 1: *The First World War,* ed. Allan Millet and Williamson Murray. Boston: Allen and Unwin.

Kier, Elizabeth. 1995. "Culture and Military Doctrine: France Between the Wars." *International Security* 19:65–93.

Kinnard, Douglas. 1985. *The War Managers.* Wayne, N.J.: Avery.

Komer, Robert. 1985. "What 'Decade of Neglect'?" *International Security* 10 (2):70–83.

Krepinevich, Andrew. 1986. *The Army and Vietnam.* Baltimore: Johns Hopkins University Press.

Kreps, David M. 1990. *Game Theory and Economic Modeling.* Oxford: Clarendon Press.

Lanning, Michael Lee, and Dan Cragg. 1992. *Inside the VC and the NVA: The Real Story of North Vietnam's Armed Forces.* New York: Ballantine Books.

Levy, Jack. 1989. "The Causes of War: A Review of Theories and Evidence." In *Behavior, Society, and Nuclear War,* volume 1, ed. Philip E. Tetlock, Jo L. Husbands, Robert Jervis, Paul C. Stern, and Charles Tilly. New York: Oxford University Press.

———. 1989. "Organizational Routines and the Causes of War." In *World Politics: Sovereignty and Interdependence,* ed. Bruce Russett, Harvey Starr, and Richard Stoll. New York: Freeman.

Liddell Hart, B. H. 1936. *The War in Outline.* New York: Random House.

———. 1972. *History of the Second World War.* New York: Capricorn Books.

Lindblom, Charles, and David Braybrooke. 1963. *A Strategy of Decision.* London: Free Press.

Littauer, Ralph, and Norman Uphoff, eds. 1972. *The Air War in Indochina.* Boston: Beacon Press.

Lloyd George, David. 1934. *War Memoirs of David Lloyd George: 1916–1917.* Boston: Little, Brown.

———. 1934. *War Memoirs of David Lloyd George: 1917.* Boston: Little, Brown.

———. 1937. *War Memoirs of David Lloyd George: 1915–1916.* Boston: Little, Brown.

McChristian, Joseph. 1974. *The Role of Military Intelligence: 1965–1967.* Washington, D.C.: Department of the Army.

MacDonald, Callum. 1993. *The Lost Battle: Crete 1941.* New York: Free Press.

McGarvey, Patrick J., ed. 1969. *Visions of Victory: Selected Communist Military Writings, 1964–1968.* Stanford, Calif.: Hoover Institution on War, Revolution, and Peace.

McNamara, Robert S., with Brian Van De Mark. 1995. *In Retrospect: The Tragedy and Lessons of Vietnam.* New York: Random House.

Mako, William P. 1983. *U.S. Ground Forces and the Defense of Central Europe.* Washington, D.C.: Brookings Institution Press.

Manchester, William. 1979. *Goodbye Darkness.* New York: Laurel.

March, Francis A. 1919. *History of the World War.* Philadelphia: United Publishers of the United States and Canada.

March, James. 1978. "Bounded Rationality, Ambiguity, and the Engineering of Choice." *Bell Journal of Economics* 9:587–608.

March, James, and Johan Olsen. 1986. "Garbage Can Models of Decision Making in Organizations." In *Ambiguity and Command: Organizational Perspectives on Military Decision Making,* ed. James March and Roger Weissinger-Baylon. Marshfield, Mass.: Pitman.

March, James, and Herbert Simon, with Harold Guetzkow. 1958. *Organizations.* New York: John Wiley and Sons.

Marder, Arthur J. 1969. *From the Dreadnought to Scapa Flow: The Royal Navy in the Fisher Era, 1904–1919,* volume 4: *1917: Year of Crisis.* London: Oxford University Press.

Mearsheimer, John. 1983. *Conventional Deterrence.* Ithaca: Cornell University Press.

Millet, Allen, Williamson Murray, and Kenneth Watman. 1988. "The Effectiveness of Military Organizations." In *Military Effectiveness:* volume 1: *The First World War,* ed. Allan Millet and Williamson Murray. Boston: Allen and Unwin.

Moe, Terry M. 1990. "Political Institutions: The Neglected Side of the Story." *Journal of Law, Economics, and Organization* 6:213–253.

———. 1991. "Politics and the Theory of Organization." *Journal of Law, Economics, and Organization* 7:106–129.

Morgenthau, Hans. 1954. *Politics Among Nations.* New York: Knopf.

Morrow, James. 1991. "Alliances and Asymmetry: An Alternative to the Capability Aggregation Model of Alliances." *American Journal of Political Science* 35:904–933.

———. 1994. *Game Theory for Political Scientists.* Princeton: Princeton University Press.

Moss, George Donelson. 1990. *Vietnam: An American Ordeal.* Englewood Cliffs, N.J.: Prentice Hall.

Mrozek, Donald J. 1988. *Air Power and the Ground War in Vietnam: Ideas and Actions.* Maxwell Air Force Base, Ala.: Air University Press.

Mueller, John. 1971. "Trends in Popular Support for the Wars in Korea and Vietnam." *American Political Science Review* 65:358–375.

Murray, Charles, and Catherine Bly Cox. 1989. *Apollo: The Race to the Moon.* New York: Touchstone.

Nash, Nathaniel C. 1993. "As World Crowds in, an Island Shields Its Culture." *New York Times,* February 6, A:2.

Neustadt, Richard, and Harvey Fineberg. 1983. *The Epidemic That Never Was: Policy-Making and the Swine Flu Affair.* New York: Vintage Books.

Nincic, Donna J., and Miroslav Nincic. 1995. "Commitment to Military Intervention: The Democratic Government as Economic Investor." *Journal of Peace Research* 32:413–426.

O'Neil, Barry. 1995. "Weak Models, Nil Hypotheses, and Decorative Statistics: Is There Really No Hope?" *Journal of Conflict Resolution* 39:731–748.

Organski, A. F. K., and Jacek Kugler. 1980. *The War Ledger.* Chicago: University of Chicago Press.

Overy, Richard. 1995. *Why the Allies Won.* London: Jonathan Cape.

Palit, D. K. 1974. *Return to Sinai: The Arab-Israeli War, 1973.* Salisbury, U.K.: Compton.

Palmer, Bruce, Jr. 1984. *The 25-Year War: America's Military Role in Vietnam.* Lexington: University Press of Kentucky.

Pape, Robert A., Jr. 1990. "Coercive Air Power in the Vietnam War." *International Security* 15:1103–1146.

Paschall, Rod. 1989. *The Defeat of Imperial Germany: 1917–1918.* Chapel Hill, N.C.: Algonquin Books.

Pear, Robert. 1992. "Disputed Military Aircraft Crashes; 7 Aboard Lost." *New York Times,* July 21, A:1.

Perret, Geoffrey. 1991. *There's a War to Be Won: The United States Army in World War II.* New York: Ballantine Books.

Posen, Barry R. 1984. *The Sources of Military Doctrine: France, Britain, and Germany Between the World Wars.* Ithaca: Cornell University Press.

Powell, Jody. 1984. *The Other Side of the Story*. New York: William Morrow.

Ranft, Bryan. 1988. "The Royal Navy and the War at Sea." In *Britain and the First World War*, ed. John Turner. London: Unwin Hyman.

Rasmusen, Eric. 1990. *Games and Information: An Introduction to Game Theory*. Cambridge, Mass.: Basil Blackwell.

Reiter, Dani. 1994. "Learning, Realism, and Alliances: The Weight of the Shadow of the Past." *World Politics* 46:490–526.

Richelson, Jeffrey T. 1994. *Presidential Directives on National Security From Truman to Clinton*. Alexandria, Va.: Chadwyck-Healey.

Ridgway, Matthew. 1967. *The Korean War*. New York: Doubleday.

Riker, William H. 1990. "Political Science and Rational Choice." In *Perspectives on Positive Political Economy*, ed. James Alt and Kenneth Shepsle. Cambridge: Cambridge University Press.

Rosen, Stephen Peter. 1991. *Winning the Next War: Innovation and the Modern Military*. Ithaca: Cornell University Press.

Roskill, S. W. 1954. *The War at Sea: 1939–1945*, volume 1: *The Defensive*. London: HMSO.

———. 1956. *The War at Sea: 1939–1945*, volume 2: *The Period of Balance*. London: HMSO.

———. 1960. *The War at Sea: 1939–1945*, volume 3, part 1: *The Offensive*. London: HMSO.

———. 1961. *The War at Sea: 1939–1945*, volume 3, part 2: *The Offensive*. London: HMSO.

Rostow, Walt, to LBJ, White House Memorandum, 1/20/67, University of California, Davis, archive no. 6-2-37.

Ryan, Paul B. 1985. *The Iranian Rescue Mission: Why It Failed*. Annapolis, Md.: Naval Institute Press.

Sagan, Scott. 1993. *The Limits of Safety*. Princeton: Princeton University Press.

———. 1994. "The Perils of Proliferation." *International Security* 18:66–107.

Schampel, James. 1993. "Change in Material Capabilities and the Onset of War: A Dyadic Approach." *International Studies Quarterly* 37:395–408.

Schlight, John. 1988. *The War in South Vietnam: The Years of the Offensive, 1965–1968*. Washington, D.C.: Office of Air Force History, U.S. Air Force.

Schmitt, Eric. 1995. "House Panel Backs B-2 But No More Seawolf Subs; Both Moves Are Opposite Military's Hopes." *New York Times, May* 24, C:18.

Schon, Donald A. 1971. *Beyond the Stable State*. New York: W. W. Norton.

Schwarzkopf, H. Norman, and Peter Petre. 1992. *It Doesn't Take a Hero*. New York: Bantam Books.

Selten, Reinhard. 1978. "The Chain-Store Paradox." *Theory and Decision* 9:127–159.

Sheehan, Neil, et al. 1971. *The Pentagon Papers: New York Times Edition*. New York: Bantam Books.

Simon, Herbert. 1957. *Administrative Behavior*. New York: Free Press.

———. 1981. *The Sciences of the Artificial*. Cambridge: MIT Press.

Siverson, Randolph M., and Harvey Starr. 1991. *The Diffusion of War: A Study of Opportunity and Willingness*. Ann Arbor: University of Michigan Press.

Smith, Steve. 1988. "Policy Preferences and Bureaucratic Position: The Case of the American Hostages Rescue Mission." In *Bureaucratic Politics and National Security*, ed. David C. Kozak and James M. Keagle. Boulder, Colo.: Lynne Rienner.

Snyder, Jack. 1984. *The Ideology of the Offensive: Military Decision Making and the Disasters of 1914*. Ithaca: Cornell University Press.

———. 1985. "Civil Military Relations and the Cult of the Offensive." In *Military Strategy and the Origins of the First World War*, ed. Steven Miller. Princeton: Princeton University Press.

Specter, Michael. 1992. "City Dwellers Want U.S. Park Funds to Go East." *New York Times*, July 27, A:1.

Stam, Allan Conrad III. 1996. *Win, Lose, or Draw*. Ann Arbor: University of Michigan Press.

Stanton, Shelby. 1985. *The Rise and Fall of an American Army*. New York: Dell.

Sternhell, Charles, and Alan Thorndike. 1946. *Antisubmarine Warfare in World War II: Report No. 51 of the Operations Evaluation Group*. Washington, D.C.: Office of the Chief of Naval Operations, Operations Evaluation Group, U.S. Navy.

Stinchcombe, Arthur L. 1990. *Information and Organizations*. Berkeley: University of California Press.

Stockman, David. 1986. *Triumph of Politics*. New York: Harper and Row.

Stokesbury, James L. 1981. *A Short History of World War I*. New York: William Morrow.

Sturdee, Doveton. 1934. "A Few Remarks on the Main Naval Strategy of the War" (appendix to chapter 3). In *The Submarine Peril: The Admiralty Policy in 1917*, ed. John Jellicoe. London: Cassell.

Summers, Harry G. 1982. *On Strategy: A Critical Analysis of the Vietnam War*. New York: Dell.

Tarrant, V. E. 1989. *The U-Boat Offensive, 1914-1945*. London: Arms and Armour Press.

Taylor, A. J. P. 1963. *The First World War*. New York: Perigee.

Terraine, John. 1989. *The U-Boat Wars: 1916-1945*. New York: Henry Holt.

Thayer, Thomas C. 1977. *A Systems Analysis View of the Vietnam War: 1965-1972*, volumes 1-8. Washington D.C.: Department of Defense.

———. 1985. *War Without Fronts: The American Experience in Vietnam*. Boulder, Colo.: Westview Press.

Tidman, Keith R. 1984. *The Operations Evaluation Group: A History of Naval Operations Analysis*. Annapolis, Md.: Naval Institute Press.

The Times. 1918. *The Times History of the War*, volume 14. London: Times.

Ultee, Maarten, ed. 1986. *Adapting to Conditions: War and Society in the Eighteenth Century*. Tuscaloosa: University of Alabama Press.

Vance, Cyrus. 1983. *Hard Choices: Critical Years in America's Foreign Policy*. New York: Simon and Schuster.

Van der Vat, Dan. 1988. *The Atlantic Campaign: World War II's Great Struggle at Sea*. New York: Harper and Row.

Van Evera, Stephen. 1984. "Causes of War." Ph.D. Diss. University of California, Berkeley.

———. 1985. "The Cult of the Offensive and the Origins of the First World War." In *Military Strategy and the Origins of the First World War*, ed. Steven Miller. Princeton: Princeton University Press.

———. 1988. "Why States Believe Foolish Ideas: Non-Self-Evaluation by Government and Society." Paper presented at the annual meeting of the American Political Science Association, Washington, D.C.

Von der Porten, Edward P. 1969. *The German Navy in World War II*. New York: Thomas Y. Crowell.

Warner, Oliver. 1975. *The British Navy: A Concise History*. London: Thames and Hudson.

Weigley, Russell. 1984. *The History of the United States Army*. Bloomington: University of Indiana Press.

Weinberg, Gerhard L. 1994. *A World at Arms: A Global History of World War II*. Cambridge: Cambridge University Press.

Westmoreland, William C. 1976. *A Soldier Reports*. Garden City, N.Y.: Doubleday.

Westmoreland, William C., and Ulysses S. Grant Sharp. 1968. *Report on the War in Vietnam: As of June 30, 1968.*

Wildavsky, Aaron. 1972. "The Self-Evaluating Organization." *Public Administration Review* 32:509–520.

Wilson, James Q. 1989. *Bureaucracy: What Government Agencies Do and Why They Do It.* New York: Basic Books.

Wirtz, James J. 1991. *The Tet Offensive: Intelligence Failure in War.* Ithaca: Cornell University Press.

Zisk, Kimberly Marten. 1993. *Engaging the Enemy: Organization Theory and Soviet Military Innovation, 1955–1991.* Princeton: Princeton University Press.

Index

Ingram Content Group UK Ltd.
Milton Keynes UK
UKHW011814190423
420445UK00001B/122